# THE ETHICS OF
# EDUCATIONAL RESEARCH

*To our wives*

*Cheryl and Angela*
*for their forbearance*

# The Ethics of
# Educational Research

EDITED BY

*Mike McNamee*
AND
*David Bridges*

**Blackwell**
Publishing

© 2002 by Blackwell Publishers Ltd.
a Blackwell Publishing company

First published as a special issue of *Journal of Philosophy of Education*, 2001
Reprinted 2004.

Editorial Offices:
108 Cowley Road, Oxford OX4 1JF, UK
  Tel: +44 (0)1865 791100
Osney Mead, Oxford OX2 0EL, UK
  Tel: +44 (0)1865 206206
350 Main Street, Malden, MA 02148-5018, USA
  Tel: +1 781 388 8250
Iowa State University Press, a Blackwell Publishing company, 2121 S. State Avenue,
Ames, Iowa 50014-8300, USA
  Tel: +1 515 292 0140
Blackwell Munksgaard, Nørre Søgade 35, PO Box 2148, Copenhagen, DK-1016,
Denmark
  Tel: +45 77 33 33 33
Blackwell Publishing Asia, 54 University Street, Carlton, Victoria 3053, Australia
  Tel: +61 (0)3 347 0300
Blackwell Verlag, Kurfürstendamm 57, 10707 Berlin, Germany
  Tel: +49 (0)30 32 79 060
Blackwell Publishing, 10, rue Casimir Delavigne, 75006 Paris, France
  Tel: +331 5310 3310

First published 2002 by Blackwell Publishers Ltd.

Library of Congress Cataloging-in-Publication Data has been applied for

ISBN 0-631-23167-6

A catalogue record for this title is available from the British Library.

For further information on
Blackwell Publishers visit our website:
www.blackwellpublishers.co.uk

# Contents

# Acknowledgements

The editors would like to thank Richard Smith and Paul Standish, the past and present editor of the Journal of Philosophy of Education, for their support and advice and also Lorna James of Blackwell for her assistance in putting this collection of material together.

They are grateful to the following learned societies for their permission to reproduce their ethical guidelines: British Sociological Association; British Psychological Society; British Educational Research Association: Social Sciences and Humanities Research Council of Canada which were current at the time of going to press. Readers should note, however, that they are subject to on-going review.

# 1

# Introduction: Whose Ethics, Which Research?

## MIKE McNAMEE

When Richard Peters wrote *Ethics and Education* (1966) he could scarcely have imagined the revolutions in ethics that have since occurred. Nor could he have imagined the way philosophers have created curricula and codes of ethics that have been incorporated in the various professional spheres within and beyond education. Whether this signals a decline in the trust that professionals might once have claimed, the diminishing of a strongly internalised sense of responsibility, or merely an extension of the natural developments of professionalisation is not yet clear.

There is a marked contrast between the professional health of philosophy of education and its robustness as an educational discipline. While the philosophy of education was in its heyday there was much work for analytical philosophers—much uncharted territory—even the (then soothing) thought that professional philosophers might come to buttress the ranks of philosophers of education in the wake of Peters' pioneering work. Nowadays a few university Education departments acknowledge the value of the contributions philosophy characteristically offers to educational practice, yet most philosophers of education feel marginalised.

One area where philosophers' ongoing professional contributions are valued is in philosophy of science and the philosophy of research methods. Many philosophers have heard the call at the beginning of such courses to teach students about to embark upon research what precisely is meant *inter alia* by 'paradigms' and 'positivism'. The links between those grand theoretical ideas are commonly lost on undergraduate students and experienced as an irrelevance by empirically-minded researchers eager to gather data unimpeded by such weighty yet abstruse considerations. The rising recognition of ethics in the training and education of new researchers has, however, marked another substantial area beyond the traditional work of

1

philosophers of education. It is scarcely conceivable that a respectable course of study at either undergraduate or postgraduate levels would now fail to include a session or two on the ethics of research. Until very recently there has been relatively little beyond the more generic research texts applying ethics to social sciences (e.g. Adelman, 1984; Burgess, 1989; Homan, 1992; Sieber, 1992), but even there little attention is paid to the philosophical character of the nature of problems encountered in the processes of educational research.[1] The present volume attempts to address that lacuna in two ways. First, it marks out a broader picture of the conceptual terrain of research ethics than might initially be thought relevant or appropriate. Second, it gives philosophical substance to professional discussions of the ethics of research and offers fresh insights into the conflicts and dilemmas recognisable in diverse educational research practices.

Changing conceptions of ethics have made their mark on this collection. The apparent common sense orthodoxy of Richard Peters' era, a development of liberal and Kantian ideas into principles of procedure, has largely been supplanted by a fractured pluralism: a focus on the present and on particular practices that stands in stark contrast to the essentially *principled* way of conceiving morality that was hegemonic for most of the last two hundred years. It was always the intention of this collection to bring together a range of researchers interested in the specifically ethical dimensions of research. Thus it includes essays by philosophers and non-philosophers alike, who discuss key issues of access and consent, voice and empowerment, virtue, conflict, the dominance of modes of reasoning in the character and conduct of research, in a way that is illuminating for all engaged in educational research. The collection thus sketches a self-consciously broad picture of ethics and of educational research. This Introduction seeks to contextualise those discussions in the literature of research ethics and, more generally, to relate them to some of the recent debates in moral philosophy.

## CONSENT, CONFIDENTIALITY AND ANONYMITY

The notion of voluntary informed consent is unquestionably at the heart of research ethics in the natural sciences following the horrifying revelations of scientific experimentation on prisoners during the Second World War. The Nuremberg and Helsinki declarations laid out the inviolable principle of consent, asserting that the subjects of research have the right to be informed of the nature and purposes of the research and autonomously to choose whether to participate in it. The principle of consent thus protected individuals' right not to be harmed nor to have their conception of their interests overridden. The right of the researched corresponded symmetrically to the duty of researchers to respect that autonomy and never to coerce or deceive.

The language here belongs paradigmatically to the terrain of what Bernard Williams (1985, pp. 174–196) has characterised as the 'institution of morality', an institution driven by a picture of rationality. Persons ought to be moved by special sorts of reasons and moved to act thus in a special way (out of duty: not pleasure, interest or inclination).

Although voluntary informed consent is conceived as an exceptionless principle in the natural sciences, it is conceived in the social sciences (under which description the bulk of educational research falls) rather more weakly as a standard procedure to protect subjects or participants. The precise nomenclature here is noteworthy. While social scientists have come both to recognise and be wary of the inescapable power dimension which standardly privileges the researcher over the researched, the use of the word 'participant' is supposed to acknowledge an ideological shift in the researcher's own ethical and political obligations to the researched. Roger Homan challenges the substance of this position in discussing the ways in which consent, and the value of autonomy that it seeks to safeguard, is often overridden in educational research.

In his essay here Homan directly attacks those researchers who merely pay lip-service to consent as an ethical issue and who seek, consciously or otherwise, to gain access to a site of research without addressing those whom the researcher wishes to investigate. He argues that researchers commonly utilise powerful gatekeepers in order to smooth the way to gaining access to participants' data. He notes the standard practice in educational research of gaining consent from a headteacher to research within a school where the researcher knows that if the person at the top of the institution gives consent it is unlikely anyone lower in the hierarchy, most notably the pupils themselves, will refuse to participate. As he puts it, the consent of those thus researched is assumed, not voluntary. But Homan goes further than this. While the potential for harm in the social sciences may not always rank as high as in, say, medical research, he invites us to consider the range of harms that may occur when issues to do with respect for the researched are not properly addressed.

Homan also notes how the conditions of informedness (which relates to the explanation of all pertinent dimensions of the research and its comprehensibility by the researched) and consensuality (that the participant is capable of a rational and mature judgement) need to be considered prior to the commencement of the research. Even where such conditions are met, trained researchers sometimes utilise the data collection phase to explore issues that are only tangentially related to the intended research, with the potential for the abuse of private spaces accessed by the researcher and the common failure to weigh up the opportunity costs borne by the researched, such as pupils and teachers.

The cautionary flavour of Homan's discussion carries over into Les Tickle's chapter. Tickle interrogates the boundaries of professional conduct in relation to the complex of such educational roles as tutor, lecturer, colleague and mentor, showing how these compound the difficulties of action researchers. He investigates the way in which a whole range of standard ethical research conditions involving gaining consent, developing trust and maintaining anonymity coalesce in his own research and in the case of Mary Chamberlain's work *Fenwomen*. In the latter case, tabloid journalists revealed the identities of those in the book and wrote lurid stories of their private lives, to the outrage of those who had agreed to co-operate with Chamberlain. In this innocent failure to safeguard what was promised to the participants, her attempt to give voice to women who had traditionally been disempowered backfired tragically.

Tickle explores two similarly problematic scenarios that arise from the tensions between on the one hand the commitment to improve the lot of those researched and on the other the principled demands of confidentiality and anonymity and the more open-ended virtue of trustworthiness. He explores how two beginning teachers were abused by those in authority over them in their schools. Where the student-teacher refused to release him from the confidentiality of their relationship he nonetheless was able, upon agreeing to anonymity, to raise the matter with colleagues and the headteachers in order to reduce the potential for abuse in the future. His second scenario concerns the mentor to a newly-qualified teacher who had been in public dispute with the headteacher. Tickle discusses how to reconcile disclosure and withholding while attempting both to ensure ongoing collaboration with the school and to redress the injustice done to a particular teacher. In particular he addresses the institutional contexts in which boundary settings and transgressions occur and shows how what are thought of as positive ethical values such as anonymity and confidentiality can effectively prevent one from pursuing what is right.

## THE ETHICS AND POLITICS OF VOICE

One is aware, reading Tickle's chapter, of his sensitivity to his membership in the intersecting and sometimes conflicting communities of education. Likewise, in her epigrammatic remarks upon community being the context in which good character is developed and judged, Amélie Rorty wites: 'no action without interaction; no interaction without politics' (1988, p. 324). This recognition of the political in judging the ethical significance of certain acts or policies is brought to the fore in very different ways in the chapters by Shirley Pendlebury and Penny Enslin, and David Bridges.

Social scientists often hold the view that universalistic ethics is no more than a hangover from the preconceptions of modernity. Williams' characterisation of the 'institution of morality' resonates with this view. Impressed by scientific theorising, philosophers of modernity, from Kant to Habermas, have been seduced by the need to systematise moral reflection into some kind of theoretically grounded system of principles. Buoyed up by the quantity of anthropological evidence most social scientists and many philosophers often characterise such theorising as the product of misguided rationalism. It is doubly noteworthy then, that in their chapter Pendlebury and Enslin argue for a form of humanist universalism, inspired by Martha Nussbaum, in the face of postmodern critiques.

Speaking on behalf of other communities, as educational researchers commonly do, requires justification against charges of imperialism, indifference or ignorance, or misplaced paternalism. Pendlebury and Enslin, in the only universalistically-inspired chapter in this volume, argue that relativism need not be entailed even where cultural and tradition-bound heterogeneity is acknowledged and confronted. In the face of the undeniable diversity of cultural practices with which they engage, educational researchers can justify their interventions to the extent that they add to the range of basic capabilities that enable the researched to live good lives. One might see this drive to cater for basic needs as the political-economical corollary of Elizabeth Anscombe's famous remark that we should give up ethics until we have better psychology.

Educational researchers' moral justification, then, for investigating and speaking on behalf of others, does not rely on some set of trans-historical identifiers of the human subject (e.g. respect for human rational autonomy) but rather on making sense of concrete circumstances. If goods such as health, education, political liberty and participation, self-respect and life itself are taken into account without endorsing specific patterns of life, then the charge that educational researchers will merely reproduce the projections of well-meaning liberal Western mindset, Pendlebury and Enslin argue, is demonstrably false. Their ethic for educational researchers is precisely this: promote the capabilities of those whom you research in terms of those things *necessary* for the quality of life. Thus, they argue, researchers, particularly in their work with marginalised or impoverished groups, can avoid the abuse of the trust given to them by their relatively powerless research participants. Of course, certain traditionalists will see in this liberal humanism the well-meaning attempt to allow a diversity of cultural traditions to flourish while nevertheless functioning to erode the values of traditions for whom a Western picture of freedom and choice is itself objectionable.

Voices critical of universalism and supportive of political ethnocentrism are brought in play in David Bridges' chapter. In particular, he offers a critique of the ethical and epistemological dimensions of the ethnocentric position: 'nothing about us without us'. He charts the political campaign of the disability theorist J. I. Charlton to empower disabled scholars in part by confining the domain of disability research to those who are thus categorised. Bridges dismisses the idea that only those who have had particular experiences are thereby qualified to talk meaningfully about them. There are other assumptions here also in need of critique. It might seem for example that 'outsiders' may import harmful analytical frameworks and promote them in their research; but who counts as 'inside' and 'outside' a field of research at any given time is unclear. Nor are the boundaries of such fields easy to define: are those going a little deaf, for example, qualified to research this area of disability?

Bridges notes the common claim that educational researchers have often moved into research sites on the promise of benefits to the host community, only to disengage themselves before any such benefits have accrued. He proposes that any claim premised on potential benefits ought to be substantiated. More commonly the arrangement is more honestly portrayed as one of host-generosity in an openly one-sided arrangement. In reciprocating that generosity there is a crucial need to respect the cultural *mores* of the host community, for the contributions and rewards are themselves culturally nuanced in a way that researchers ought to acknowledge (and not merely out of politeness).

In recognising the phenomenon of 'ventriloquy' where the researched are merely the vehicle for the researcher's message, the chapters by Pendlebury and Enslin and Bridges illustrate the possibilities for subtle forms of disrespect. In tightly framing the contexts, in prioritising the questions or areas of research, researchers can silence or marginalise the very concerns and cares that those, whom they claim to speak on behalf of, wish to express most forcefully. Given that educational research so frequently attempts to raise the profile or position of disempowered groups it is ironic that so little care is taken to understand them 'from the inside'. Nevertheless, Bridges argues that 'outsider research' can be justified on grounds of the promotion of the interests of the researched and the benefit in knowledge and understanding gained by the researcher and the relevant educational communities. To fail to acknowledge this may effect an ethical and epistemological isolationism that benefits no one.

## CODES AND VIRTUES, PRINCIPLES AND PHRONESIS

If these chapters implicitly take the view that moral reflection is to be made concrete in particular practices, it is worth noting some further anti-theoretical moral sentiments that serve to situate Robin Small's chapter. A central purpose of any moral theory is to systematise the justification of practices and judgements. The word 'principles' is commonly used to capture the idea of rules that cohere to form a systematic whole. The form of a principle, an exceptionless rule to put it crudely, is however, problematic as a starting point for ethical judgment and system-building, as many philosophers have recently pointed out. On a naïve view in which moral problems are solved by appeal to universal principles, one moves in a computational or deductive fashion. One begins with a universal principle that when applied to a particular problem provides a solution that all rational persons must assent to.

If this is something of a caricature it is nevertheless a caricature that informs and indeed dominates in institutional life, irrespective of the philosophical criticism it has been subjected to. So, for example, a failure to gain the consent of one's research subjects or participants signals a failure to observe the principle of respect for autonomous agents: to use them only as means towards a researcher's ends. Here it seems we have a major premise, 'One must respect the autonomy of research participants as autonomous agents', and a minor premise, 'The researched have not been asked for their consent'. Then the conclusion that the research(er) is unethical is deduced straightforwardly from the major premise, which itself is based on the moral principle of respect. Both Pring and Small object to this naïve deductivist picture of principle-led moral decision-making. While many philosophers have noted that principles underdetermine action—one has always to understand when and how a principle is to be applied—Joseph Dunne makes the powerful point that:

> In contrast to this deductivism, the phronetic approach takes as its point of departure the *problematicity* of minor premises; the hardest thing about being virtuous, perhaps, is just being able to *see* what is really significant in different situations. Whereas in the deductivist approach, the challenge in ethical life is mainly a matter of the will, for the phronetic approach it is very much a matter of a particular kind of knowledge. (Dunne, 1993, p. 308)

This does not of course oblige us to jettison the idea of principles altogether. It does however point us to the need to think through the relations between principles and particularity. The felt need for principles if we are to avoid caprice or unfounded intuitions is well taken. It is founded on the need for good reasons for action. This strain of thinking is properly called anti-theoretical in that it is deeply sceptical of the picture of reasons grounded in a system of universal principles connected to a deductive decision procedure.

Small argues that we should adopt an alternative to the naïve deductive model of principled decision-theoretic moral action, and that codes of ethical or professional conduct in educational research are only ever relatively finished products. As such they are an imposition of a *status quo* by an institution. He finds the authoritarian nature of their execution inimical to the philosophical temper. Where a code attempts to cater for the range of research styles that different disciplines have developed it is bound to falter. A code can at best represent some inelegant consensus and not a fully coherent theoretical structure awaiting application. In negotiations upon different patterns of language, affect and judgement discourse will always be power-infiltrated. There seems to Small to be little prospect of ethically defensible procedures to develop codes in the first place, even before one confronts problems of implementation.

Small turns to the British philosopher Ross's deontological account of right action. Unlike the Kantian picture of categorical or unexceptionless duties, Ross gives a picture of *prima facie* duties whose conditional nature enables their subjection to other duties in particular circumstances. The duties comprise four very general ones (justice, beneficence, self-improvement and non-maleficence) and three that arise under more particular circumstances (fidelity, reparation and gratitude). In that codes of conduct characteristically attend only to our interaction with others, the duty of self-improvement sits a little oddly with this list. Nevertheless, the principle of right action drives the spirit of such codes where the rule-governed approach appears felicitous. One might think of such a code as a set of moral traffic rules designed to prevent the harms that befall careless, incompetent or wanton drivers. What appeals to Small is the conditionality and pluralism of Ross's list and its respect for conflict in the lives of agents who, as a matter of fact, have relatively few moral intuitions expressed as general principles.

In the light of Ross's duties, Small unpacks two recent large-scale codes of conduct. He too problematises the applicability of codes to particular cases. Having earlier criticised the deductive model he examines the 'problem-solving' approach espoused by Jonsen and Toulmin (1988) where paradigm cases supplant principles as the source of our reflections. In this sense the ruminations of the researcher or board/committee member(s) are phronetic (practically wise) in the Aristotelian sense: they are carried out by persons whose mode of reflection is an open-ended, flexible, non-formulaic congress of thought, feeling and judgement to arrive at their 'conclusions'. What is less Aristotelian is Small's proposed alternative to the problems of applying codes. Instead of strong normative interventions by philosophers he proposes a more formal, procedural, role. In whatever grip universities, schools and other institutions have been held by simplistic pictures of ethical code application, they must be released from it. This is precisely the aim of Small's essay, along with another: to make more circumspect the philosopher's role in the development of bureaucratic measures for ethical control of the workforce.

While the foregoing essays focus on the duties of researchers to operate at a level of ethical sensibility to particular cultures there is also a need to consider ethical issues at a more individual level. While moral philosophy had neglected the ethics of virtue, and educational researchers such as Kohlberg had derided the virtues so roundly, the resurrection of virtue ethics has been little short of spectacular in the last twenty years. Richard Pring's chapter specifically addresses the range of moral and intellectual virtues and the temptations educational researchers face.

He does so first by the use of four examples that draw attention to key issues such as trust, deception and negotiation: issues that figure frequently in any lecture in the ethics or mechanics of methods in research design. It is easy enough, however, when discussing these issues with real-life examples to ignore situational characteristics beyond the standard frame of tenured faculty, dedicated students, morally unproblematic topics and so on. In the selection of examples Pring pays close attention to the *manner* in which particular circumstances alter our judgements.

Pring observes that politics, inescapable in the production of knowledge, transforms our ethical appraisals of character and context. The researcher has obligations to create beneficial effects from (and in) the research. Nevertheless, the estimation of effects to the researched and to the research team cannot be easily registered as mere utilitarian cost or benefit. One must, for example, make estimations of the short- and long-term effects of publishing or withholding data in order to maintain good working relationships with one's educational partners. Equally, one has duties towards research sponsors just as one has to the reputation of the research team and one's own university or school. All these considerations have to be brought to bear in an estimation of value where there is no single or undisputed currency.

What concerns Pring most in the appraisal of these examples is the role that principled deliberation must play. In Aristotelian fashion he argues that we must circumscribe the role that principles play in the shaping of our moral deliberations. He articulates the indeterminacy of principles when pressed into the service of context-sensitive judgement. He illustrates clearly the potential for conflict in a principled fashioning of ideas such as the public's right to know, a subject's right to anonymity, a researcher's promise to observe confidentiality—all of which might cohere or conflict with, say, a commitment to improve the lot of the researched or to make good on the promises made in research bid to a sponsor.

One of the salient distinctions drawn out variously in his examples relates to the moral bonds that may develop in the investigation of certain research problems and contexts. There will clearly be cases where the relationships between the researcher and the researched is genuinely one of partnership and equal negotiation; where the newly fashionable term 'research participant' as opposed to the power-ridden 'research subject' is genuinely felicitous. The *democratic* researcher, Pring argues, illustrates how many aspects of good research practice are the products of relationships characterised by the virtues. In contrast to the dominant focus on principles of right action Pring makes a plea for the virtues of the educational researcher to be taken seriously: courage to get at the truth where the truth hurts, humility in the face of justified criticism, modesty in the self-evaluation of the merits of one's research, empathy for the plight of the researched, trustworthiness to the vulnerable whether researched or one's co-researchers.

Before leaving this topic it is worth noting considerations critical of the very idea of virtuous character and the virtues. Stanley Milgram's (1974) research into obedience to dishonest, deceptive, untrustworthy authority is well-known. Milgram is himself widely charged with being disrespectful of his research subjects who were deceived into thinking that they were administering electric shocks to willing volunteers in a scientific experiment purporting to investigate the effects of punishment on learning. Across a variety of research protocols, 65% of the subjects administered shocks up to 450 volts even though at 300 volts the apparent subject of the research (an actor the other side of the laboratory wall) had moved from wimpering to screaming and even to pounding the wall. It is widely believed that, when debriefed, the subjects who had been exhorted to continue in the face of the apparent harm visited on the innocent subjects were outraged. What is less commonly noted is that in the follow-up to the debrief process where the subject and the actor were 'reconciled', 83.7% of the subjects later reported that they were 'glad' or 'very glad' that they had participated in the study whereas only 1.3% were sorry or very sorry (Milgram, 1974, pp. 194–195). This fact can be taken to direct our moral attention in two ways. One might, like a consequentialist, point to the overwhelmingly positive effects registered in the subject's feedback and also to the benefits of improved social scientific awareness of obedience to authority. By contrast, one might in deontological fashion point to the abuse of the subjects' autonomy. And it is right to observe, of course, that one could arrive at those same conclusions with no awareness whatever of the existence of moral theory.

A point of deeper import, however, attends to the very notion of character itself. The recent trend of neo-Aristotelian scholarship resuscitating the ethics of virtue is predicated on the existence of a strong concept of character. Ethics is not first and foremost grounded in duty or consequence but in character comprised of one's enduring traits:

> ...the attitudes, sensibilities, and beliefs that affect how a person sees, acts, and indeed lives. As permanent states, these will explain not why someone acted this way *now*, but why someone can be counted on to act in a certain way. In this sense, character gives a special sort of accountability and pattern to action. (Sherman, 1989, p. 1)

And that is surely what Pring and those charged with the promotion or regulation of ethical research are after. It is the idea that a firm character will bring about good conduct now and in the future in a reliable and accountable way. Yet it is precisely here that the substance and methods of Milgram's work are relevant. First, it appears that people in certain circumstances will behave in ways contrary to folk psychology. Second, one may not be able to interrogate such behaviour without recourse to deception. If we recognise a general norm that deception may be justified where the deceptive methods are exclusively necessary and the investigation of sufficient general merit then we may not be excessively perturbed at limited disrespect or insignificant harm. But the first criticism, disturbing as it is, has been buttressed recently by philosophical and psychological research. And, if true, it forces us to cast aside completely the idea that what one wants first and foremost is researchers of good character.

Harman (1999) argues that character traits presupposed in virtue ethics simply do not exist. He draws upon Darley and Batson (1973),[2] who recruited seminarians at Princeton Theological Seminary. The subjects (to call them 'participants' would be misleading) were assigned to give a talk either on equal opportunities or on the parable of the Good Samaritan. They were sent from their site ('Jerusalem') to the place of their talk ('Jericho'). In between the two locations was a confederate of the researchers, distressed and slumped in a doorway. Might one expect all the seminarians to stop and help? Would the topic of the talk in any way direct their action? It did not. 63% of those in no hurry stopped whereas only 45% of those who were in a hurry did. The key variable is apparently the hurry that the subjects were in. So much for our reliance upon virtuous character. Harman follows Darley and Batson, and Ross and Nesbitt (1991), in arguing that a belief in generally virtuous character operating consistently across domains commits the 'fundamental attribution error' (or Fundamental Attribution Tendency as Ross and Nesbitt put it) to 'ignore situations factors and overconfidently assume that distinctive behaviour or patterns of behaviour are due to an agent's distinctive character traits' (1999, p. 315).

Millgram and others conclude that trait-globality does not exist. Virtue-theorists who focus solely or predominantly on 'interiority' are misguided, though not necessarily because of the non-existence of trait-globality. If persons are not fundamentally prey to whims, those concerned with the ethics of character nonetheless need to pay close attention to the situations in which choices are made. Nor are all persons equally prone to those situational forces. It follows that those of us concerned with promoting ethically-sound research cultures need to understand what does make people vulnerable to manipulation. As Flanagan puts it: 'locating the source of certain counter-moral tendencies puts us in a position to construct social life in ways that weaken the tendencies and thereby keep them from realizing their damaging potential' (1991, p. 314). Second, a point must be made too about the intellectual virtues Pring alludes to. In his critique of Harman's selective use of scientific data, DePaul notes that Ross and Nesbitt themselves observe how trait-based predictions, favoured by virtue ethicists and folk psychologists alike, in certain circumstances offer 'good prospects for accuracy' (1991, p. 138) across situations: where predictions are based on a 'large, diverse sample of past observations and pertain not to a single action or outcome but to an average expected over the long haul' (*ibid.*). As DePaul concludes, it is likely that this is all reasonable theories of virtue require of the idea of personality traits.[3]

Philosophers in the field of virtue ethics, again particularly inspired by Aristotle, have begun to attend to the role which moral perception can play in moral action. One should note here that there are different versions of the idea of moral perception.[4] Some writers emphasise the role of emotion; on the other hand there are cognitivist theories of ethics and emotions like Kant's where reason plays the role of final authority.[5] Others, such as Sherman, hold that, in her phrase, we 'see through the emotions' (1999, p. 44). And later:

> We can think of them [emotions] as modes of attention enabling us to notice what is morally salient, important, or urgent in ourselves and our surroundings. They help us to track the morally relevant 'news'. They are a medium by which we discern the particulars . . . In addition to their role as modes of attention, emotion plays a role in communicating information to others. They are modes of responding. Putting the two together, emotions become modes both for receiving information and signalling it. Through the emotions we both track and convey what we care about. (1999, p. 40)

It is precisely the spirit of these remarks that drives my own chapter, which brings to the fore the emotion of guilt felt in the conflict of professional obligations and personal commitments. It is not uncommonly the case that when one investigates the life-worlds of teachers or pupils the range of knowledge that comes into one's compass far exceeds that anticipated in the research design.

I discuss the role conflict of the educational researcher who stumbles upon an unprofessional though not illegal relationship between teacher and pupil, highlighting that it is not clear to whom we turn in times of conflict. I draw upon the whistle-blowing literature in related professions to see how it might illuminate the angst felt by a female teacher-researcher in the hypothetical case study I present in my chapter. The first problem the researcher experiences is the multitude of roles that she occupies in the context of her research. She has obligations to the pupil, her colleague and the school. But the sources of value-conflict are not exhausted by other-related obligations. Her projects and commitments, such as her feminist commitments and her career aspirations implicated in the research, create further tensions. I attempt to make clear how the picture here is not reducible to standardisation without remainder. It is this *particular* researcher with the *particular* configuration of obligations and interests that must be addressed.

It is precisely this heightened awareness to particularity that the whistle-blowing literature, with its focus on standard conditions and solutions framed as obligations, misses. Its legalistic notion of the impartial spectator posture and its tests of reasonableness (as if under the aspect of eternity) are irreconcilable with the tests of utility that are also present. I try to draw out why the conflict is felt so deeply by using the notion of 'guilty knowledge': the feelings of guilt that attach when one comes to know of harm visited on innocent others, and has no unqualified sense of which way to act. Each way out of the conflict appears to harm some person or institution. I use the notion of moral salience as opposed to that of decision-theoretic procedure to estimate the significance of the various aspects of the conflict. As Dancy puts it:

> To justify one's choice is to give the reasons one sees for making it, and to give those reasons is just to lay out how one sees the situation, starting in the right place and going on to display the various salient features in the right way; to do this is to fill in the moral horizon. (1993, p. 113)

My chapter does not offer guidance to the researcher as to how she must act. It attends rather to the processes of moral deliberation and shows how the felt guilt is a way of registering the significance of the potential consequences. I draw on Williams's idea that some theoretical perspectives, imbued with a spirit of rationalism, cannot make sense of the idea of a moral cost or moral remainder that is not cancelled even where in good faith one does the 'right thing'. So the space of conflict is taken up by feelings of subjective guilt: one stumbles across wrongdoing, and to prevent it one must harm others. The guilt is a function of sensitive perception of moral significance. By drawing the distinction, after Greenspan (1996), between moral and causal responsibility we can help the researcher see how blame does not necessarily attach to them, whichever option they choose. What we cannot do is have our regret annulled by the corresponding benefits, and indeed it is the recognition of this that shows the ethical maturity of the researcher.

The notion of integrity, clearly at stake in these matters, is taken up in Christopher Winch's chapter. Winch addresses an issue close to the hearts and minds of many educational researchers. If good research is partly characterised by good, virtuous, researchers, then what are the virtues of educational research? Winch argues that issues of accountability are properly framed in deontological language and, second, that the internal professional ethics of educational researchers demands of them certain commitments immanent in the traditions of research. Without specifying particular instances of these professional norms, he asserts that what is entailed in educational research is a commitment to the pursuit of truth, enduring worth, clarity and enlightenment.

Winch argues that in the heated debates about the quality of educational research, unnecessary confusion has arisen because of a failure explicitly to articulate the variety of aims of educational research and the professional responsibilities of those engaged in it. He sets these out as (i) to produce knowledge about education; (ii) to help formulate educational policy; (iii) to improve the workings of education; and (iv) to contribute to radical changes in society. His list, like any list, is open to dispute. What is less open to dispute, in the UK at least, is the increasing dominance of one type of educational research (and by implication, one type of educational researcher too) which merges aims (ii) and (iii) and sidelines the need for, and perceived value of, broader normative pictures about the disputed nature and aims of a worthwhile education. So, although the formulation of educational policy might be conceived of as a primary arena for philosophical exploration of a rather abstract kind (as has been effected famously by Plato, Rousseau and others), it has been hijacked more recently by those who wish to take for granted a *particular* set of educational aims and then to research the most efficient and effective methods by which such aims may be translated into educational practice.

Winch argues that fulfilment of the aim to produce knowledge about education cannot simply issue in a responsibility to generate knowledge that necessarily has immediate application. Despite political and economic demands educational research ought also to feel the pull of standards inherent in the relevant disciplines researchers are committed to and necessarily draw on. Those who press philosophy into the service, for example, of developing codes of professional practice can feel keenly, as Small observes above, their own normative commitments about the nature of ethics and philosophy clashing with a bureaucratic institutional culture that wants easily applied universal rules of conduct. It is here that Winch teases out one very important aspect of professional ethics for educational researchers who receive funds for their work.

It will be clear that anyone who accepts funds to conduct a given research project has a duty *ceteris paribus* to carry out the research to the best of their ability. Again, like Pring above, Winch notes the clear temptation to deliver (at least some of) what the funder wants to hear. While, however, Pring appears to endorse a picture of integrity where the courage to adhere to one's beliefs about the pursuit of truth is particularly prominent, Winch takes a more moderate view, arguing that there is a vice in attempting to hold 'excessively true to oneself'. He implies that this betokens a lack of wisdom: a failure to put one's own normative commitments into a broader context.

What may be most at odds between the two pictures in play here is the level of situatedness that is implicit. Winch oscillates between the idea of educational researchers developing a detached or at least impartial view of their own characteristic biases, whereas Pring and McNamee more consciously foreground the context of conflict in research. What is at least clear is their joint recognition that the conflict that arises does so within *particular* contexts and that the particularity must be foregrounded. Although the various styles of educational research generate and preserve their own partial norms, there are those that will work better than others to promote of the good and the right. Here one cannot stand back from normative critique of particular traditions or paradigms within educational research.

## SCIENTISTIC AND STATISTICAL SEDUCTION

Philosophers of education have characteristically felt under assault by critics who have undermined the value of distinctively philosophical research. David Carr's chapter by contrast presses a deeply sceptical line of argument against empirical educational research. He offers stark contrasts between the values of philosophical reflection on professional practice and those scientifically-oriented scholars for whom the criterion of usefulness is ultimate and for whom the dominance of instrumental reasons goes largely unchallenged. As a foil, he begins with a question concerning the balance between educational theory and practice. Observing the kinds of distinctions philosophers characteristically want to make between the contenders for the title 'theory', and the ambiguities built into everyday understandings of 'professionalism', he disparages the idea that the generalisations of empirical social scientific research have any real value in the face of the untidy particularities of educational practice. He reserves his strongest criticism for those who peddle a technicist line; for research designed to foster the idea that a simple set of pedagogical or management skills can bring teachers and learners the educational goals they aim for.

While research ethics texts across the spectrum of the natural and social sciences characteristically urge a picture of right conduct, Carr looks to the broader normative issues of what constitutes good research more generally. He interrogates with particular effect the inherent normativity of education and thereby of educational research. Much contemporary research, in reducing the act of teaching to neutral, off-the-peg toolkits, robs educational engagements of their depth. It is as if such research is 'a solution in search of a problem' (Olsen cited in Goodin, 1995, p. 5). It makes teaching and learning analogous to car maintenance or other technically-driven modes of action. The point resonates all the way through Dunne's own account of phronesis in education:

> The most crucial clarification about teaching occurs at the level at which we decide what kind of interaction it is. A decision at this level has the heaviest consequences not only for how we understand but also how we go about doing it. The concepts of 'technique' and 'practice' may seem like high level abstractions, but the different orientations that each of them establishes ramify into the most minute details of how a teacher will set about the task. (Dunne, 1993, p. 367)

Carr similarly insists that a richer view of teaching and learning will conceive of the logic of teaching and learning in ways more akin to caring human relations where the clear separation of means and ends is not merely inappropriate but meaningless. It is a folly, he maintains, to suppose that empirical research can 'discover' new modes of teaching and learning. Better to attend to the pre-scientific, pre-theoretical, features that characterise 'normal' human association. It would of course be a truism to say that anyone deprived of trusting, caring and co-operative relations would thereby be disabled in respect of personal development. Nevertheless, attending to the fabric of essentially human relations does not entail empirical enquiry as usually conceived. Thinking through the contours of human association at a general level allows us to perceive at least some of the crucial qualities of human relationships and development that, whether normal or abnormal, authorise a wide range of instantiation. Richard Wollheim (1984, p. xiv) has captured this point succinctly in his remark that 'normality is the name for a tortuously effected and ill-defined achievement'. Conceptions of 'normal' agency do not privilege empirical educational research.

Carr regards much of the 'reflective practitioner' literature as misconceived. Like Pring and others, he believes that practical choices and judgements in research, as in professional practice, ought to be conceived of as phronetic in character. The rich, context-sensitive deliberations required are logically incapable of codification. Their character will be inimical to technical elucidation and hence not susceptible to experimental methods. All educational research, then, that aims at delivering universal skills of pedagogy is in need of unmasking.

The limits of empirical social scientific explanation are explored in a rather different, though still critical, vein by Paul Smeyers. He seeks to unpack philosophically what goes on under the general headings of qualitative and quantitative research and argues that what is required is a form of intellectual modesty. As educational researchers we must understand the limits of forms of explanation at a deeper level. In so doing he makes links between the ethical, broadly conceived, and the philosophy of science.

Smeyers argues that there will always be a suspicion concerning the rigour of qualitative research while respect for law-like explanation still lingers. Such wariness continues to be propagated in subtle fashion by labels like 'hard' and 'soft', or 'natural' and 'human' sciences. A battery of statistical measures, impenetrable to the uninitiated, which sustain a picture of rigour and detached rationality, often supports the hegemonic power of natural science. But the positivistic strain in educational research may well be the product of a deeper longing to explain regularities of behaviour, to predict and to manipulate in accordance with them. And this is not just the folly of politicians or policy-makers who want standardised solutions to educational problems. Sceptics from within and outside educational research have asked whether the proliferation of non-generalisable case studies in the pages of educational journals constitutes a form of intellectual indulgence. Like Carr, Smeyers evokes the Wittgensteinian scepticism towards theories of human conduct. How can we understand fundamental educational questions, such as what is important for human beings, by recourse to scientific analysis? Instead, he argues for a proper recognition of the uniqueness of educational situations, partly constituted by the beliefs and interpretations of the actors in them.

In order to shake a little the foundations of a belief in the quantitative drive in educational researchers, Smeyers presents an extended discussion of the idea of causality in social explanation. He distinguishes between statistical and functional types of explanation and sets out the interplay between causal processes and statistical explanation. He offers a critique of the seduction involved in thinking that if events can be causally *explained* then they are causally *determined*. He goes on to expose the inherent limitations of statistical explanations based on high inductive probability. This, he argues, naturally leads us to the conclusion that different modes of explanation are necessarily required for different domains. Educational research must focus on both the mechanistic and the intentional aspects of human conduct. Understanding what things are like and understanding what they mean or signify entail different modes of research, different framings of problems, different potential solutions. Carr's scepticism towards empirical educational research led him to the conclusion that the resources and mode of analytical philosophy of education had not been fully mined; its death (as it were) had been greatly exaggerated. In contrast, Smeyers notes the fact that as philosophy of education is paying greater attention to the empirical than in the days of analytical hegemony, so too social scientific research is becoming more philosophical.

The impartiality of natural sciences aspiring to the objective 'view from nowhere', as Nagel has put it, is one that is mirrored in the aspirations of traditional moral philosophy. In both sets of views, there exists a powerful taken-for-granted assumption concerning the rationalist background. One of the most pervasive presuppositions of empirical research relates to the core notion of 'data' and how it relates to the idea of a background: the idea of what is 'given' before researchers may meaningfully commence their investigations. This naturalness of the background is the starting point for the final chapter, by Paul Standish.

The 'naturalness' or 'normalness' of the backgrounds of educational research are both diverse and messy by contrast to other more homogenous forms of enquiry such as mathematics. Teasing them out is difficult work and of a kind not normally valued within the instrumental mindset that values only 'useful' external outputs. Standish observes the operation of this mindset in a diverse range of educational contexts, not least in the requirement that doctoral students go through standardised research training régimes comprising generic research skills. Supervisors and research committees frame questions and methods so tightly at the beginning that options are foreclosed, unaware (or uncaring of) how methods determine the reach of data and, more generally, how the ends appear unproblematically to be anticipated by received means and methods.

Like Smeyers, Standish wants to subvert the manipulative and controlling influences of the researcher over the researched, and to challenge the relations between subject and object. He argues that a more respectful and patient attention to the problem can lead to a heightened receptiveness where the problem itself can come partly to lead the researcher. In these situations the quality of passivity dawns upon us, as he puts it; a meaningful picture of ourselves as researcher emerges, as we wait for the words or ideas to flow in and through us. And with this is a deeper picture of research engagement. But the dominant technicist approach to research *training* does not sit easily with such qualities of openness or passivity, nor with the *inefficiency*, the time-costs, of such depth. Standish connects his discussion of openness to the objects of research with the phenomenological tradition's insight into language and meaning. The languages of educational research speak us, he argues. From a proper account of our relations with the backgrounds, the 'grammar' of research as it might be put, must emerge a sense of our humility, as against the shallowness of a background of purportedly value-neutral, effective, ends-neutral educational research.

## DISPARATE VOICES: POLYPHONY NOT CACOPHONY

The aim of this collection was to bring about a collection of voices to situate and problematise the ideas of ethics in the contexts of educational research. It was not an aim to speak in a single voice or even tone. The orchestration of them in this introductory essay has focused more on their resonance than on their discord. It is true that different theoretical commitments to the natures of ethics and educational research can be found here. To this extent there is polyphony. The discord is not so great as to render the collection a cacophony, a metaphor often invoked to describe ethics in a postmodern age.

I remarked in the opening paragraph that there is some, perhaps anachronistic, dispute about standards of conduct and identity in modern professional life for educational researchers. Raimond Gaita has recently remarked how 'People say nowadays that a bit of ethics would do the professions and business some good. The very way they acknowledge the importance of morality appears to highlight its foreignness to their daily concerns. And yet I am reasonably confident that most people's ordinary living is not entirely consistent with this' (1999, p. 6). Non-specialised normative discourse about the quality and shape of our lives called 'ethics' is indeed, I think, properly conceived of as everyday discourse. Unlike Gaita, however, I am not convinced that the conversations of fellow professionals regarding the values of education and educational research are genuinely flourishing in our schools and universities. And this is not unrelated to the difficult times that philosophy of education has been through in recent years. Perhaps philosophers are battle-hardened. Perhaps the arid soil in which they have managed to survive has itself given them the confidence to show the richness of their work.[6]

## NOTES

1. In recent contrast, see the philosophical work of Bridges (1998), Griffiths (1998) and Pring (2000).
2. DePaul (1999) notes that Harman's analysis relies upon the later recounting of the experiment by Ross and Nisbett (1991). A fuller discussion, which situates the Fundamental Attribution Error in a wider arena of social psychological challenges to lay personality theory, is to be found in Flanagan (1991, pp. 276–315).
3. DePaul goes on to defend a Platonic theory of virtue against the empirical research and Harman's construal of it and of virtue theory.
4. Contrast Herman's (1993, pp. 73–93) Kantian account, with Sherman's (1989, pp. 44–50) Aristotelian account and Dancy's particularism (1993, pp. 112–119). See also Bakhurst's (2000, pp. 157–177) attempt to reconcile the particularist Dancy and the virtue-theoretical work of MacIntyre.
5. Though Herman (1997, pp. 115–186), against the tide of more recent writings, attempts a fairer hearing for Kant on virtues and emotions.

## REFERENCES

Adelman, C. (ed.) (1984) *The Politics and Ethics of Evaluation* (London, Croom Helm).

Bakhurst, D. (2000) Ethical particularism in context, in: B. Hooker and M. Little (eds) *Moral Particularism*, pp. 157–177 (Oxford, Oxford University Press).

Bridges, D. (1998) Research for sale: moral market or moral maze?, *British Educational Research Journal*, 24.5, pp. 593–607.

Burgess, R. (ed.) (1989) *The Ethics of Educational Research* (Lewes, Falmer).

Dancy, J. (1993) *Moral Reasons* (Oxford, Blackwell).

Darley, J. M. and Batson, C. D. (1973) From Jerusalem to Jericho: a study of situational and dispositional variables in helping behaviour, *Journal of Personal and Social Psychology*, 27.

DePaul, M. (1998) Character traits, virtues and vices: are there none? Unpublished paper presented at the World Congress of Philosophy. Boston, USA.

Dunne, J. (1993) *Back to the Rough Ground* (Indiana, University of Notre Dame Press).

Flanagan, O. (1991) *Varieties of Moral Personality: Ethics and Psychological Realism* (London, Harvard University Press).

Gaita, R. (1999) *A Common Humanity: thinking about love, truth and justice* (Melbourne, Text Publishing).

Goodin, R. E. (1995) *Utilitarianism as a Public Philosophy* (Cambridge, Cambridge University Press).

Greenspan, P. (1996) *Practical Guilt* (Oxford, Oxford University Press).

Griffiths, M. (1998) *Educational Research for Social Justice: getting off the fence* (Buckingham, Open University Press).

Harman, G. (1999) Moral philosophy meets social psychology: virtue ethics and the fundamental attribution error, *Proceedings of the Aristotelian Society*, Vol. XCIX, pp. 315–332.

Herman, B. (1993) *The Practice of Moral Judgment* (London, Harvard).

Homan, R. (1992) *The Ethics of Social Research* (London, Macmillan).

Jonsen, A. R. and Toulmin, S. (1988) *The Abuse of Casuistry: a history of moral reasoning* (Berkeley, University of California Press).

Milgram, S. (1974) *Obedience to Authority* (London, Tavistock).

Olsen, J. P. (1972) Public policy-making and theories of organisational choice, *Scandianavian Political Studies*, 7, pp. 45–52.

Pring, R. (2000) *Philosophy and Educational Research* (London, Continuum).

Rorty, A. O. (1988) *Mind in Action* (Boston, Beacon Press).

Ross, L. and Nisbett, R. (1991) *The Person and the Situation: strategies and shortcomings of social judgement* (New York, McGraw Hill).

Sherman, N. (1989) *The Fabric of Character: Aristotle's theory of virtue* (Oxford, Clarendon Press).

Sherman, N. (1997) *Making a Necessity of Virtue* (Cambridge, Cambridge University Press).

Sherman, N. (1999) Character development and Aristotelian virtue, in: D. Carr and J. Steutel (eds) *Virtue Ethics and Moral Education*, pp. 35–48 (London, Routledge).

Sieber, J. E. (1992) *Planning Ethically Responsible Research* (London, Sage).

Williams, B. (1985) *Ethics and the Limits of Philosophy* (London, Fontana).

Wollheim, R. (1984) *The Thread of Life* (Cambridge, Cambridge University Press).

# 2

# The Principle of Assumed Consent: the Ethics of Gatekeeping

## ROGER HOMAN

*The obligation to inform and obtain the consent of human subjects is axiomatic in social and medical research. Yet educational researchers are often reluctant to inform their subjects: class teachers and headteachers, for example, are often used as gatekeepers, and investigators sometimes do not so much seek consent as assume it. This chapter discusses the principle of informed consent, in particular that of children. It proposes guidelines for gatekeepers who may be called upon to authorise research and to grant to investigators access to children in their care.*

## I INTRODUCTION: 'GATEKEEPERS'

Gatekeepers are those who give access to a research field. Their role may be in allowing investigators into a given physical space, or it may go further in granting permission for research to be conducted in a particular way. That a project may be deemed legitimate does not mean that the proposed method of enquiry is acceptable: understanding of adolescent smoking habits is useful for the formulation of health-education strategies but it does not follow that investigators should be given permission to spy on teenagers in private places. In an organisation such as a factory or business a manager might give access to the building but it would be unlikely for such a person to consent to the conduct of interviews without in some way consulting the employees, let alone fellow managers whose experience may yield a specialist insight and more informed judgement of consequences for the reputation of the company. Prior consultation with respondents, however, is often by-passed in educational research, especially where children are concerned: the view may be taken that children would not understand what is being asked of them or it may be that headteachers and others regard the interests and rights of children to be invested in themselves. In educational research, then, it is frequently the case that the principle of informed consent, which is central to the ethical control of all social research, is directed not at those whose behaviour is the subject of an enquiry but at one who takes a decision on their behalf. It is not uncommon that this is the very person who is conducting the research. Consent is assumed rather than informed.

In the context of educational research, moreover, the very concept of gatekeeper is more complex than this. First, there is often the problem inherent in insider research that the investigator may draw upon data observed and banked, whether systematically or unconsciously, in the course of experience prior to the start of the enquiry. At that stage the status of the consent of participants would not have been informed, nor would their participation have been willing. Second, pupils are themselves made the unwitting gatekeepers to fields that are spatially removed from that of the interview or questionnaire but are in educational terms proximate to it: they may reveal data relating to their home and family, or to previous classroom experience and teachers, or to relationships within the peer group. The younger children are the more candid and trusting they may be and the less defensive of their privacy: those who have worked in infant classrooms will know that much of the information that is offered exceeds that which is sought. Gatekeeping in these circumstances is implicit, invisible and consequently little regarded in the literature of educational research. This chapter, therefore, is about vicarious and assumed consent. It is about the assumption of the right to grant or withhold consent by those who are not the subjects of research.

## II    INFORMED CONSENT

### The principle

The principle of informed consent is a standard feature of ethical procedure in social research. It is the requirement that human subjects be informed of the nature and implications of research and that participation be voluntary. In educational research, as we shall demonstrate below, this is widely compromised. The entitlement to give or withhold consent is often assumed by gatekeepers such as headteachers. If in schools there is a belief that children would not understand, in universities there may be an expectation that students will participate in research by tutors that compromises the right to decline.

Informed consent is a standard principle in a variety of professional practices as well as social research: it is the formulation of a widely recognised moral obligation to respect others and take into account their interests. Its intention is to ensure that human subjects are aware that they are taking part in research with all its hazards and that their participation is voluntary. The principle comes to social and behavioural research from medical practice. Its formulation in the Nuremberg Code was prompted by the revelation that internees of concentration camps had been regarded as legitimate research subjects for non-therapeutic investigations; some prisoners of war, for example, had been partly frozen in the course of a research project on frost-bite. Distanced by time, place, social setting and professional culture, most if not all educational and social researchers would be alarmed by such a research procedure. But it demonstrates a feature of many kinds of research with human subjects: there is a tendency of investigators to justify the methods they choose on the basis of an anticipated beneficial outcome and not in terms of the inconvenience or harm suffered by their subjects. Pupils or students taking part or declining to take part in research may not be frozen in the physical sense but, as we shall see, a number of harmful effects may ensue; they may suffer the loss of educational time; they may emerge from research with depressed self-esteem, or be corrupted by the nature of the enquiry. The spirit of the Nuremberg Code of 1946 is therefore highly applicable to educational research:

> The voluntary consent of the human subject is absolutely essential. This means that the person involved should have legal capacity to give consent, should be so situated as to be able to exercise free power of choice without the intervention of any element of force, fraud, deceit, duress, over-reaching or any other form of constraint or coercion; and should have sufficient knowledge and comprehension of the elements of the subject matter involved as to enable him to make an understanding and enlightened decision. (Reynolds, 1982, p. 143)

Fraud and deceit might well be identified in misleading information given in order to secure consent: investigators may ask to be granted a couple of minutes when they mean half an hour or express interest in recreational activities because they know that mention of sex and drugs might affect the response rate. There are few in modern times who would adopt the strategy of Henle and Hubble (1938) who concealed themselves under students' beds in order to record their conversations and measure the incidence of egocentricity; however, there are more subtle ways in which students are rendered powerless to refuse. Duress and coercion may be found where tutors who have responsibility for the pastoral care and assessment of students ask them to take part in their own research projects: objectivity could be compromised as much by this kind of favour as by consensual relationships.

For operational purposes the principle of informed consent may be expressed in four elements, two that relate to the processes of informing and two that relate to the voluntariness of the consenting party:

*Informed*

1. That all pertinent aspects of what is to occur and what might occur are disclosed to the subject;
2. that the subject should be able to comprehend this information.

*Consent*

3. That the subject is competent to make a rational and mature judgement;
4. that the agreement to participate should be voluntary, free from coercion and undue influence.
(Homan, 1991, p. 71)

Of course, the benefits of educational research are reckoned to be such that we need not wait for subjects to achieve maturity of judgement and comprehension of research purpose and procedures: vicarious judgements are made by parents or more usually by teachers acting *in loco parentis.*

*Implications for gatekeepers*

Those who give clearance for children or students to go scrambling over cliffs or canoeing or pot-holing exercise responsibilities at two levels. First, they give their consent that young people visit a particular environment. Second, they judge that those instructors to whom their students will be entrusted are skilled and responsible professionals. Such are the known hazards of outdoor pursuits that schools no longer take the responsibility upon themselves: the advised practice is to inform parents of risks and to secure their written agreement to participation (Department for Education, 1994; United Kingdom Activity Centre Advisory Committee, 1994). The gatekeepers of educational environments who agree to the conduct of educational research exercise similar responsibilities: they grant the investigators access and trust in their professional care and motives. Seldom, perhaps, do they appreciate how comparable are the hazards and how enduring may be the effects. Indeed, it is unlikely that researchers entering fields with which they are not previously acquainted will be poorly qualified to estimate attendant hazards. The purpose of this chapter, then, is to indicate the range and gravity of gatekeepers' responsibilities and to suggest measures that they might take before granting consent.

## III  CODES OF PRACTICE

### The operation of codes

A common feature of ethical codes is the pivotal role of the principle of informed consent. Many of the other protocols are regarded to be enshrined in it. Privacy, it is supposed, will not be intruded if the subject is given appropriate information including the entitlement to defend it by declining to take part. Covert research is precluded by the very informing of consent and deception will not occur if the information given is honest. So it is thought. But in practice the process of informed consent is a way of dodging some of the responsibilities that are laid upon researchers elsewhere in the codes. Once a subject who is informed of a particular risk agrees to participate, investigators may feel that their moral duty has been discharged: the subject's signature on a piece of paper may be held to indemnify the researcher. And once subjects know that research is being conducted and participation is voluntary, the investigator may deploy trained skills to penetrate the private domain unnoticed. In these cases the informing of consent is an abdication of responsibility rather than an honouring of it.

The giving of consent by gatekeepers, however, is a different kind of problem. The requirements of the codes are satisfied in the sense that consent has been informed and granted, albeit not by the subjects who are thereby deceived. The gatekeeper is in a position to rule that the principle of informed consent, upon which the professional bodies and university research committees set such store, need not apply. In educational research, gatekeeper and investigator may for contrary reasons agree to exempt themselves from informing pupils of the nature of research: the gatekeeper feels an entitlement to act *in loco parentis* while the investigator (for example, Wiener 1970 cited below) may merely desire private data that would be distorted if subjects were fully aware of the form of the enquiry.

### Ethics in educational research

For all that the codes elaborate a broad agenda of ethical issues, the published reports of educational research barely touch on the way these are resolved in practice. Articles in the *British Educational*

*Research Journal* commonly include a Methods section, but it invariably has to do with principles of quantitative analysis rather than issues relating to the engaging and informing of human subjects. In 250 pages of the recent *Inside the Primary Classroom* (Galton *et al.*, 1999) there is a single line of thanks to the teachers and pupils who gave free access and the only methodology is a short appendix on training in systematic observation techniques.

## IV   ISSUES IN EDUCATIONAL RESEARCH

### Costs and hazards

One of the arguments of this paper, issuing in the advice that gate-keeping requires proper training, is that the hazards of educational research are rather more varied and problematic than is commonly supposed. Our purpose here is to illustrate some of the habits and effects that persist even when the requirement of informed consent in its codified form is satisfied.

*Corruption.* School and family have evolved their own ways of controlling and phasing the exposure of young people to the outside world. Peer groups, some media and some educational researchers may rush in where angels and covert researchers fear to tread. So Udry and Billy (1987, p. 852) asked children aged 11 and above how often they experienced sexual intercourse. The problem was not that they failed to adopt the normal procedures: in fact, they were utterly scrupulous in informing and obtaining the written consent of parents, even visiting the homes of all 1405 of their potential respondents (Udry and Billy, 1987, p. 844). The issue relating to this project is rather that there is a message being conveyed even in the asking of the question: while we may suppose that a majority of eleven-year olds are not sexually active, the innocent will suppose that such activity must be current in their age-group or else the question would not have been asked.

*Privacy.* One of the grounds on which subjects might decline to participate is that they would not want to reveal private data or admit a researcher into a private domain. Sometimes subjects are inveigled into disclosures they might subsequently regret. Interviewers and those who design questionnaires are skilled practitioners trained by the methods manuals to soften reluctant subjects and to place sensitive questions where they will meet least resistance (Denzin and Lincoln, 2000, p. 660). Furthermore, private places often have more than one resident but the consent of only one is necessary to give a researcher access to the data that belong to it. For example, those completing a questionnaire for Shere Hite (1977) found themselves giving details of the habits of their sexual partners: her subjects agreed to be respondents but functioned as informants. By definition a social field has more than one occupant and each may control a gate to it. What is at issue, we suggest, is a matter of child protection: researchers who approach children with open-ended designs and exploit whatever data they elicit fail in a moral responsibility to respect the privacy of the child and home and to support the child in safeguarding it.

Children are particularly susceptible to intrusions of private space and behaviour by researchers. In the course of his classic study Kinsey and his collaborators relaxed his eight-year old subjects with games, puzzles and 'romping' before asking them intimate questions (Kinsey, Poleroy and Martin, 1948, p. 58). These days, romping is not advised, but children are still vulnerable to invasions. Those who take part in studies of learning to read may be asked about how, when and what they read at home and about other ways in which time at home is occupied: indeed, child interviewees may volunteer such data even if they are not asked. The effective subjects of such studies are not only the children but also those who control their time at home. This has at least two implications for our understanding of the nature of gatekeeping. First, the member of a school staff who admits researchers is giving access not merely to the classroom where the enquiry is conducted but to the homes of the children; the gatekeeper can hardly claim to be acting *in loco parentis* if the parents are in a significant way the subjects of the study. Second, the child who is invited to give information concerning family or home becomes the gatekeeper of that private space, exercising discretion on what to reveal and what to withhold: this is a considerable responsibility and there may be many instances in which private data about third parties are disclosed within a trusting relationship.

There is a particular issue concerning the use of video-recording. It is likely that the intending observer and the subjects to be observed will have very different estimations of what is visible. The trained observer will have a repertoire of psychological techniques, on the basis of which meanings are attached to body language, twiddling of the fingers, playing with a pencil, movements of the eye, adjustments of the seating position. Little do subjects know when they or their proxies give consent how much of their private life can be discerned in their public behaviour. Nor, even, would those conducting field research know at the time what data they are collecting: Marshall and Rosman (1989, p. 86) commend film as a method of data collection because:

It can be used in the future to take advantage of new methods of seeing, analyzing and understanding the process of change. Film is an aid to the researcher when the nature of what is sought is known but the elements of it cannot be discovered because of the limitations of the human eye.

If the nature of data is unknown even to the investigator—and thus to the gatekeeper—at the time of collection, the ethic of informing consent is a poor safeguard of privacy: what is also needed is a developed sense of moral responsibility on the part of researchers themselves.

A further aspect of the invasion of privacy is the access afforded to observed and recorded data. Teachers conducting investigations in their own professional environments may grant themselves access to data collected under another warrant or when the defences were down and may use such received data in sampling as well as in analysis.

*Time out.* While subjects may learn something as a result of participation in a study, it remains the case that research often encroaches upon time normally allocated to more formal teaching and learning. Hence there is a cost in educational terms that must be set against such incidental learning and against whatever bnefits the research itself brings.

*Emotional harm.* In the post-war period the case of behavioural research to have attracted the most consistent and universal condemnation has probably been that of Stanley Milgram (1974). Milgram's subjects knew that they were taking part in a research project but believed that they were administrating the experiment, not being the subjects of it. Having, as they thought, inflicted severe electric shocks upon innocent subjects, they discovered tendencies in themselves that caused them subsequent discomfort: one of Milgram's well-composed subjects was observed to be reduced to a 'twitching stuttering wreck who was rapidly approaching a point of nervous collapse' (Abse, 1973, p. 30). Such after-effects are not widely recognised in educational research. One of the better-known cases of an investigation which could have done emotional damage to child participants is the Oak School experiment reported in the classic study *Pygmalion in the Classroom* (Rosenthal and Jacobson, 1968). In these experiments teachers were asked to have high expectations of a randomly selected group of pupils: those not selected in this way may have suffered long-term effects, in terms of their own expectations and achievements, and perhaps diminished self-esteem, because of the way they were treated by their teachers.

*The myth of voluntariness.* Because consent is sought and because participants are entitled to withhold, it is supposed that participation is voluntary. It becomes fashionable to honour participants by referring to them as *partners in research* instead of *subjects*. Often this vocabulary expresses an ideal rather than a reality. Consent is given in a fleeting moment at the outset of an enquiry. Thereafter a bond of loyalty is cultivated, defences are broken down, the subject is made to feel that all is in a good cause that will be lost if there is a withdrawal from later questions: subjects may even forget that they are being observed. The skills of field researchers are thus deployed to render the subjects less conscious of the continuing research.

Research with children and students is often attended by factors or conditions that give the lie to the voluntariness of participation. Where the investigator is a member of teaching staff, the bond between researcher and subject may not need to be cultivated. Children and students may respond willingly to a request to help their teacher. Testing and the completion of questionnaires may be indistinguishable from routine classroom assignments. Apprehensions and inhibitions may be overcome for fear of being regarded as unco-operative and affecting the teacher–student relationship outside the research act. Such considerations as these bear upon the granting of consent; while students are formally free to withhold consent, the psychological and emotional reality is that freedom is compromised.

## Consent by children

Stephen Ball barely exaggerates when he views current practice in educational research and observes, 'No one consults the children' (1985, p. 39). The procedure for informing consent and for making it clear that participation is voluntary is often suspended in research with children. The guidelines of the British Educational Research Association recommends a 'respect for democratic values' in which participants are entitled to be informed but the right of approval or disapproval rests with teachers or parents:

> Care should be taken when interviewing children and students up to school leaving age: permission should be obtained from the school and, if they so suggest, parents.

The motives for declining to consult child participants are complex and many of them would apply equally in research with adults.

First, it is reckoned—and with good reason—that the quantity of information will affect the rate and disposition of response. The more individuals know about what is involved the less inclined they will be to take part. If investigators want to learn about adolescents' experiences of sex, drugs and substance abuse, they had better say that they were doing a survey on 'leisure'; and a self-completion questionnaire for secondary school children that includes items on religion, country of origin and residence in Britain may be introduced:

> This is a project about language. We are trying to find out how people learn and use different languages and we hope you may be able to help us. (Linguistic Minorities Project, 1983, p. 65)

The telling of a 'cover story' (McNeill, 1985, p. 61) and the avoidance of such elements in an enquiry as will deter participants are standard advice in the methods manuals and a normal practice in questionnaire design (Homan, 1991, pp. 76–77; 1992, p. 327). The fear of refusal may even incline investigators or gatekeepers to avoid seeking consent. At 'Bishop McGregor school' there was a history of negative responses to letters that had been sent out to parents: Robert Burgess (1984, p. 196) wanted to send an explanatory letter to parents but the headteacher took the granting of consent upon himself.

There is also concern that the informing of consent may lead to responses that are 'reactive', that is, they may be significantly affected by awareness of the nature of the research. If children know what the researcher is getting at, they may offer 'creative' responses to please and confirm expectations (or still more creative responses to confound them). Adults may do this too, of course, but it is in research with children especially that this is taken to provide a rationale for restricting the amount of information that is given, that is, for compromising the informing of consent, as the following statements indicate:

> We would prefer the children not to have any previous information about the subject matter of the survey as this could influence their replies and I should be obliged if you could ask any members of your staff whose timetable might be interrupted not to mention the main purpose of our visit to the children. (Wiener, 1970, p. 218)

> Because of the experimental nature of the tests, basic principles of test construction do not permit us to discuss the test or test scores either with parents or the children themselves. (Rosenthal and Jacobson, 1968, p. 66)

And Ball quotes Lynda Measor's words: 'I asked that no introduction be made about me. I didn't want teachers telling kids what I was' (Ball, 1985, p. 40). Ironically, though, the possibility of a reactive response may be greater with adults than with children because of their greater sophistication. None of this alters the fact that, if to be informed and to choose whether or not to participate are rights, we have to ask why they are differentially accorded to adults and children.

Investigators may value an hour of classroom time too highly to occupy much of it with detailed explanations and answering the inevitable questions. A standard procedure with adults is to give prior written notice and information but this habit is unusual in classroom research.There is a perceived likelihood that children will not understand the nature or purpose of research even if it is explained carefully: the British Psychological Society (2000, pp. 8–9), for example, brackets children with 'participants who have impairments that will limit understanding and/or communication such that they are unable to give their real consent'.

Whatever the personal motives of educational researchers, their outward justification is to be gaining insights that will benefit teachers and learners. Respect for truth and the right to know may thus overwhelm respect for any potential respondents who are inclined to obstruct. The sense that there is a greater good in educational research than the entitlement of pupils to opt out is often shared by gatekeepers such as headteachers who give vicarious consent for investigators to proceed.

Furthermore, it is arguable that children are not the subjects of classroom research: they only happen to be there at the time. The investigation, it might be supposed, is not about children but about some aspect of learning such as motivation or special needs, or about a curriculum area like mathematics or numeracy. The focus of Wheldall (2000) is not upon the forty low-progress readers who submitted to a battery of assessments, but upon the effectiveness of a particular literacy intervention programme. The children in Year 6 interviewed by Reay and Willam (1999) are the source of the data but ultimately the subject of their study is the ritual of assessment and its impact upon the self-esteem of pupils: even the comment by Hannah in that study—'I'll be a nothing'—is there to tell us not about Hannah but about the impact of impending SATs.

The reverse is also true: where children and students are the subject of research, however, they are not always directly involved. Studies that are said to be of teachers' attitudes, views or perceptions may draw upon the mediated 'experience' of teachers—that is, upon years of covert observation by teachers acting in role, not knowing that they were collecting data and therefore not informing their students that they were being researched. Such studies use teachers as surrogate informants. It is recognised that these studies will depend upon teachers' constructions of reality rather than those of the investigator, but some data may nevertheless remain fairly raw. The use of demographic and secondary data and of records of which at least some are in the public domain allows the remote study of groups of students: by these means we have research findings on students enrolling for mathematics degrees (Kitchen, 1999) and the effects of birth-season and sex on the assessment of children with special educational needs in an English comprehensive school (Wilson, 2000). The use of statistical data that were not originally collected for research purposes is common in this kind of research.

The reluctance of educational researchers to seek the informed consent of children contrasts sharply with prevailing practice in medicine and health care where there has evolved a different attitude to the competence of minors. The high-profile Gillick case in the mid-1980s issued in an important judgement. Mrs Gillick, concerned that girls under 16 might seek contraceptive advice without involving parents, wanted a judgement that such girls could not make competent decisions for themselves. The judgement forthcoming was that competence was not a matter of age but of maturity. In 1990 the Department of Health ruled that parents could not prevail over a competent child declining treatment (Montgomery, 2001, p. 178). The 1989 Children's Act for England and Wales continually makes the point that adults must take account of the feelings and views of children; 'if the child is of sufficient understanding to make an informed decision, he may refuse to submit to a medical or psychiatric examination or other assessment' (Part V Section 43 (8)).

On the basis of interviews with child patients, Priscilla Alderson argues forcefully that children are much wiser than they are given credit for and that parents and professionals claiming to act in their interests are not always benign:

> Consent or refusal, the act of exercising self-determination, is the key to all other rights. Many adults are loath to entrust the right to children because of old prejudices that minors cannot make informed, wise decisions. Low expectations are self-fulfilling, continually reinforcing beliefs in adults and children that it is unwise and unkind to entrust children with major decisions. High expectations are self-fulfilling, encouraging children to develop mature competence. (Alderson, 1993, p. 190)

## V   CONCLUSION: FIVE BARS FOR GATEKEEPERS

The notion that educational research is not about the observation of pupils and students but about the collection of data they happen to bear is problematic. If it is held to excuse the securing of consent, it may equally justify the intrusion of private space: the tapping of adolescents' telephone calls may be said to be acceptable if all the investigator wants to do is to quantify the use of subordinate clauses.

In December 1999 the *Daily Sport* newspaper printed photographs of the Prime Minister's son and other young people at a seasonal social function called the 'Mistletoe Ball'; it then used such headlines as 'Don't look, Mum' and 'Teenage toffs get raging horn'. This publication was referred by Downing Street to the Press Complaints Commission. On 22 December 1999 the *Sport* defended its action on the grounds that its photographer was invited by the organisers of the event to take photographs there. The responsibility for intrusion and even for publication was thus said to lie with the gatekeeper. Whether or not such a defence is convincing, it is an indication of the way in which investigators may believe that the one who gives permission accepts responsibility. In view of the nature of responsibility borne by gatekeepers, it is appropriate to formulate and discuss a number of principles that they might usefully observe.

## *Insider researchers should not be their own gatekeepers*

The effect of the principle of seeking the consent of human participants in research is to mark a boundary, not merely in spatial terms but in terms of the delineation of data. A community such as a classroom or school is closed to the outside world, but offers relative freedom to resident professionals. They will be inclined to perceive that community as a public domain and suppose that they have an entitlement to all its data. Teachers have a privileged access to, for example, children's chronological ages, family backgrounds, friendship patterns, achievement scores and reputations. But these data have not been acquired as research data and the usual procedure of informing consent did not apply before enquiry, testing or observation. There are, moreover, issues of validity and accountability that are raised when an enquiry is founded upon a history of acquaintance and subliminal observation not available to an outsider.

A number of points may be made against the adoption of this principle. There is a public interest argument in favour of enriching research by whatever means: the long-term good of children and their education is less likely to be well served if exclusions are made upon privileged insights. Nor is the classroom the only situation in which insightful research may rest upon the foundation of a common experience or a privileged bond: Janet Finch (1984) demonstrates the possibility that researchers who are women may elicit a richer response from women subjects.

## *In licensing research, gatekeepers should avoid acting exclusively in the professional interests of themselves, their colleagues or their collaborators, or upon the assumption that an overriding public good is to be served by their enquiry*

The case of the headteacher who gave his own consent rather than risk the refusal of parents makes the point. Such are the economic conditions and pressures in which educational researchers operate in the present time that they may be motivated less by a desire to serve the public good by measuring the correlation between two variables than they are by a personal desire to secure further employment under a research contract or to publish a book or paper or to obtain a university degree by dissertation or to bring credit upon the institutions that employ them. The pursuit of one's own career or the loyalty to a colleague in such a pursuit may engender in the gatekeeper an unbalanced view of the probable costs and risks of an enquiry against its beneficial outcomes.

We can also envisage circumstances in which the interests of pupils may be served by research but where a disservice is done to the school. A school in the process of correcting some shortcoming may want to spare itself too close and uncomfortable a scrutiny, even though such an appraisal might illuminate the needs of its pupils.

### *Responsible gatekeeping is not for the untrained*

The formal authority for granting or refusing access to a research field may reside with a member of a management group, a head or deputy, a head of department or senior teacher. With the benefit of hindsight we can see that Milgram's subjects let themselves in for disturbed nights and that half of the children who took part in the *Pygmalion in the Classroom* study may be going through life with lower self-esteem or an aversion to formal education. Milgram himself was blamed for not taking the advice of experienced professionals who could have foreseen the personal consequences of his experiments (Baumrind, 1964). If one whose business is research cannot foresee consequences, it is arguably unfair to expect such foresight of a member of a school or college management group who may have no experience of research practice. He or she needs to be aware of the kinds of hazard that attend educational research, to have learned the lessons of the mistakes of other practitioners and to consider imaginatively the possible consequences of the enquiry being proposed. The moral responsibilities of allowing research among children and students are grave and it is therefore not surprising that professionals should look for codes that will indemnify them.

### *Gatekeepers should not unload the ultimate responsibility upon those who cannot assess consequences, notably children and parents*

The informing of participants on the nature, purpose and implications of research is a widely established ethical protocol. It should be seen as an addition to the exercise of moral judgement by those conducting research, not as a substitute. Participants are not in a position to give consent to a procedure of which not even the investigator may foresee the consequences; to elicit such consent and to interpret it as clearance for an enquiry to continue, therefore, is an abdication of moral responsibility.

There are further complications in the requirement of consent by participants who are students or pupils normally taught by the investigator. It may be that an attitude of trust or loyalty or a climate of reciprocal favour is made to apply in the giving of consent. Pupils may overcome apprehension or misgivings only because in other situations the teacher has secured their trust. Students or parents of pupils may be disinclined to refuse to participate for fear of losing favour or gaining a reputation for being unco-operative. Compliance with a teacher's research in a situation associated with the assessment of work may be compared with compliance in consensual relationships, on which many guidelines have been written.

*Gatekeepers called upon to grant consent should not act without considering carefully the reasons why that entitlement is being withheld from the subjects themselves*

Since the giving or withholding of consent is perceived as the right of human subjects of research, gatekeepers should endeavour to act in empathy with the subject and not in the interests of the investigator. There might be a legitimate case for withholding such information as would have a reactive effect upon the data: the explanation 'We are really looking at your sentence structures' so closely resembles the way in which a teacher might formulate a specific target that respondents would be likely to try hard to please at a time when the investigator could be looking for the norm. On the other hand, the withholding from parents of a questionnaire about children's reading habits might not be justifiable on the grounds that it is a survey of provisions at home using children as informants.

The purpose of this paper has been to explore ethical issues relating to the role of gatekeepers and its conclusions in that regard are set out above. There is evidence that researchers' ethical obligations lapse when they work with children. At a time when the autonomy of the child is stressed in statutory provisions and guidelines, there is a risk that educational researchers may by default dishonour the rights of children as research participants: they may betray the trust of children and collect confidential data, they may assume a right of access to school records, they may exploit children as surrogate informants, they may use their power to withhold information about the research to which adults would be entitled.

*Correspondence:* Professor R E Homan, School of Education, University of Brighton, Falmer, East Sussex BN1 9PH, UK. Email: r.homan@bton.ac.uk

## REFERENCES

Abse, Daniel (1973) *The Dogs of Pavlov* (London, Valentine Mitchell).

Alderson, Priscilla (1993) *Children's Consent to Surgery* (Buckingham, Open University Press).

Ball, S. J. (1985) Participant observation with pupils, in: Robert Burgess (ed.) *Strategies of Educational Research: Qualitative Methods*, pp. 23–53 (Lewes, Falmer).

Baumrind, Diana (1964) Some thoughts on ethics of research: after reading Milgram's 'Behavioral study of obedience', *American Psychologist*, 19, pp. 421–423.

British Psychological Society (2000) *Code of Conduct, Ethical Principles and Guidelines* (Leicester, British Psychological Society).

Burgess, Robert (1984) *In the Field: an Introduction to Field Research* (London, Allen & Unwin).

Denzin, Norman K. and Lincoln, Yvonna S. (eds) (2000) *Handbook of Qualitative Research*, 2nd edition (London, Sage).

Department for Education (1994) Safety in Outdoor Courses, Guidance *Circular 22/94* (London, DfE).

Finch, Janet (1984) 'It's great to have someone to talk to': the ethics and politics of interviewing women, in: C. Bell and H. Roberts (eds) *Social Researching: Politics, Problems and Practice*, pp. 70–87 (London, Routledge).

Galton, Maurice, Hargreaves, Linda, Comber, Chris and Wall, Debbie (1999) *Inside the Primary Classroom: 20 Years On* (London, Routledge).

Henle, M. and Hubble, M. B. (1938) Egocentricity in adult conversations, *Journal of Social Psychology*, pp. 227–234.

Hite, Shere (1977) *The Hite Report: a Nationwide Study of Female Sexuality* (London, Tammy Franklin).

Homan, Roger (1991) *The Ethics of Social Research* (London, Longman).

Homan, Roger (1992) The ethics of open methods, *British Journal of Sociology*, 43(3), pp. 321–332.

Kinsey, A. C., Poleroy, W. B. and Martin, C. E. (1948) *Sexual Behaviour in the Human Male* (Philadelphia, Saunders).

Kitchen, Ann (1999) The changing profile of entrants to mathematics at A level and to mathematical subjects in higher education, *British Educational Research Journal*, 25(1), pp. 57–74.

Linguistic Minorities Project (1983) *Linguistic Minorities in England: a Report by the Linguistic Minorities Project for the Department of Education of Education and Science* (London, University of London Institute of Education).

McNeill, P. (1985) *Research Methods* (London, Tavistock).

Milgram, Stanley (1974) *Obedience to Authority* (London, Tavistock).

Marshall, Catherine and Rosman, Gretchen B. (1989) *Designing Social Research* (London, Sage).

Montgomery, Jonathan (2001) 'Informed consent and clinical research with children', in: Len Doyal and Jeffrey S. Tobias (eds) *Informed Consent in Medical Research*, pp. 173–181 (London, BMJ Books).

Reay, Diane and Willam, Dylan (1999) 'I'll be a nothing': structure, agency and the construction of identity through assessment, *British Educational Research Journal*, 25(3), pp. 343–354.

Reynolds, P. D. (1982) *Ethics and Social Science Research* (Englewood Cliffs NJ, Prentice-Hall).

Rosenthal, Robert and Jacobson, Lenore (1968) *Pygmalion in the Classroom: Teacher Expectations and Pupils' Intellectual Development* (New York, Holt Rinehart).

Stacey, Margaret (1980) *Methods of Social Research* (Oxford, Pergamon).

Udry, J. R. and Billy, J. O. G. (1987) Initiation of coitus in early adolescence, *American Sociological Review*, 52, pp. 841–855.

United Kingdom Activity Centre Advisory Committee (1994) Outdoor Adventure Activity Procedures: code of practice (London, ACAC).

Wheldall, Kevin (2000) Does Rainbow Repeated Reading add value to an intensive literacy intervention program for low-progress readers? An experimental evaluation, *Educational Review*, 52(1), pp. 29–36.

Wiener, R. S. P. (1970) *Drugs and Schoolchildren* (London, Longman).

Wilson, Geoffrey (2000) The effects of season of birth, sex and cognitive abilities on the assessment of special educational needs, *Educational Psychology*, 20(2), pp. 153–166.

# 3

# Opening Windows, Closing Doors: Ethical Dilemmas in Educational Action Research

LES TICKLE

*The chapter records personal accounts of the author's dealings with dilemmas encountered in the research methods literature and in the field of practice, as an action researcher and teacher educator. It draws on Mary Chamberlain's* Fenwomen *to illustrate some of the dangers of ethnographic research. Using data from two instances, one in a pre-service initial teacher-training programme and the other in teacher induction, the author draws out the tensions between the 'need to know' in order to act professionally, and the 'need to protect' in order to do the same.*

## INTRODUCTION: RESEARCHER ACTION

A memorable but little known piece of research that continues to serve me as an exemplar when teaching about research methods, as well as serving as a guardian against wrong-footedness or wrong-doing in my work with teachers, is Mary Chamberlain's *Fenwomen* (Chamberlain, 1983). This oral history was written explicitly from a feminist perspective, in order to give voice to the women of Isleham village in Cambridgeshire, to allow women to speak for themselves through the research:

> The woman's story must be told, but it must be seen in a perspective of its own. In our present society she cannot compete on the same page as the ploughboy. (*ibid.* 1983, p. 12)

The research is ethnographic and politically activist, and is literary and poetic in its presentation. Captivating description sets the scene, and reflects the emotional agenda of the author:

> Black fen they call it round here. Black for the dark peaty soil; black for the mood of the area, for its history and for its future. (1983, p. 11)

The methodological justifications offered are succinct: stories of the women stand as extracts from life histories, testimonies that 'appeared intact and related to individuals . . . as well as a class of experience' (1983, p. 1). This is research that exemplifies the hermeneutic principle and methodological standpoint of researchers who wear their prejudices on their sleeves rather than pretending to objectivity. It is a case that tests out the principles of reflection and action upon the world in order to transform it, and of feminism's re-visioning of the man-made world (Crotty, 1998, pp. 151, 160). Mary Chamberlain was explicit about her part in seeking to change the lives of the women of Isleham, and clear about wanting to articulate their experiences. Giving them voice was her means of an (albeit maternalistic) attempt to empower them, by acting on their behalf.

Educators also operate as activists intent on bringing about change in, and sometimes on behalf of, those they serve. They engage in practical action aimed at achieving ends intended to benefit those they educate. In the field of action research, Carr and Kemmis (1986), Elliott (1991), Schon (1983), Sockett (1994), McKernan (1991) and others have argued that because educational activity aims to bring about beneficial change, and because the nature of practices which realise those aims are inevitably value-driven, the process of reflexivity constitutes a particular kind of research, a process of *praxis*. This is educational engagement which bonds practical pursuit of what is good with deliberation directed towards 'the discernment of right ends' (Carr, 2000, p. 75). Deliberation about both the aims and the means of education is intended to develop practical wisdom. Here, just as in Mary Chamberlain's work, researcher and activist go hand in hand, in the same person, and it is in that spirit that I see my own work as a teacher, teacher educator, and action researcher.

## CONSENT, CONFIDENTIALITY AND TRUST

In the second edition of her book, Mary Chamberlain celebrated the approach that she had adopted with a number of justifications: the foregrounding of her politicised partiality; the use of oral history as consistent with the women's movement's usual means of communicating their life-stories; because it is the only way of discovering some aspects of the past; because of its integrity in using individuals' memories and stories for the capturing of human experience such as anguish, bitterness and joy; and because of the poetics and the politics of the approach, the 'magic and melody of words' and the 'silences and highlights, the confusions and distortions' of what is not just a description but 'a discourse'. These qualities are celebrated for their potential to create democratic history through the participation of the common people in the process of authoring the history. For these and other reasons, Mary Chamberlain claimed, rightly in my view, that such methods are uniquely powerful. It is these qualities that create an exemplar for my research methods courses.

Nevertheless she also reports how the power got out of hand, as celebrations of a rather different kind were held in the weekly national tabloid *News of the World*, known for its coverage of gossip and scandal, and the regional daily *Cambridge Evening News*, with its coverage of local events and personalities. Even prior to the publication of the book, a different view of the nature and substance of the research was out. Headline stories about village love-lives, sex and family secrets were written by journalists with their own purposes and audiences in mind. There was harrying of villagers by the press. Mary Chamberlain recorded in her preface that the women of the village who had trusted her were outraged.

Sympathetic political and scholarly intentions towards the women who had revealed their stories had been turned into hurtful events and experiences as the revelations were interpreted and reinterpreted in the public domain. The identity of the village, which was barely anonymised as Gislea in the book, had been easily detected. The identities of individuals living there, with personal details recorded and photographs of village life included as illustrations, were not difficult for reporters to uncover. It is this part of the story which serves as the warning against wrong-footedness or wrongdoing in my own and my students' research. It is a warning which hangs mainly on the relationship between the aims of the researcher and the methodological principles which are adopted in the conduct of the research, especially with regard to power in the control, use and distribution of data.

Whatever social contract had been negotiated by Mary Chamberlain, or understood by the women of the village, it is evident from the preface to the second edition of *Fenwomen* that the ethical intentions of the scholar, in terms of both her activist aims and her research procedures, were badly let down either by misunderstanding about the conditions under which the data were obtained and what the women had consented to, or by pernicious populist journalism. Whichever it was, it appears that three key conditions of the ethnographer, the use of confidentiality, anonymity and openness, were in tension in Isleham/Gislea. It seems that these conditions were muddled, or their boundaries transgressed, in a way which resulted in disclosure, hurt, outrage and distrust, and which consequently undermined the activist aims, leaving the women feeling vulnerable and powerless in the face of an exploitative media pack.

We are left by Mary Chamberlain to imagine the agreements she had reached with the women about the use of data, and about how she handled the village meeting in which she was called to account by them. We may presume that what she went through as she faced their anger was coloured by emotion on her part. How deeply she felt and for how long, how the experience affected her later research practices, what happened to her relationships with individual women, and so on, are matters left to speculation. Such speculation on the real world of the researcher provides a connecting point to the complex nature and the nuances of consent, trust, confidentiality, (dis)empowerment, disguise, revelation and so on as they were played out in her interactive and reflexive moments. It is those kinds of nuances, the part played by concern for the well-being of research participants, and by respect for their right to protect themselves against the consequences of revealing information, that I want to explore in two instances from my work in teacher education.

Conventionally in qualitative research the conditions under which consent is negotiated for access to and the use of data are those of openness, anonymity or confidentiality. These are usually recommended to enable researchers to achieve certain purposes. Openness is a condition which ensures that all participants and interested parties have free access to information, and dissemination of the research is unrestricted. Anonymity is used to prevent individuals from being identified when the data is released. A promise to disguise names, places and events is involved so that information from participants may be more forthcoming, without jeopardising publication. Confidentiality provides complete protection by guaranteeing that the data will not be reported to anyone else in any form. It is intended to reassure participants that they can reveal what they otherwise might not, in order to help the researcher to understand their perspectives more fully, and with particular sensitivity to their feelings (of vulnerability, for example), their relationships with others in the research field, their right to the privacy of personal experiences, and so on. Whichever condition is invoked by researchers or by their informants, consent from those involved in and contributing to the research provides authority over the use of data. In the application of the conditions lies the issue of trust, especially the trust that the data provided, and any restrictions attached to its dissemination and use, will be respected by the researcher. A procedure for gaining 'informed consent' is often recommended to, or required of, researchers.

In my own examples below I shall explore the tensions and the dilemmas which these commonly cited research conditions—gaining consent, establishing trust, being open, listening in confidence, and anonymising people and places in research reports—created for me, as a teacher educator engaged in action research. I will focus on the detail of incidents with two students, one in pre-service, the other in her induction year. I had major responsibilities for researching and developing both of their programmes of study, and undertook action research in relation to my role as a support tutor. The two cases, like Mary Chamberlain's work, highlight the tensions created by those research conditions as they were played out in the handling of data in my work. My declared activism and educational purpose were to facilitate teachers' professional development, and to maximise the opportunities through which their professional practice could grow in quality. An action research disposition towards my work and their experiences involved opening windows on their lives and learning, and on my own and my colleagues' tutoring, as a means of increasing our capacity for practical wisdom.

Where Mary Chamberlain apparently discovered herself unexpectedly embroiled in reflection on and appraisal of her conduct, in action research such methodological scrutiny is an integral characteristic, because the research evidence relates directly and often immediately to judgements within educational practice. It is an essential ingredient of practical wisdom. However, certain features of Chamberlain's oral history and my action research raise similar issues and concerns in relation to the handling of data, arising from the relationship between research and action. But also, there are other clear differences in the contexts of her work and mine. First, her honest and illuminating reporting has contributed to an ever-growing and now familiar literature which has sensitised researchers like me to ethical considerations. Second, accountability through academic scrutiny and sponsor-scrutiny of our work has increased in recent years. Third, the professional and political context of teacher-educators' work means that research is carried out in sites which depend heavily on the goodwill of 'partnership' schools. These extrinsic factors add to the intrinsic, human elements which keep ethical considerations in focus in teacher-education research sites. But there is a more fundamental difference between the two.

Those research procedures and conditions reflect an inherent link between quite different concerns in an educator's work—those of the activist, intent on the pursuit of good educational practice and practical wisdom, and those of the action researcher, intent on uncovering evidence through the use of ethical research methods. The research methods literature is replete with advice on 'establishing trust', usually under the heading *ethics*. In the ethnographic literature the bond of trust is a device for becoming accepted by those who provide data, for opening windows on information (Bogdan and Biklen, 1998, p. 88; Fetterman, 1998, p. 140). Warnings are given about breaking confidences, or using information which was created under confidentiality rules (Brown and Dowling, 1998, p. 65). It is seen as a matter of 'fairness' and regarded as a 'more than pervasive' issue in the extent to which it deserves and gets consideration (Ely *et al.*, 1991, p. 93). Here are important considerations about the power and rights of individuals over information about their experiences, and the understandings which are reached (or not) between participants and researchers, and the portrayal of participants and their thoughts conveyed in research reports.

In action research, however, there is a more complex tension. Openness, anonymity and confidentiality may be invoked to suit particular situations because of the interactions, relationships and micro-politics of close-knit institutions like schools, colleges and training institutions. For the action researcher, each may in its own way both open windows and close doors, precisely because the research is directly associated with professional action within a given—and continuing—social situation. The practitioner researcher has an integrated role, as actor and as information gatherer. Indeed, intelligent practice commonly depends upon rigorous research. But the integrated role is particularly difficult where access to information and consent over its use depends on the promise of confidentiality, or even anonymity. Such agreements are useful for non-participant researchers seeking to understand social life. They can remove the information and themselves from the situation. But the action researcher is tied in, involved, one of a community of practitioners. And because information from other participants may be needed to take effective action, or even to act at all in some circumstances, issues of access, consent and the use of real names (which anyway will usually either be known to others in the institution or will need to be made known) are complex and problematic.

Where openness and trust exist, and the actions have no undesirable potential consequences, research and action go hand in hand without contention. In education, however, just as in Mary Chamberlain's work, contentiousness is endemic and power is unequally distributed within relationships. Furthermore, in educational circumstances the need to know, to understand what is happening, and the need to act in order to affect what is happening, occur in tense combination. That, perhaps, is why some of the action research literature contains such glaring contradictory advice. McNiff, Lomax and Whitehead (1996, p. 34), for example, insist that 'You will not reveal anything of a personal or compromising nature', while also letting 'all interested parties know what you are doing', at the same time as you should 'not reveal the real names of people'. Sometimes the need (or desire) to know will result in the promise not to reveal—without which the information will not be got. Such advice highlights the ethical and decision-making complexities in educational action research. So how do these questions and judgements appear in practice, and what do the conditions look like 'in the field' for the action researcher? Let me consider that question through some incidents in the lives of two novice teachers.

## CASE-STUDY: SUSAN

Sue was twenty-one years old; a student teacher in the third year of a four-year undergraduate course, preparing to teach in primary schools. The course design, and the tutors, explicitly intended that the students should develop action research as an orientation to professional learning. Elements of the programme introduced students to issues and practice in interpretive case-study and action research methods, via assignments undertaken in schools, and through seminars and tutorials.

As a consequence of modelling a research stance towards curriculum and teaching, the programme was the subject of a substantial, participative, continuous internal evaluation in which students, tutors and partnership schools were expected to engage. The arrangements for this were based on principles of democratic evaluation (MacDonald, 1976) and action research (Elliott, 1991; McKernan, 1991), with a notion that we would act as a 'learning community'. In short, this implied that the condition of openness would prevail, in a spirit of problem-solving in a professional, collegial venture with a broad aim of understanding educational practice with a view to improving it. As tutors, our research into the learning and practical experiences of students adopted ethnographic methods, while the closely connected research of our practice as teacher educators used action research methods (see Tickle, 1987). The students in turn devised projects researching the learning experiences of their pupils, or aspects of curriculum, or other issues and provisions within their schools; and they devised action research projects related to their own practices as aspirant professionals.

Sue's school placement for the third and final year of teaching practice, at the end of which she would be judged for recommendation for Qualified Teacher Status, was in one of the University's partnership schools. The headteacher, senior staff and other teachers had encouraged and enjoyed close links with the University over several years, through regular involvement in a partnership scheme, and professional relationships between liaison staff were, mutually, deemed to be excellent. Set in a suburban, modern, housing estate on the edge of the city, educating 8–12 year-olds from a relatively affluent area, this school had a good reputation. The staff were regarded as committed and caring. They provided many activities to supplement the mainstream curriculum—in drama, music, sport, environmental education, field trips and the like. Among these, the science/geography/personal and social education dimensions of the curriculum were enhanced by an annual, week-long summer camp for Year 7 pupils (aged 11–12).

Sue was teaching a Year 7 class and the camp fell mid-way into her period of school placement. She was told about it by her supervising class teacher during preparations for final practice and instructed not to plan teaching for that week but advised that she would be able to join in the camp as a staff member. That arrangement was approved by the link tutor, one of many such arrangements in which student teachers participated, especially during the summer term. Shortly after the end of the practice period, another student who was attached to the same school told me, in an oblique way, that Sue had had a 'terrible time' with the class teacher, especially during the camp. She would not elaborate, and I speculated that the story was sensitive, to the point that Sue had not wanted me to hear about the problem. We knew each other well and usually had an open, friendly and communicative relationship, and on next seeing her, I asked about the camp without revealing the conversation with her friend. She froze, saying she did not want to talk about it. I expressed puzzlement at that, but she would not enlarge upon the remark.

The programme of research into student experience and learning had explicitly intended that both students and tutors would be open in their deliberations about the course. This incident appeared to deny that aim in several respects, and particularly to deny access to evidence that would help me act. Sue claimed the right to privacy and to protect the information and, it seemed, the right to protect herself against the possible consequences of revealing it. Yet if something untoward had happened to Sue, I had a responsibility for her welfare, and that of other students who might be placed in similar circumstances.

The tutorial and research roles were clearly fused at this point, the fusion creating a dilemma about rights, respect and commitment to students' independence on the one hand, and on the other the need to know more in order to judge an appropriate course of professional action. Access to the data which Sue appeared to be guarding was needed if I was to help her, or others, should there be just cause to act on her or their behalf. At least, that is how I saw my educational responsibilities, though I recognise the possible charges of paternalism, interventionism, or misplaced heroism which might be raised in response to this view. However, as I saw the situation, action as the 'adult partner' seemed both necessary and justified, to uncover what lay behind the reported trauma, in order, in due course, to judge appropriate action. There was also a desire to gain the fullest picture of student experiences, for the purpose of informed programme development, which might only be possible if the apparently vulnerable student was guaranteed that her story would be heard confidentially.

Several times over the following six weeks I asked Sue to tell me what had happened at camp. She eventually agreed, on condition of strict confidentiality. I accepted that condition. She had, she said, experienced a week of being used by the class teacher as the camp 'skivvy', left alone at base with the chores, preparing and clearing away four meals each day, and prevented from engaging in learning and teaching activities with the pupils. When she had asked to be allowed to participate with the pupils her request was refused. When she had eventually complained directly to the teacher in question she had been told emphatically to remember that her teaching practice report was due to be written soon (by the class teacher herself), implying that sanctions would follow if she voiced her complaint further.

I judged the events so serious that I asked Sue to release me from the confidentiality agreement, in order to enable me to talk with the senior staff of the school, and to ensure that similar things would never happen to any other student. She explained that she was fearful of spoiling her chances of employment in the locality if it became known that she had complained. She refused my request but went so far as agreeing that I might inform my immediate, course-team colleagues, provided the information was anonymised and that they agreed that the report would go no further. That condition was applied and the agreement gained from colleagues, so that I was able at least to take limited action by making them aware of the incident and of Sue's concern about reporting it. Later, I discovered (without enquiring) that the headteacher knew about the event. Though he did not say how he knew, he indicated that action had been taken to ensure that students would not be placed under the supervision of the same teacher again.

The sensitivity of the conversation with the headteacher simply confirmed that the condition of openness had been surrendered; the possibility of educational action on my part was lost, and even the research advantage of gaining information by agreeing to the condition of confidentiality was severely limited, because I could not further my enquiries in the school. In reporting this tale now, after more than fifteen years, my privileged access to Sue's story is being used by breaking the trust in which it was held, via a mechanism of anonymity, in an attempt to raise the issues openly. That way, perhaps, other action researchers might consider the implications of conditional access to information, trust, and informed consent, from the perspective of the fieldworker's experience of events played out in practice. The experience was even more intense in the second case, to which I shall now turn.

## CASE-STUDY: DIANE

Using action research methods in a teacher induction programme, I found myself involved in a serious breakdown in relationships between a newly qualified teacher and her headteacher/tutor. The school in which Diane worked was a small, modern, single-storey building, designed for five- to eight-year olds, with playground and recreation field alongside. Set in the midst of a housing estate in a small market town, the young population of the area had grown in numbers beyond the intended capacity of the building. There were a hundred and twenty children in places built, furnished and staffed for ninety. The headteacher, deputy head and one other experienced teacher had been joined in September by Diane, newly qualified with specialist expertise in music. She mainly taught the reception class, but took other classes for music, and led assembly for the whole school.

My role as external support tutor to newly qualified teachers (NQTs), and the headteacher's in-school support tutor role, were based on principles which aimed to encourage practice-based inquiry among all participants. An interpretative perspective, using both action research and ethnographic case study approaches and methods underpinned the development both of individuals within the programme, and the programme itself (see Tickle, 1994). As part of the negotiation for the research, it had been agreed that all aspects of conversations, interactions or reports of experiences should be open to all those concerned within the project, unless otherwise requested by an individual participant. The inclusion of the 'conditional consent' clause was in recognition of the potential threat of disclosure in the assessment of the probationary period of the NQTs.

It was only two weeks into the first term that Diane phoned to ask for help, insisting before going further that the conversation should be in confidence. With that assurance, she revealed a serious breakdown in her relationship with the head, sparked by a staffroom incident which Diane considered minor, but for which she had been severely reprimanded. Over the following two weeks, numerous telephone calls, meetings, visits to the school and conversations with Diane, the head and the Local Education Authority school liaison officer revealed an emerging and increasingly dramatic story of conflict, grief, decline in self-confidence, feelings of inadequacy, aggravation and grievance. A diary entry recorded my thoughts at the time:

> I was left with a serious dilemma, and a number of questions about the role I had accepted, its boundaries, and the moral obligations of it. First, I felt responsibility towards Diane, wanting to ensure that she did not suffer either short-term or long-term consequences because of the behaviour of the headteacher. I had seen no evidence that Diane was a failure in classroom teaching and that had been confirmed by both the head and the LEA officer. Nor had I seen any evidence that Diane was 'peculiar'—a charge made to her by the head. Indeed she seemed to have some interesting views, and talked openly and lucidly about her experiences in school, displaying all the doubts and uncertainties that I took to be very normal. I had told her on the phone . . . . that the notion of being peculiar in any case assumes some sort of norm, some collective identity from which she distinctly deviated. So I regarded her as a victim who was in a relatively powerless position in employment, and whose major power was in the form of resignation from that employment. She was willing to use that power, and that in itself suggested to me a good deal of courage, given that it was likely to wreck her chosen career. While I wanted to intervene on her behalf I knew that that power relationship was between her and her employer . . . My role explicitly was defined as concerned with the development of classroom teaching skills and the capacity for reflective thinking about teaching. I had already moved beyond that in attempting to arbitrate the relationships problem at the request of the headteacher. (But since Diane took the view that she could not pursue that attempt, and would terminate all efforts by resignation, there seemed little I could do.)

The events culminated in Diane submitting her resignation from the job after six weeks, because of the way she was treated by the head.

I have reported Diane's case eslewhere (Tickle, 1994, pp. 94–103), including the view that she was competent in the classroom, had good relationships with pupils, and contributed to the work of the whole school through her musical, pedagogical and organisational expertise. After her resignation, not just from the school but from the profession, it transpired that Diane was not the first NQT to be submitted to what I interpreted as unjust and damaging managerial treatment in this school by that head. Yet the LEA officer argued that he must 'stand by the head'. With no formal power to act, but with a determination to prevent a recurrence of the injustice, I was again faced with the dilemma between the need to know what was occurring in order to understand the experiences of new teachers, and the professional responsibility of acting on behalf of one of them in particular. The agreement with Diane not to reveal the story she told gave me access to data, enabled me to counsel Diane, but prevented its use in acting to change the situation. The consequence of not revealing the story was that remedial action was prevented, both in

Diane's own case and in that of others who might find themselves in similarly difficult circumstances.

Again, the struggle between enclosure and disclosure was enacted. In this case the anonymity clause enabled me to cite aspects of these events in an internal project report. While this amounted to a belated betrayal of the confidentiality agreement with Diane, the potential consequences to her of disclosure had been removed with her resignation from post and withdrawal from the profession. On the other hand, I judged that the safeguarding of others and of their learning, through the development of the school-based professional tutor role, could potentially be enhanced by disclosure of this case (along with other cases). The report, however, was subsequently withdrawn following complaints from another headteacher and member of the project steering group that the school and headteacher could be identified. My attempt to anonymise the school and personnel had failed. I was left with the residual dilemma and sense of powerlessness.

## INSIGHT AND INACTION

Although the case records of the two instances are presented only in outline here, they and others are backed by 'thick' data, which reveal further detail and nuances of tutor–student–school relationships, and especially the experiences of students and new teachers (see Tickle, 1987; 1994; 2000). While the vignettes disguise some detail, they serve to illustrate the social interactions of the action researcher, and some of the judgements, tensions and dilemmas that can arise in the immediacy of events. Now, long after these incidents, and in the spirit of Mary Chamberlain's Preface to the second edition of *Fenwomen*, I want to reflect on some of the choices made, their implications, and the issues which emerged with regard to the practical pursuit of the conditions associated with confidentiality, anonymity, openness, consent, trust and disclosure.

Much of the data came my way as part of the intensive and extensive professional activities of the programmes which we were involved in—with the addition in Susan's case that I actively sought data because of my professional concern for her well-being and for the (re)constructive evaluation of the course. Within the day-to-day activities there were inevitable micro-political and interpersonal risks and opportunities, in seeking to effect changes and in observing the professional behaviour of others. In those risks and opportunities there was a fragile trust within which access to situations—and data—was granted and information transmitted, held and acted upon. That fragility was conditioned at least in part by dimensions of perceived and actual power (and powerlessness) in the relationships of the personnel, which were crucial to the decisions made both about the sharing of information and about the actions which themselves might betray it. The vulnerability of Susan and Diane, who were subject to performance assessment as teachers, was a crucial factor. Judgements were also, perhaps, affected by my own experiences of 'interpersonal sensitivity' in the culture of teaching, with its attendant assumptions about autonomy, codes of professional conduct, and avoidance of conflict. Additionally, there were institutional boundaries whose necessary transgressions, with different senses of role, belonging, guest status and attendant courtesies were to be respected. Thus, as insights increased with the accumulation of sensitive data, so did the fragility of the decision-making and the dilemmas of *praxis*.

The benefits that confidentiality brought in hearing what would otherwise have remained untold—benefits both of gaining insight and of being in a position to take informed action—were emasculated by the very conditions which were there to guide right action in both inter-personal relations and research procedures. Greater knowledge about the nature of the problems faced by Susan and Diane, and the circumstances which gave rise to them, enabled me to act in only limited ways through personal counselling, rather than by tackling openly the more senior staff involved regarding their alleged actions. It also meant that I was unable to make enquiries of those staff or among others in the schools: that the research itself was curtailed because their accounts could not be verified. Nor could the perspectives of other personnel be gathered, limiting the portrayal of situations in their full complexity. Control over the data operated as a partial enabling mechanism for professional action related to the individual, but as seriously disabling with regard to the wider project's development and the common good, which might have been possible through the broader illumination of experience and the dissemination of information. Being educationally impotent, prevented without the betrayal of trust from acting in ways which might have altered the circumstances and alleviated the difficulties, immediately for the two and longer-term for others who might follow them, left a severe sense of frustration and failure. However, wrong-footedness was an evident possibility. Caught between these, substantial efforts to re-negotiate seemed to provide a way out. Yet these were also rejected by Susan, and denied by the urgency of events in the case of Diane. Wrongdoing—in terms of conscious betrayal and the breaking of rules of conduct in research—was something I postponed until the consequences for each of them had disappeared. Indeed, the information from Susan has been held in trust until now, and even now is anonymised. Consequences for myself in terms of being, and being seen to be, trustworthy were, and remain, a major consideration. Consequences in terms of the failure to gain a fuller picture of events, to open windows more widely, to maximise my effectiveness as a researcher, were also, and continue to be, deeply felt.

## ON REFLECTION

Had I been working merely as an ethnographer with a focus on the experiences of novice teachers, the denial of access to further data, the attempt to re-negotiate the agreement with Sue, the threat of consequences for reporting Diane's experiences, and so on, would not need to have arisen, in so far as my window on the experiences of the individuals was well and truly opened. The illumination of their world seemed bright, even if the worlds themselves were not; the detail in their stories revealed life-history events, captured the human experience of anguish and provided a record of individual testimonies, as Mary Chamberlain had put it. But doors were closed to me both as an educational practitioner intent on developing the teacher education practices in the programmes concerned, and in gaining insight into the views of other participants. Within both of these intentions there was a reflection of Mary Chamberlain again (though there is no indication that she wanted to talk to the men of Isleham, or the landowners). Again the difference seems to be that it is in relation to my activist role that some kind of resolution to the ethical dilemmas which I faced needed to be found. Indeed, one possible resolution has emerged, not from my deliberations about ethnographic research practices, but rather from reflection about my educational aims and pedagogical practices.

In my relationship with Susan, Diane and their peers, there was a hope that I might successfully 'speak for those who cannot openly speak for themselves' (Sparks, 1994, p. 97); or more accurately, that I might act on behalf of those who felt unable to act for themselves. It was that which was prevented, and which led me to feel that I was betraying my own set purposes, failing to achieve the educational goal by maintaining the research ethic, to a degree that has kept alive the intensity of these cases in my mind for many years. In hindsight, and as a result of reflection on these instances, my own educational pre-dispositions have re-aligned more with those who search for and try to establish enabling conditions, practices and social relations that are geared to maximising (in this case, professional) self-fulfilment. The realignment was furthered by my re-reading of Abraham Maslow's (1973) paper 'What is a Taoistic Teacher?', in which he expresses his own belief in and respect for the tendency towards self-actualisation, which in pedagogical terms involves a willingness to trust learners, and requires the teacher to adopt a particular kind of responsibility which negates manipulation, or shaping learners into some pre-determined form, or acting on their behalf. Rather, according to this point of view, practice which enables the uncovering of the maximum potential of the particular individual's own actions is favoured (Maslow, 1973, p. 150). This presumes a concept of the educator who can be entrusted with the kind of responsibility that evolves consciousness, as Mentor was in the education of Telemachus (Vernant, 1983). Bruner (1977) talked of it as a social relationship stabilised by the adult partner. Maslow put it in terms of the best helpers of other people being those who are the most highly evolved, most fully developed in motivation, self-direction, autonomy, responsibility and *capabilities in trusting others* (my emphasis) (Maslow, 1973, p. 153).

I now see that the kind of parenting disposition in evidence in my work with Sue, Diane and their peers was essentially protective and interventionist in ways that were contrary to their own wishes, and to those aims of self-fulfilment. One conclusion is that in my educational practices I should substitute the protective parenting with a new position arising from concerns with the self, to go beyond the point of speaking and acting on behalf of others, to make it possible for others to speak for and act on behalf of themselves (Tickle, 1999; 2000). In trying to resolve the dilemmas the limits of my rights and the responsibilities of my tutees will have to be re-positioned so that the students can benefit educationally, in terms of self-fulfilment and the adoption of their own responsibilities—for example, in taking actions that would prevent others from suffering what they had endured. What this will mean for my teacher education practice is finding ways from within the individuals to confront the power relations in the situations described, to empower novice teachers to act openly, to contend the use of confidentiality. The risk in this repositioning is to increase the possibility of denied access to data, to close windows as well as doors. Then I would have to depend on the conviction that the educational ethic should take precedence over the research ethic, to live with the essential optimism which Maslow offers, to have faith in his existential, phenomenological conception of mankind, in which there is 'great hope for the potentialities of the person (with which) comes a great trust in . . . the wisdom of self-choice' (Maslow, 1973, p. 150). Where there is this trust in human beings, he asserts, there is a willingness to leave them alone.

But, as is evident in these very ideas, the educator's role is not to leave people literally alone, isolated, vulnerable, without the mature support which educating presumes. Rather it is a matter of realising a particular pedagogy. So, as an ethnographer *and* action researcher, one result of this reflection is the development of my own use of educational *auto*biography in which I have begun to test out the limits and consequences of being open, of revealing sensitive data to others. Given that there is another story to be told about this process, as well as about the life experiences themselves, here I simply want to attest that it is both personally and methodologically challenging. However, I also want to attest that a further result in my work as a teacher educator is the encouragement of the use of autobiography by teachers, in ways which potentially offer empowerment of greater subtlety than that which ethnography, oral history, and some forms of action research have sometimes espoused. It offers the option to individuals both to investigate situations and to speak and act on their own behalf, to adopt phenomenology and *praxis* that are genuinely rooted in first-person experiences. Through them, it provides the potential to engage in personal and professional *self*-development in a form where the power of revelation and informed action remain at the discretion of the individual, to be deployed on the basis of judgements about educational advantage and advancement.

This difference has important implications for the research methods that interpretive research encourages, and which have often been adopted in action research. In autobiographical research, the judgements, actions and courage involved in *praxis*, and attendant questions of moral wisdom relating to the purposes of the work, are retained by the individual whose action-research it is. Answers to the questions of access to data, negotiation of how data are gathered and recorded, agreements about their interpretation, use and reporting are self-negotiated. In this sense the research is entirely insider research. The professional as a self-determining and self-actualising educator would need to take on those responsibilities and that empowerment, and their consequences. This of course would be a tall order to fill for people like Susan and Diane, in the face of the actual power relations they are caught up in. In that sense, the issue boils down to one of the development of moral and professional courage, together with self-respect and self-trust.

It would also be a tall order to fill for people like Mary Chamberlain, who would need to rethink their role. The pedagogical implications for teacher educators like myself are just as considerable. I have begun to explore those in detail elsewhere (Tickle, 1999; 2000), but perhaps the most poignant recognition for me at the stage of writing this paper is the need to transfer the *sense* of power, away from the well-intentioned hero/ethnographer. Indeed, only now do I recognise even the gendered language of 'emasculation' and 'impotence' which I have included in this report. To explore what this will mean in my research, and to work out the practical implications of empowerment within new kinds of pedagogical relationships, is the next challenge for this 'adult partner'.

*Address for correspondence:* Les Tickle, School of Education and Professional Studies, University of East Anglia, Norwich NR4 7TJ, UK.
Email: l.tickle@uea.ac.uk

## REFERENCES

Bogdan, R. C. and Biklen, S. K. (1998) *Qualitative Research in Education* (Needham Heights MA, Allyn & Bacon).
Brown, A. and Dowling, P. (1998) *Doing Research, Reading Research* (London, Falmer Press).
Bruner, J. (1977) *The Process of Education* (Cambridge MA, Harvard University Press).
Carr, D. (2000) *Professionalism and Ethics in Teaching* (London, Routledge).
Carr, W. and Kemmis, S. (1986) *Becoming Critical: Knowing Through Action Research* (Lewes, Falmer Press).
Chamberlain, M. (1983 edn) *Fenwomen* (London, Routledge & Kegan Paul).
Crotty, M. (1998) *The Foundations of Social Research* (London, Sage).
Elliott, J. (1991) *Action Research for Educational Change* (Milton Keynes, Open University Press).
Ely, M., Anzul, M., Friedman, T., Garner, D. and Steinmetz, A. M. (1991) *Doing Qualitative Research: Circles Within Circles* (London, Falmer Press).
Fetterman, D. (1998) *Ethnography* (London, Sage).
MacDonald, B. (1976) Evaluation and the control of education, in: D. Tawney (ed.) *Curriculum Evaluation Today: Trends and Implications* (London, Macmillan).
Maslow, A. (1973) What is a Taoistic teacher?, in: L. Rubin (ed.) *Facts and Feelings in the Classroom* (London, Ward Lock).
McKernan, J. (1991) *Curriculum Action Research* (London, Kogan Page).
McNiff, J., Lomax, P. and Whitehead, J. (1996) *You and Your Research Project* (London, Routledge).
Schon, D. (1983) *The Reflective Practitioner* (New York, Basic Books).
Sockett, H. (1994) *The Moral Base for Teacher Professionalism* (New York, Teachers College Press).
Sparks, A. C. (1994) Self, silence and invisibility as a beginning teacher: a life history of lesbian experience, *British Journal of Sociology of Education*, 15(1), pp. 93–118.
Tickle, L. (1987) *Learning Teaching, Teaching Teaching* (Lewes, Falmer Press).
Tickle, L. (1994) *The Induction of New Teachers: reflective professional practice* (London, Cassell).
Tickle, L. (1999) Teacher self-appraisal and appraisal of self, in: R. P. Lipka and T. M. Brinthaupt (eds) *The Role of Self in Teacher Development* (Albany, State University of New York Press).
Tickle, L. (2000) *Teacher Induction: the way ahead* (Buckingham, Open University Press).
Vernant, J.P. (1983) *Myth and Thought Among the Greeks* (London, Routledge & Kegan Paul).

# 4

# Representation, Identification and Trust: Towards an Ethics of Educational Research

SHIRLEY PENDLEBURY and PENNY ENSLIN

*Crudely put, educational research is unethical when it misrepresents or misidentifies—and so betrays—its putative beneficiaries or the goods and values they hold dear. How can researchers guard against these vulnerabilities? While acknowledging the vulnerabilities of educational research to abuses of trust and representation, and that there is no Archimedean point from which to approach research into people's practices, we defend a universalist conception of research ethics in education. This universalist conception is developed via an examination of a central debate in feminism, contrasting Alcoff's positionality, Caughie's performative conception and Nussbaum's universalist conception of feminism.*

Educational research is conducted in many ways for many purposes. Whatever its form or purpose, it is vulnerable to abuse. In some respects its vulnerabilities are those of any research whatsoever; in others they are the special vulnerabilities of research that seeks to interpret the meanings and implications of human practices or to improve the quality of people's lives. Where educational research has these concerns at its heart, it is especially vulnerable to abuses of representation, identification and trust. Crudely, we can say that educational research is unethical when it misrepresents or misidentifies and so betrays its putative beneficiaries or the goods and values that they hold most dear. We take this crude claim as a starting point in marking out the terrain for our argument.

On the first and most obvious reading, the claim seems to imply that ethically sound educational research involves a commitment to some sort of relativism. Yet that very commitment itself raises the question: 'Ethically sound from whose point of view?' To see what is at stake here, consider two illustrative sketches exemplifying some key ethical issues in research that are related to concerns about representation and identification.

Our first sketch refers to Harlan Lane's work on the deaf community. In his book *The Mask of Benevolence*, Lane (1992) remarks that our representations of others determine the outcomes of our ethical judgements. The point is a crucial one in his defence of the right to speak on behalf of the deaf community as an enabling condition for advocacy. Against the dominant 'audistic' model, which privileges orality and so represents the deaf community as disabled, Lane proposes that the deaf be represented as a cultural and linguistic minority. Casting the deaf as disabled, he argues, is a form of paternalism that permits hearing professionals to speak for a group seen as unable to speak for themselves. However, as deaf critics have been quick to point out, Lane's project of discursive intervention may itself be open to the very charge of paternalism it seeks to expose, since it appears to speak *for* the deaf.

While Lane acknowledges that his position as a cultural outsider limits what he can say on behalf of and about the deaf, he insists that his project is possible without lapsing into paternalism. His defence depends on a distinction between two ways of coming to know a culture: one can come to know a culture *from the inside* as a 'native speaker' or *from the outside* as a trained and attentive listener. Lane makes no pretence at being a 'native speaker'; to do so would be to engage in 'mimicry', to speak *as* a member of the deaf community and so to suggest an insider's knowledge that he cannot possibly have. Nor, he protests, is he attempting to speak *for* the deaf since this would be to engage in the paternalism he rejects. Rather he positions himself, self-consciously, on both sides of the cultural divide, taking the dual perspective of a trained and attentive listener. Risky and difficult though it may be to sustain, this dual perspective makes advocacy possible without either paternalism or mimicry. Indeed the dual perspective rests on a self-conscious awareness of the ways in which the representations that structure our relations to others can result in paternalism. Yet, as Pamela Caughie (1999) points out, such awareness can also lead to guilt, collective indifference or silence in just those situations where an ethics of responsibility, or even just plain decency, may call for intervention.

The Lane example raises important questions about who can say what, with what authority, as well as about the necessity for, and conditions of, trust in research on or with human subjects. (The distinction between the 'on' and 'with' is important. The 'on' makes the research subject a research object, the 'with' implies a participatory relationship with at least a degree of reciprocity.) As our second sketch shows, questions of this kind arise as much for researchers who are members of the communities they investigate as for those—like Lane—who are outsiders.

In setting out to conduct an ethnographic study of the lived experiences of pupils at a rural school in his village in South Africa's Northern Province, Collin Phurutse (2000) worries about an ambiguity in his own identity. Although he is a member of the community in which he conducts his research, he is also a researcher with responsibilities to a scholarly community of practice with its own goods and standards, tools and artefacts. Compare his position with Lane's. Phurutse is both an insider and an outsider. Being an insider means that he can claim, without recourse to mimicry, to be a native speaker and to have the special insights of the native speaker into the practices and understandings of the community. Also, his insider status seems to issue a warrant of trustworthiness and an imperative to serve the interests of the community and protect its self-understandings. As a special kind of outsider—one with the critical lens of a researcher—he is driven by other imperatives which arise from his membership in a research community and which may, from the perspective of the villagers, cast doubt on his trustworthiness.

This dual identity poses several ethical dilemmas for Phurutse, dilemmas made more stark by the unique socio-economic and political circumstances in which he works. For present illustrative purposes we mention two, both linked to the notion of voice. Phurutse is concerned that his research should 'give voice to view points and persons who have hitherto been marginalised or silenced' (p. 12)—in this case a poor rural community in South Africa. We take his commitment 'to give voice' as a moral commitment that arises from his concern to honour the beneficiaries of his research (i.e. the teachers and pupils in the village) and the values they hold dear. At the same time, he correctly sees the risks of romanticising the culture of the community if he simply leaves them to speak for themselves through extensive quotation in his research texts. A properly critical stance requires him to step outside, as it were. This brings us to a second, related dilemma. In important ways, Phurutse's critical stance is enabled by the literature on situated learning from which he has developed a conceptual framework for his research. Yet the way in which this literature characterises concepts like participation casts the rural teachers in Phurutse's study as authoritarian and incompetent, and the learners' experiences as alienating. His own experiences as a learner in a poor rural school and the accounts of teachers and pupils in his study give a very different picture. To ignore people's own understandings of their lived experiences, Phurutse thinks, would be to further disempower an already marginalised community, yet to accept them uncritically would be to fall into the trap of romanticising culture. He cannot resolve the dilemmas without a deep and astute situational appreciation.

Both Lane's case and Phurutse's remind us that there is no view from nowhere, no Archimedean point from which to approach research into people's practices. This could be taken to imply a rejection of a universalist conception of research ethics, yet this is exactly what we will deny in this paper. Our denial is not a failure to acknowledge the strength of some culturally situated arguments. We recognise how positions of power can blind one to people's predicaments. We recognise, too, that researchers *are* in a position of power that may tempt them to betray the trust of those researched. Research, like teaching and many other human practices, requires that the researcher be entrusted with a range of discretionary powers, yet in granting such discretionary powers the truster opens the way for the trusted to use her discretionary power for questionable, and even harmful, ends. As Annette Baier (1994) observes in her work on trust and social life, trust is a double-edged sword whose benefits entail the risks of abuse. To elaborate:

> If part of what the truster entrusts to the trusted are discretionary powers, then the truster risks abuse of those and the successful disguise of such abuse. The special vulnerability which trust involves is vulnerability to not yet noticed harm, or to disguised ill will. What one forgives or tactfully averts one's eyes from may be not well-meant but ill-judged attempts to care for what is entrusted but, rather, ill-meant and cleverly disguised abuses of discretionary power. To understand the moral risks of trust, it is important to see the special sort of vulnerability it introduces. Yet the discretionary element which introduces this special danger is essential to that which trust at its best makes possible. (Baier, 1994, pp. 103–104)

While trust is necessary for research to thrive, Baier reminds us that not all the things that thrive when there is trust among people are things that should be so encouraged. Conspiracy, exploitation and oppression can also thrive in the soil of trust. A trusted researcher can use her research to justify the continuation of morally reprehensible practices, to disguise and thus entrench oppression, to get people fired, to get schools and colleges closed down, to justify inequalities, to deflect attention from much required action or intervention.

While acknowledging these vulnerabilities of educational and other social research and the extent to which they compel one into a relativist position, we will nonetheless defend a universalist conception of research ethics in education. We will develop this conception via an examination of a central debate in feminism. Alcoff's (1991–92) notion of positionality epitomises one side of the debate; Nussbaum's (1999) universalist conception of feminism epitomises the other. A third position is Caughie's (1999) performative conception, which claims to address weaknesses in the other two.

## THE POSITIONAL RESPONSE TO DILEMMAS IN RESEARCH ETHICS

Lane's defence of his discursive intervention in characterisations of the deaf exemplifies one of the primary moral dilemmas in research: the problem of speaking for others. This is a dilemma because, as Linda Alcoff (1991–92) argues, it can lead to two equally objectionable responses. On the one hand, it can result in an unself-conscious appropriation of anothers' position ('paternalism' or 'imperialism'); on the other, it can result in a guilty retreat from the practice of speaking for ('collective indifference' or 'silence'). The former arises from the speaker's or researcher's desire for mastery; the latter from the speaker's or researcher's desire to be immune to criticism. Alcoff attempts to mediate between these two responses by specifying criteria (in the form of imperatives) for determining the validity of efforts to speak for others. The first is to resist the impulse to speak for another; the second is to interrogate the effect of one's own location on what one says, as well as the effect of what one says on the material and discursive contexts of the speech situation. Both Lane (1992) and Phurutse (2000), in different ways and for different reasons, follow this second imperative.

Alcoff's second imperative involves the concept of *positionality*,[1] which defines human subjects in terms of their social locations, historical experiences and external contexts, rather than in terms of some or other assumed essential attributes. The positional stance is intended to mediate between two opposing views: a humanist view of the subject as an autonomous, rational agent and a post-structuralist view of the subject as a linguistic performance or, in Caughie's words, between 'humanism's universal subject and poststructuralism's depersonalised subject' (Caughie, 1999, p. 32).

Postionality has become something of a touchstone for good qualitative research writing in education. Along with her research topic and tasks, the critically reflexive researcher introduces herself, often at some length. She does so less for the purposes of confession or to bring into the open the idiosyncrasies of personality and temperament than to acknowledge her autobiography as one marked by gender, sexuality, class, ethnicity and so on, and to acknowledge the possible effects that her position may have on the form and outcomes of the research (see Usher, 1996).

Debates over issues of identification and representation are commonly presented in terms of speaking 'as' and speaking 'for', practices which raise interesting and difficult questions for the ethics of research in education. A researcher's right to speak on behalf of certain cultural or social groups may be defended as an enabling condition for advocacy. But exercising the right in a morally defensible manner may seem to necessitate a dual perspective that comes from positioning oneself, self-consciously, on both sides of a cultural divide. As we have seen, this is precisely what Lane attempts to do in offering a positional defence along the lines suggested by Alcoff. In a sense, Phurutse does something similar. The trouble, or so Caughie (1999) thinks, is that the positional defence results in a caveat syndrome—an effort that writers (or teachers or researchers) make in order to save themselves from their own ethical practices and from the risks they have taken in boundary crossing. On these grounds, Caughie (1999) questions the usefulness of the positional stance in responding to ethical dilemmas of writing, teaching and research. She thinks that the notion of positionality inhibits the writing and entails the binary logic of the 'other'. Here's the gist of her argument:

> In... these efforts to speak and write across 'politically charged boundaries' of identity and identification, efforts that I term 'passing', we return again and again to discomforting questions about who has the right to speak, who can represent or identify with another, and to our necessary implication in the very practices we critique. Again and again we offer in response solutions, disclaimers, imperatives, and caveats in a hopeless effort to save ourselves from criticism, or at least to get the jump on it so that our accusers can't accuse us of anything we didn't already know'. (Caughie, 1999, p. 37)

If a researcher's efforts to escape criticism for writing across 'politically charged boundaries' are hopeless, what does this mean for an ethics of responsibility in research? Caughie offers one kind of answer, Nussbaum another. We consider Caughie's answer first. It is seductive but ultimately not a strong enough reason to reject a universalist stance.

## A PERFORMATIVE RESPONSE

Caughie's worry about the positional stance in writing, teaching and, by implication, research is that it involves the desire 'to control our identifications and the effects of performativity, neither of which, by definition, we can control' (p. 37). Indeed, the very question 'Who has the right to speak?' assumes one knows in advance what identities, identifications and political commitments are and should be. The question obscures the way identifications and political commitments work. But this does not mean that just anyone has the right to make identifications across politically charged boundaries. Rather 'it is to call for a narrative explanation that can "unknot" the overdeterminations that structure any defense of one's right to speak' (Caughie, 1999, p. 38).

Caughie advances her argument via a brief account of Eve Kosofsky Sedgwick's *Epistemology of the Closet* (1990). Here Sedgwick 'identifies' as a gay man, while acknowledging that our identifications and the effects of performativity are beyond our control. In 'identifying' as a gay man, Caughie claims, Sedgwick passes in an ethical sense. This means that she neither passes *as* a gay man nor writes from the *position* of a gay man, and thus has no need to confess or defend a transgression; rather she writes 'through an identification *whose meaning and value lie in the writing itself*' (p. 38) (our emphasis). But just as we cannot control our identifications or their trajectories, so we cannot control how our writing (or, by implication, research) is received or what effects it will have. Nonetheless our writing (and research) carry an implicit ethics in their performance precisely because they do have effects.

On the performative account, the value of one's teaching or writing or research practice lies not in the claims one makes for it but in contributions it makes. Of course, this view of the value of research is not confined to a performative account; there is a universalist response to ethical dilemmas in research which also takes the value of research to lie in the contributions it makes or fails to make. However, the positional and performative responses both suggest reasons for rejecting a universalist response. Part of our task in the next section will thus be to sketch a universalist account that it need not be vulnerable to the weaknesses of some straw-dog version's universalism, that is, the view from nowhere and the universal subject.

## A UNIVERSALIST RESPONSE

As we said earlier, positionality mediates between 'humanism's universal subject' and the depersonalised subject of poststructuralism. The fact that mediation is seen to be required implies problems with the two polar extremes. Yet problems with the notion of a universal subject may too easily be seen as grounds for rejecting a humanist universalism. Humanist universalism is commonly rejected precisely on the grounds that it tries to adopt a view from nowhere, presuming to represent the other while assuming unacknowledged Western values. Martha Nussbaum's (1999) account of humanist universalism provides a way of working with ethical dilemmas in research that concern feminists like Alcoff.

Nussbaum's brand of humanism begins from the idea of the equal worth of human beings, in virtue of their basic human capacities for choice and reasoning, and at the same time acknowledges the specificity of circumstances—natural, social, political and historical—that make people's lives different. It is a feminist humanism whose salient features are that it is *'internationalist ... liberal, concerned with the social shaping of preference and desire*, and ... *concerned with sympathetic understanding'* (p. 6). While acknowledging differences in concrete circumstances and their significance in the texture of people's lives, this brand of humanism assumes considerable commonality in what people must have in order to be capable of living well.

Nussbaum (1999) rejects the argument that a sensible interest in specificity must lead to a normative cultural relativism in which ultimate standards of what is right and wrong must be derived from a group's internal traditions. Instead she argues that the central human capacities and functions, and basic human needs and rights, can be given in a fully universal way and should guide feminist thought and planning, with appropriate attention to specific circumstances.

Universalist views, applied to women and other socially marginalised groups, are often suspected of being projections of well-educated Westerners onto people of diverse backgrounds. Nussbaum answers this worry through a method that emphasises local knowledge, is open to many voices and collaborates with people from many different places and positions. The universals she claims are the yield of collaborative labour over many years. For our purposes, the most important part of Nussbaum's response is her insistence on 'the universal importance of protecting spheres of choice and freedom, within which people with diverse views of what matters in life can pursue flourishing according to their own lights' (p. 9). With this insistence, she defends her brand of universalism from the charge that it imposes foreign values upon others. The charges of cultural dominance can hardly stick on activities that support those basic capacities and opportunities necessary for choosing a flourishing life, so long as people are then free to choose for themselves how best to flourish.

Nussbaum proposes a set of central human capabilities that all citizens should have, and that public policy should aim to promote as part of the good life. These capabilities are to do with 'health, education, political liberty and participation, self-respect, and life itself' (p. 30). She proposes that each nation has an obligation to ensure that each citizen reaches a basic level of functioning. But she goes further than this, arguing that governments and individuals are morally obliged to promote justice for all, across international boundaries. In defending this position, Nussbaum calls for support for international human rights and for international agencies that promote them:

But the goal should always be to put people into a position of agency and choice, not to push them into functioning in ways deemed desirable. I argue that this is no mere parochial Western ideology but the expression of a sense of agency that has deep roots all over the world; it expresses the joy most people have in using their own bodies and minds. (Nussbaum, 1999, p. 11)

Consider two examples that Nussbaum borrows from Martha Chen (1995) to illustrate her brand of universalism and what it means to respect people's agency and choice. Both are examples of women living in traditional non-Western societies. Saleha Begum struggled, during the 1970s, against community norms in Bangladesh that prohibit women from working outside the home, even if conforming to these norms threatened their survival. In her case, her disabled husband could not provide as local tradition assumed he would. After working in the fields at night so that she would not be seen, Saleha and a team of women demanded employment on a food-for-work programme sponsored by the government. At first local officials refused to agree, on the grounds that tradition prohibits Bangladeshi women from working outside the home. With help from other organisations the women won. Later, they asserted their independence further by attending educational programmes, and learning new agricultural and social skills. In Nussbaum's terms, Saleha's capabilities were undermined by traditions that prohibited paid work, threatening her basic nutrition, among other things. The point is pertinent for an ethics of educational research: we cannot dismiss educational research on the grounds that it fails to respect tradition or culture if in so doing it supports people who resist traditional or oppressive practices that undermine their capabilities.

Metha Bai, a widow and mother of two small children, was similarly forbidden to work outside her home in Rajasthan, India, even though her survival depended on it. Hers is a story of age-old traditions about widowhood in India. It will not do simply to claim that she has 'the right to work' without an understanding of the traditions and how they are embedded in caste and Hindu family practices. Rights talk has no purchase in the absence of concrete local knowledge. As a widow whose upper-caste norms prohibit paid work, Metha Bai yearned for autonomy and choice. Her longing for autonomy illustrates one of the ways 'in which abstract value can be instantiated in a concrete situation, through rich local knowledge' (Nussbaum, 1999, p. 48). Again, here is an example of how cultural tradition is opposed to women's flourishing. Metha Bai too saw the injustice of such cultural traditions. However, although deeply critical of tradition that reduced her quality of life, she was reluctant to be seen to resist:

What, then, is 'the culture' of a woman like Metha Bai? Is it bound to be that determined by the most prevalent customs in Rajasthan, the region of her marital home? Or, might she be permitted to consider with what traditions or groups she wishes to align herself, perhaps forming a community of solidarity with other widows and women, in pursuit of a better quality of life? (Nussbaum, 1999, p. 37)

Nussbaum's questions remind us of the risks of romanticising 'culture' at the expense of enabling people to pursue a better quality of life. Her universalism yields an account of research ethics that is neither insensitive to tradition nor merely a projection of one dominant set of values on another. This account also rejects the idea that universalism inevitably results in, and at the same time conceals, injustice and betrayal.

## IMPERATIVES FOR ETHICAL RESEARCH IN EDUCATION

We began this paper with the crude claim that educational research is unethical when it misrepresents or misidentifies and so betrays its putative beneficiaries or the goods and values that they hold most dear. What does our analysis and discussion suggest about how researchers can guard can against these vulnerabilities? The work on positionality and performativity provides a rich elaboration of the issues at stake and of possible ways of addressing them. But, as we have shown, there is a universalist approach to these issues which escapes the criticisms commonly levelled against universalism and provides some more morally compelling answers to ethical dilemmas in research.

Drawing from our discussion of Nussbaum's brand of universalism, we extract a strong imperative for researchers who are sensitive to the pitfalls of paternalism, misrepresentation and betrayal: *your research must promote those human capabilities, including agency and choice, that are necessary for the quality of life of those who have participated in the research. This is especially important if your research is intended to inform public policy.*

To elaborate, the goal is not to push people into functioning in ways deemed desirable by the researcher or the policy makers or research funders, but to put them in a stronger position to exercise their agency in the light of their circumstances and professional obligations. Research that informs policy should enable the development of central human capabilities. For Nussbaum, as we have shown, a sense of agency and the longing to exercise it is no mere Western ideology but has deep and ubiquitous roots. Universalism requires attention to, and respect for, difference and it requires an acknowledgement that people's pursuit of flourishing must be according to their own lights and not according to yours. One aspect of genuine agency is knowing when, whom and how to trust and when to call for 'trust-busting' procedures (Baier, 1994).

*Address for correspondence:* Shirley Pendlebury, Department of Education, University of Witwatersrand, 1 Jan Smuts Avenue, Johannesburg, PO WITS 2050, South Africa. Email: 022pen@mentor.edcm.wits.ac.za

## NOTE

1. *Positionality* is a close relative of the concept of 'situated knowledges' as articulated by Donna Harraway (1988) and other feminist theorists who insist that all knowledge claims are partial perspectives. See also Caughie (1999).

## REFERENCES

Alcoff, L. (1991–92) The problem of speaking for others, *Cultural Critique*, 20, pp. 5–32.

Baier, A. (1994) Trust and antitrust, in: *Moral Prejudices: Essays on Ethics* (Cambridge MA, Harvard University Press).

Caughie, P. (1999) *Passing and Pedagogy: The Dynamics of Responsibility* (Chicago, University of Chicago Press).

Chen, M. (1995) A matter of survival: women's rights to employment in India and Bangladesh, in: M. Nussbaum and J. Glover (eds) *Women, Culture and Dvelopment: A Study of Human Capabilities* (Oxford, Clarendon Press).

Harraway, D. (1988) Situated knowledges: The science question in feminism and the privilege of partial perspective, *Feminist Studies*, 14, pp. 575–599.

Lane, H. (1992) *The Mask of Benevolence: Disabling the Deaf Community* (New York, Knopf).

Nussbaum, M. (1999) *Sex and Social Justice* (New York/Oxford, Oxford University Press).

Phurutse, C. (2000) Cultural involvement and marginalisation: 'Lived experiences' of learners in the rural community of ga-Phaahla. Paper presented at Kenton Ebayi, 27–29 October, Port Elizabeth.

Sedgwick, E. (1990) *Epistemology of the Closet* (Berkeley, University of California Press).

Usher, R. (1996) Textuality and reflexivity in educational research, in: D. Scott and R. Usher (eds) *Understanding Educational Research* (London, Routledge).

# 5

# The Ethics of Outsider Research

DAVID BRIDGES

*This chapter examines criticisms made by or on behalf of 'disempowered' groups against outsider research into their experience: that outsiders cannot properly understand and represent their experience and are exploitative and disrespectful, and that having outsiders articulate your views for you is intrinsically disempowering. I argue that 'outsider research' can contribute to the better understanding of the researcher, of the community engaged in the research and of the wider community. Nevertheless the claim 'nothing about us without us' expresses an ethical and epistemological truth in educational research: as a statement about the kind of relationship which should obtain between researcher and participants.*

## I INTRODUCTION

The relationship between researcher and researched has become a matter of intense controversy in a number of apparently different contexts. These have, nevertheless, certain key features in common: they are all contexts in which groups of people who define themselves as 'disempowered'[1] resist the 'intrusions' of researchers from outside their own community or at least the current terms of such intrusion. In the recent literature these groups have included women, people with disabilities, gays and lesbians, and indigenous people in societies dominated by white former colonialists.[2] Cases have been made out of, and on behalf of, each of these communities that are critical of research into their experience conducted by people from outside their communities. It is argued, *a fortiori*, that research into this experience should be conducted by people from within the community. 'Nothing about us without us' is, for example, the striking slogan that has

71

emerged from the disability camp (see Charlton, 1998). In this essay I shall explore more closely the nature of these arguments and the ethical and epistemological costs of sustaining them. I shall argue for the importance of retaining a role for outsider research in such communities, though one which must operate under appropriate ethical constraints and on the basis of proper human respect and care.

I shall from the start, however, observe that the distinction, the polarity, which I am sustaining here between the insider and the outsider researcher should itself be challenged. Even with generalised identities like 'disabled', 'blacks' or 'working-class' it is not always very obvious who is inside and who outside the group. However, as we add more descriptors to define the identity of any given community (for example, black, middle-class, female, graduate) we are more likely to create people who stand in relation to it in some respects as an insider and in some as an outsider (for example, they are black, middle-class and female but not graduates or they are female graduates but not middle class or black). Griffiths refers to Kay Haw's (1996, 1998) research on Muslim girls as an illustration of the 'different set of ways in which researchers have to negotiate a complex set of insider-outsider identifications' (Griffiths, 1998, p. 138). In this instance, Haw was partly an outsider in her research setting (white, non-believing, but of Christian heritage) and partly an insider (female, ex-teacher, British). Besides, as Razavi (1992) acknowledges, the insider researcher will always be something of an outsider in his or her own community by virtue of becoming a researcher, especially in any community which is itself culturally remote from the world of academe. 'By virtue of being a researcher, one is rarely a complete insider anywhere' (Razavi, 1992, p. 161). This said, I will nevertheless fall back on the crude distinction, because even in the individual experience of 'a complex set of insider-outsider identifications' we are pulled by the demands and expectations of these different roles.

The arguments in support of the exclusion of outsider researchers from disempowered communities seem to me to be of three kinds:

(i) epistemological arguments that an outsider *cannot* understand or represent accurately a particular kind of experience, and also about the inappropriate explanatory frameworks which outsiders bring with them to their research that provide the grounding for the argument that they *should not* attempt to do so;

(ii) more directly ethical arguments to do with exploitative or disrespectful behaviour of researchers;

(iii) ethico-political arguments about the disempowering effects of having others articulate your views for you.

In the following sections I shall represent and comment on each of these in turn.

## II  ONLY INSIDERS CAN PROPERLY REPRESENT THE EXPERIENCE OF A COMMUNITY

First, it is argued that only those who have shared in, and have been part of, a particular experience can understand or can properly understand (and perhaps 'properly' is particularly heavily loaded here) what it is like. You need to be a woman to understand what it is like to live as a woman; to be disabled to understand what it is like to live as a disabled person etc. Thus Charlton writes of 'the innate inability of able-bodied people, regardless of fancy credentials and awards, to understand the disability experience' (Charlton, 1998, p. 128).

Charlton's choice of language here is indicative of the rhetorical character which these arguments tend to assume. This arises perhaps from the strength of feeling from which they issue, but it warns of a need for caution in their treatment and acceptance. Even if able-bodied people have this 'inability' it is difficult to see in what sense it is 'innate'. Are all credentials 'fancy' or might some (e.g. those reflecting a sustained, humble and patient attempt to grapple with the issues) be pertinent to that ability? And does Charlton really wish to maintain that there is a single experience which is *the* experience of disability, whatever solidarity disabled people might feel for each other?

The understanding that any of us have of our own conditions or experience is unique and special, though recent work on personal narratives also shows that it is itself multi-layered and inconstant, i.e. that we have and can provide many different understandings even of our own lives (see, for example, Tierney, 1993). Nevertheless, our own understanding has a special status: it provides among other things a data source for others' interpretations of our actions; it stands in a unique relationship to our own experiencing; and no one else can have quite the same understanding. It is also plausible that people who share certain kinds of experience in common stand in a special position in terms of understanding those shared aspects of experience. However, once this argument is applied to such broad categories as 'women' or 'blacks', it has to deal with some very heterogeneous groups; the different social, personal and situational characteristics that constitute their individuality may well outweigh the shared characteristics; and there may indeed be greater barriers to mutual understanding than there are gateways.

These arguments, however, all risk a descent into solipsism: if our individual understanding is so particular, how can we have communication with or any understanding of anyone else? But, granted Wittgenstein's persuasive argument against a private language (Wittgenstein, 1963, perhaps more straightforwardly presented in Rhees, 1970), we cannot in these circumstances even describe or have any real understanding of our *own* condition in such an isolated world. Rather it is in talking to each other, in participating in a shared language, that we construct the conceptual apparatus that allows us to understand our own situation in relation to others—and this is a construction which involves understanding differences as well as similarities.

Besides, we have good reason to treat with some scepticism accounts provided by individuals of their own experience and by extension accounts provided by members of a particular category or community of people. We know that such accounts can be riddled with special pleading, selective memory, careless error, self-centredness, myopia, prejudice and a good deal more. A lesbian scholar illustrates some of the pressures that can bear, for example, on an insider researcher in her own community:

> As an insider, the lesbian has an important sensitivity to offer, yet she is also more vulnerable than the non-lesbian researcher, both to the pressure from the heterosexual world—that her studies conform to previous works and describe lesbian reality in terms of its relationship with the outside—and to pressure from the inside, from within the lesbian community itself—that her studies mirror not the reality of that community but its self-protective ideology. (Kreiger, 1982, p. 108)

In other words, while individuals from within a community have access to a particular kind of understanding of their experience, this does not automatically attach special authority (though it might attach special interest) to their own representations of that experience. Moreover, while we might acknowledge the limitations of the understanding which someone from outside a community (or someone other than the individual who is the focus of the research) can develop, this does not entail that they cannot develop and present *an* understanding or that such understanding is worthless. Individuals can indeed find benefit in the understandings that others offer of their experience in, for example, a counselling relationship, or when a researcher adopts a supportive role with teachers engaged in reflection on or research into their own practice. Many have echoed the plea of the Scottish poet, Robert Burns (in 'To a louse'):

> O wad some Pow'r the giftie gie us
> To see oursels as others see us![3]

—even if they might have been horrified with what such power revealed to them. Russell argued that it was the function of philosophy (and why not research too?) 'to suggest many possibilities which enlarge our thoughts and free them from the tyranny of custom . . .It keeps alive our sense of wonder by showing familiar things in an unfamiliar aspect' (Russell, 1912, p. 91). 'Making the familiar strange', as Stenhouse called it, often requires the assistance of someone unfamiliar with our own world who can look at our taken-for-granted experience through, precisely, the eye of a stranger. Sparkes (1994) writes very much in these terms in describing his own research, as a white, heterosexual middle-aged male, into the life history of a lesbian PE teacher. He describes his own struggle with the question 'is it possible for heterosexual people to undertake research into homosexual populations?' but he concludes that being a 'phenomenological stranger' who asks 'dumb questions' may be a useful and illuminating experience for the research subject in that they may have to return to first principles in reviewing their story. This could, of course be an elaborate piece of self-justification, but it is interesting that someone like Max Biddulph, who writes from a gay/bisexual standpoint, can quote this conclusion with apparent approval (Biddulph, 1996).

People from outside a community clearly can have *an* under-standing of the experience of those who are inside that community. It is almost certainly a *different* understanding from that of the insiders. Whether it is of any value will depend among other things on the extent to which they have immersed themselves in the world of the other and portrayed it in its richness and complexity; on the empathy and imagination that they have brought to their enquiry and writing; on whether their stories are honest, responsible and critical (Barone, 1992). Nevertheless, this value will also depend on qualities derived from the researchers' externality: their capacity to relate one set of experiences to others (perhaps from their own community); their outsider perspective on the structures which surround and help to define the experience of the community; on the reactions and responses to that community of individuals and groups external to it.[4]

Finally, it must surely follow that if we hold that a researcher, who (to take the favourable case) seeks honestly, sensitively and with humility to understand and to represent the experience of a community to which he or she does not belong, is incapable of such understanding and representation, then how can he or she understand either that same experience as mediated through the research of someone from that community? The argument which excludes the outsider from understanding a community through the effort of their own research, *a fortiori* excludes the outsider from that understanding through the secondary source in the form of the effort of an insider researcher or indeed any other means. Again, the point can only be maintained by insisting that a particular (and itself ill-defined) understanding is the only kind of understanding which is worth having.

The epistemological argument (that outsiders *cannot* understand the experience of a community to which they do not belong) becomes an ethical argument when this is taken to entail the further proposition that they *ought not* therefore attempt to research that community. I hope to have shown that this argument is based on a false premise. Even if the premise were sound, however, it would not necessarily follow that researchers should be prevented or excluded from attempting to understand this experience, unless it could be shown that in so doing they would cause some harm. This is indeed part of the argument emerging from disempowered communities and it is to this that I shall now turn.

### III   OUTSIDERS IMPORT DAMAGING FRAMEWORKS OF UNDERSTANDING

Frequent in the literature about research into disability, women's experience, race and homosexuality is the claim that people from outside these particular communities will import into their research, for example, homophobic, sexist or racist frameworks of under-standing, which damage the interests of those being researched.

In the case of research into disability it has been argued that outsider researchers carry with them assumptions that the problem of disability lies with the disabled rather than with the society which frames and defines disability. 'The essential problem of recent anthropological work on culture and disability is that it perpetuates outmoded beliefs and continues to distance research from lived oppression' (Charlton, 1998, p. 27). By contrast: 'a growing number of people with disabilities have developed a consciousness that transforms the notion and concept of disability from a medical condition to a political and social condition' (Charlton, 1998, p. 17). Charlton goes on to criticise, for example, a publication by Ingstad and Reynolds Whyte (1995), *Disability and Culture*. He claims that, although it does add to our understanding of how the conceptualisa-tion and symbolisation of disability takes place, 'its language is and perspective are still lodged in the past. In the first forty pages alone we find the words suffering, lameness, interest group, incapacitated, handicapped, deformities. Notions of oppression, dominant culture, justice, human rights, political movement, and self-determination are conspicuously absent' (Charlton, 1998 p. 27).

Discussing the neo-colonialism of outsider research into Maori experience, Smith extends this type of claim to embrace the wider methodological and metaphysical framing of outsider research: 'From an indigenous perspective Western research is more than just research that is located in a positivist tradition. It is research which brings to bear, on any study of indigenous peoples, a cultural orientation, a set of values, a different conceptualization of such things as time, space and subjectivity, different and competing theories of knowledge, highly specialized forms of language, and structures of power' (Smith, 1999, p. 42).[5]

This position requires, I think, some qualification. First, researchers are clearly not immune from some of the damaging and prejudicial attitudes on matters of race, sexuality, disability and gender which are found among the rest of the population, though I might hope that their training and experience might give them above-average awareness of these issues and above-average alertness to their expression in their own work. Even where such attitudes remain in researchers' consciousness, this intelligent self-awareness and social sensitivity mean on the whole that they are able to deploy sufficient self-censorship not to expose it in a damaging way. Researchers may thus remain morally culpable for their thoughts, but, at least, communities can be spared the harm of their expression. It is also a matter of some significance that researchers are more exposed than most to public criticism, not least from critics from within these disempowered communities, when such prejudices do enter and are revealed in their work. If they employ the rhetoric of, for example, anti-racist or anti-sexist conviction, they are at least in their public pronouncements exposed to the humiliation of being hoisted by their own petard. It is difficult to see the fairness in excluding all outsider researchers on the *a priori* supposition of universal prejudice. It is better, surely, to expose it where it is revealed and, if absolutely necessary, to debar individuals who ignore such criticism and persist in using the privilege of their research position to peddle what can then only be regarded as damaging and prejudicial propaganda. Secondly, it is plainly not the case that Western research is located exclusively (as is implied) in a positivist tradition, even if this tradition has been a dominant one. Phenomenology, ethnography, life history, even, more recently, the use of narrative fiction and poetry as forms of research representation, are all established ingredients of the educational research worlds in the UK, USA or Australasia. Contemporary research literature abounds with critiques of positivism as well as examples of its continuing expression.

I have placed much weight in these considerations on the importance of any research being exposed to criticism—most importantly, perhaps, but by no means exclusively by the people whose experience it claims to represent. This principle is not simply an ethical principle associated with the obligations that a researcher might accept towards participants in the research, but it is a fundamental feature of the processes of research and its claims to command our attention. It is precisely exposure to, modification through and survival of a process of vigorous public scrutiny that provides research with whatever authority it can claim. In contemporary ethnographic research, case-study and life-history research, for example, this expectancy of exposure to correction and criticism is one which runs right through the research process. The methodological requirement is for participants to have several opportunities to challenge any prejudices which researchers may bring with them: at the point where the terms of the research are first negotiated and they agree to participate (or not); during any conversations or interviews that take place in the course of the research; in responding to any record which is produced of the data gathering; in response to any draft or final publication. Indeed, engagement with a researcher provides any group with what is potentially a richly educative opportunity: an opportunity to open their eyes and to see things differently. It is, moreover, an opportunity which any researcher worth his or her salt will welcome.

Not all researchers or research processes will be as open as are described here to that educative opportunity, and not all participants (least of all those who are self-defining as 'disempowered') will feel the confidence to take them even if they are there. This may be seen as a reason to set up barriers to the outsider researcher, but they can and should more often be seen as problems for researchers and participants to address together in the interests of their mutual understanding and benefit.

Notwithstanding these considerations, one of the chief complaints coming out of disempowered communities is that this kind of mutual interest and benefit is precisely what is lacking in their experience of research. It is to this consideration that I shall now turn.

## IV    OUTSIDERS EXPLOIT INSIDER PARTICIPANTS IN THE COMMUNITIES THEY RESEARCH

Ellen describes how fieldwork has become 'a rite of passage by which the novice is transformed into the rounded anthropologist and initiated into the ranks of the profession'—a ritual by which 'the student of anthropology dies and a professional anthropologist is born' (Ellen, 1984, p. 23). This is a reminder that research can carry benefits to the researcher which go beyond those associated with the 'pure' pursuit of understanding. As participants in research become more aware of this, their attitudes towards research and researchers can, understandably, change. The following observation was made by a woman from a community that had experienced several waves of enthusiastic researchers:

> The kind of behaviour researchers have towards locals tells us that they just want to exploit them and take from them their ideas and information. It also tells us that they don't really care at all. They want the information to use in front of a group of people at home, so that they can be seen as clever academics. Then in the end they publish books, reviews, articles etc in order to spread their popularities. So what is this, and what is research really about? Not all researchers are exploiters, but most are, and I think it is time up now for this, and that these researchers should also be exploited by local people. (Florence Shumba, quoted in Wilson, 1992, p. 199)

Researchers who are sensitive to this issue typically look for ways to counter the imbalance of benefit. They will sometimes discuss with participants ways in which the research could be designed to benefit all parties, by, for example, ensuring that it addresses issues on which the participants need information as well as the researchers or by providing data that the research participants can use independently and for their own purposes. In the absence of any other perceived benefit, some schools in the UK have responded to researchers' requests for access and time for interviews by proposing to charge by the hour for teachers' time. Of course sometimes participants will be persuaded to participate on the grounds that some other people whose interests they care about—pupils in schools, for example, or children currently excluded from education—will secure the benefit of the research, but there has to be the link between something which they perceive to be a benefit (albeit altruistically) and the commitment which they are asked to make.

These illustrations of the terms of engagement between researchers and their participants present a picture of a trade in benefit, the negotiation of a utilitarian equation of mutual happiness and, perhaps, pain, though one in which higher satisfactions (e.g. new insights and the improvements to the future education of children) have a place alongside lower ones (a bit of self-publicity or cash in the school fund). Questions of exploitation, in Kantian terms of treating people as means rather than ends (see Kant, 1964)[6] come in if, as is sometimes alleged, researchers use their positions of authority or their sophistication to establish relationships in which the benefits are very one-sided in their favour.

This distinction between the utilitarian principle and the Kantian one is crucial here. The utilitarian principle might require us to measure in the scales a much wider community of benefit. If, for example, the researcher could show that, even though the Maori community he or she was researching experienced the inconvenience of the research without the benefit, thousands of other people would benefit from it, then the utilitarian equation might provide justification for the research. But this is precisely one of the weaknesses of the utilitarian principle of the greatest happiness of the greatest number—at least when it is applied with this sort of simplicity. It requires either a broader take on the utilitarian principle (which might observe that a programme of action which allocates all the benefits to one group and all the 'pain' to another will not be conducive to the greatest aggregation of happiness) or the invoking of something closer to the Kantian principle, which would demand that we do not exploit one group of people to the exclusive benefit of another. Researchers seeking collaboration with participants in disempowered communities have essentially two forms of appeal— to their self-interest or to their generosity. Either they need to see some benefit to themselves which is at least roughly commensurate to the effort that is required of them (or in some cases the value of what they have to offer); or they need knowingly to contribute out of their own benevolence towards the researcher or others whom they believe the research will benefit.

In this second case, the researcher is placed in something of the position of the receiver of a gift and he or she needs to recognise consequently the quite elaborate ethical apparatus that surrounds such receipt. There is a particular 'spirit' in which we might be expected to receive a gift: a spirit of gratitude, of humility, of mutuality in the relationship. There may also be a network of social expectations, which flow from such giving—of being in thrall to the giver, of being in his or her debt—but on the whole anyone contributing to an educational research project would be naïve to assume that such 'debts' might be repaid. Most of the time, researchers are in fact inviting the generosity of their participants, and perhaps there is something more ethically elevated in responding to such generosity with a true spirit of gratitude and a recognition of the mutuality of relationship which binds giver and receiver, than in seeking to establish a trade in dubious benefits. Smith (1999) provides a wonderful picture of the combination of spirit and benefits that might be involved in establishing this relationship (as well as a whole new angle on the notion of 'empowerment'!) when she outlines the range of issues on which a researcher approaching a Maori community might need to satisfy them: 'Is her spirit clear? Does he have a good heart? What other baggage are they carrying? Are they useful to us? Can they fix up our generator? Can they actually do anything?' (Smith, 1999, p. 10). Perhaps all educational researchers should be required to satisfy participants on these questions.

I conclude that the possibility that outsider educational research may be conducted in an exploitative manner is not an argument for obstructing it comprehensively, but it is an argument for requiring that it be conducted under an appropriate set of principles and obligations and in a proper spirit. 'Qualitative researchers', argued Stake, 'are guests in the private spaces of the world. Their manners should be good and their code of ethics strict' (Stake, 1998, p. 103). Any community may legitimately reject a researcher (insider or outsider) who fails to establish and conduct relationships under these requirements.

In this field, ethics is never far removed from politics. This essay has focused on the relationship between educational researchers and communities that are self-defined as 'disempowered' but has not really addressed the issue of power. At the heart of the objections to outsider research is a view that such research, far from challenging and removing such disempowerment, operates to reinforce it. It is this argument which I shall now address.

## V　OUTSIDERS' RESEARCH DISEMPOWERS INSIDERS

At least one of the arguments against outsider research into self-defined 'disempowered' sections of the population is made independently of the measure of sensitivity and care, which the outsider researchers demonstrate in its conduct. 'If we have learned one thing from the civil rights movement in the US', wrote Ed Roberts, a leading figure in the Disability Rights Movement (DRM), 'it's that when others speak for you, you lose' (quoted in Driedger, 1989, p. 28). Roberts' case is in part that for so long as such groups depend on outsiders to represent them on the wider stage, they will be reinforcing both the fact and the perception of their subordination and dependency as well as exposing themselves to potential misrepresentation. They have to break the vicious circle of dependency—and that means taking control for themselves of the ways in which their experience is represented more widely:

> The DRM's demand for control is the essential theme that runs through all its work, regardless of political-economic or cultural differences. Control has universal appeal for DRM activists because their needs are everywhere conditioned by a dependency born of powerlessness, poverty, degradation, and institutionalisation. This dependency, saturated with paternalism, begins with the onset of disability and continues until death. (Charlton, 1998, p. 3)

Outsider researchers sometimes persuade themselves that they are acting in an emancipatory way by 'giving voice to' neglected or disenfranchised sections of the community. Their research may indeed push the evident voice of the researcher far into the background as he or she 'simply presents', perhaps as large chunks of direct transcription and without commentary, what participants have to say. But, as Reinharz has warned, this is by no means as simple as it might appear:

> To listen to people is to empower them. But if you want to hear it, you have to go hear it, in their space, or in a safe space. Before you can expect to hear anything worth hearing, you have to examine the power dynamics of the space and the social actors . . .
>
> Second, you have to be the person someone else can talk to, and you have to be able to create a context where the person can speak and you can listen. That means we have to study who we are and who we are in relation to those we study . . .
>
> Third, you have to be willing to hear what someone is saying, even when it violates your expectations or threatens your interests. In other words, if you want someone to tell it like it is, you have to hear it like it is. (Reinharz, 1988, pp. 15–16)

Even with this level of self knowledge, sensitivity and discipline, there is a significant temptation in such situations to what is sometimes called ventriloquy: the using of the voice of the participant to give expression to the things which the researcher wants to say or to have said. This is a process which is present in the selection of participants, in the framing of the questions which they are encouraged to answer, in the verbal and visual cues which they are given of the researcher's pleasure or excitement with their responses, and, later, in the researcher's selection of material for publication. Such ventriloquy, argues Fine, disguises 'the usually unacknowledged stances of researchers who navigate and camouflage theory through the richness of "native voices"' (Fine, 1994, p. 22).

The argument that insiders within 'disempowered' communities (or any other communities for that matter) should be researching and, where appropriate, giving public expression to their own experience is surely uncontroversial. In a context in which insider research has been negligible and hugely subordinated to waves of outsider research, there is a good case for taking practical steps to correct that balance and spare a community what can understandably be experienced as an increasingly oppressive relationship with research.

There are, however, at last three reasons in principle for keeping the possibility of outsider research open: (i) that such enquiry might enhance the understanding of the researcher; (ii) that it might enhance the understanding of the community itself; and (iii) that it might enhance the understanding of a wider public. There is no doubt a place for researching our own experience and that of our own communities, but surely we cannot be condemned lifelong to such social solipsism? Notwithstanding some postmodernist misgivings, 'There is still a world out there, much to learn, much to discover; and the exploration of ourselves, however laudable in that at least it risks no new imperialistic gesture, is not, in the end, capable of sustaining lasting interest' (Patai, 1994, p. 67). The issue is not, however, merely one of satisfying curiosity. There is a real danger that if we become persuaded that we cannot understand the experience of others and that 'we have no right to speak for anyone but ourselves', then we will all too easily find ourselves epistemologically and morally isolated, furnished with a comfortable legitimation for ignoring the condition of anyone but ourselves. This is not, any more than the paternalism of the powerful, the route to a more just society.

How can we reconcile the importance of (1) wider social understanding of the world of 'disempowered' communities and of the structures which contribute to that disempowerment, (2) the openness of those communities and structures to the outsider researcher, and (3) the determination that the researcher should not wittingly or unwittingly reinforce that disempowerment? The literature (from which a few selected examples are quoted below) provides some clues as to the character of relations between researcher and researched which 'emancipatory', 'participatory' or 'educative' research might take.

To begin with, we need to re-examine the application of the notion of 'property' to the ownership of knowledge. In economic terms, knowledge is not a competitive good. It has the distinctive virtue that (at least in terms of its educative function) it can be infinitely distributed without loss to any of those who are sharing in it. Similarly the researcher can acquire it from people without denying it to them and can return it enriched. However, it is easy to neglect the processes of reporting back to people and *sharing* in knowledge and the importance which can be attached to this process by those concerned. For Smith, a Maori woman working with research students from the indigenous people of New Zealand, 'Reporting back to the people is never a one-off exercise or a task that can be signed off on completion of the written report'. She describes how one of her students took her work back to the people she interviewed. 'The family was waiting for her; they cooked food and made us welcome. We left knowing that her work will be passed around the family to be read and eventually will have a place in the living room along with other valued family books and family photographs' (Smith, 1999, pp. 15–16).

For some, what is required is a moving away from regarding research as a property and towards seeing it as a dialogic enquiry designed to assist the understanding of all concerned:

Educative research attempts to restructure the traditional relationship between researcher and 'subject'. Instead of a one-way process where researchers extract data from 'subjects', Educational Research encourages a dialogic process where participants negotiate meanings at the level of question posing, data collection and analysis . . . It . . . encourages participants to work together on an equal basis to reach a mutual understanding. Neither participant should stand apart in an aloof or judgmental manner; neither should be silenced in the process. (Gitlin and Russell, 1994, p. 185)

For others, it is a matter not simply of a kind of professional principle of respect for others but also a requirement of care: 'The research encounter needs to be imbued with more than a simple desire to collect data from a "subject". As researchers, one facet of our research capability must be to exhibit a sense of care and concern to understand the "other's possibility"' (Tierney, 1994, p. 105). Noddings expands: 'Apprehending the other's reality, feeling what he feels as nearly as possible, is an essential part of caring . . . For if I take on the other's reality as possibility and begin to feel its reality, I feel also that I must act accordingly; that is, I am impelled to act as though in my own behalf, but in behalf of the other' (Noddings, 1986, p. 16).

For many within the field that I have been reviewing, however, respect, care and dialogic relations are not enough. Research must be conducted in such a way that it contributes actively to the creation of a more just society and researchers should adopt what have been offered as emancipatory research methods: 'Thus, I am arguing that the researcher/author has three tasks: the researcher engages the researched in a reflexive encounter; the research "act"—the book, article or presentation—brings to light the inequities of power that may exist; and the researcher actively works for care and change' (Tierney, 1994, p. 111). Compare Fine (1994, p. 29):

Participatory activist research . . . assumes that knowledge is best gathered in the midst of social change projects; that the partial perspectives of participants and observers can be collected by researchers in 'power sensitive conversations' (Haraway, 1988, p. 590), which need to be transformative—they cannot be just a pluralistic collection of voices but need to be a struggle.

It is on this argument not enough for researchers to seek to understand the worlds of the disempowered; they must also seek (as Marx would have urged) to change them. This, however, might be a step too far. Researchers' prime responsibility (*qua* researcher) is, surely, to seek honest and as far as possible truth-like understanding of whatever is the focus of their enquiry. Even while advancing the case for educational research in the cause of social justice, Griffiths acknowledges that 'educational research is about getting knowledge' or, more specifically, 'better knowledge', as she calls it (Griffiths, 1998, p. 129). This pursuit will certainly require of researchers an alertness to the prejudices that they bring to their enquiry and a reflexiveness, which will allow the enquiry itself to challenge these assumptions. Such enquiry should, as I have already acknowledged, be conducted under a moral imperative of respect for participants, that is a requirement to treat them as ends rather than as a means to ends, and under a responsibility to anticipate and avoid possible harm to participants (and I would include in this their disempowerment). Of course, one of the ways in which the researchers may contribute to challenging or correcting social injustice of one kind or another is by representing it, or participants' perceptions of it, honestly, vividly and accurately in their research products and making these public. Another way will be through their own reflective 'dialogic' or 'educative' engagement with the researched community. This much is a proper requirement of the research as research and of the researcher as researcher ('proper' in the sense that it is difficult to see how it could claim to be research unless it did these things and 'proper' in that these are the kind of things that one might reasonably expect a researcher to be competent to do).

To impose on researchers a further obligation to work as part of the research process for political change of a kind which will address any perceived injustices reported in the research is, however, to raise expectations which run, dangerously perhaps, beyond their competence as researchers. Educational researchers are not obviously any more competent than anyone else to define the proper ordering of a just society; nor discerning as to the best path towards such a society; nor skilled in managing the political processes by which such a social order might be achieved. Perhaps among the number of educational researchers there are some who happen to have, in addition to their research skills, this combination of political wisdom and political acumen and perhaps these can appropriately apply this combination of talents to their field of enquiry, but should we wish that the political naïvety and ineptness which may be more commonly associated with sound research skills in the educational research community be thrust upon the disempowered as a matter of general principle? This really would give them grounds for seeking the researchers' exclusion.

And yet this conclusion is misleadingly at odds with much of what I have been arguing in the course of this paper, and when I read, for example, Griffith's (1998) advocacy of a framework for 'educational research for justice' I find in her 'ten principles' much that resonates with what I have defended here as ethical requirements falling upon the educational researcher going about his or her business of trying to understand the world, or more particularly other people's experience of it. The principles and aspirations which I have attached to even a single-minded research endeavour reflect necessary if not sufficient conditions for a more just society—or at least, and more modestly, for greater justice in that part of its activity which lies in proximity to the practice of educational research. Commitment to, for example: sensitive and reflexive understanding of the experience of others; respect for others as persons; listening to others in conditions of respect and care; mutuality of benefit and gratefulness for giving relationships; openness to criticism and the exposure of prejudice— such commitments may not directly challenge wider social and economically formed structures of oppression, but they are the sort of principles which have the capacity to render such structures visible and to display them as intolerable.

The claim *'nothing about us without us'* ought to be an ethical as well as an epistemological truism in educational research as a statement about the kind of relationship which should obtain between researcher and participants. It does not however provide a basis for excluding the outsider researcher from genuine and respectful enquiry.

*Correspondence:* David Bridges, Centre for Applied Research in Education, University of East Anglia, Norwich NR4 7TJ, UK. Email: d.bridges@uea.ac.uk

## NOTES

1. More accurately, some of their members define them as disempowered; not all would necessarily agree. Dangerously, perhaps, I shall take this self-designation as given for the purpose of this discussion. I shall even resist the temptation to examine the notions of empowerment and disempowerment. These are usefully discussed in relation to educational research in Morwenna Griffiths' book, *Educational Research for Social Justice* (1998).
2. In treating these together I fall into something close to what one writer describes as 'the new feminist mantra (of) integrated analysis of race, class, gender, ethnicity, sexuality' (Patai, 1994, p. 61). This arises simply from the observation that the issues are defined and discussed in very much the same terms across these different spheres of activism and enquiry.
3. This transcribes (with some loss) into Standard English as 'Oh would some Power give us the gift to see ourselves as others see us!'
4. This is not to imply that insider researchers are incapable of some of that externality too. An Iranian researcher, writing about her enquiry into absentee landlords in her own country, explains: 'The fact that I am "one of them" does not mean that I am incapable of analysing them . . . This, I think, arises from being a researcher, which makes total immersion very difficult; it distances the researcher even from her or his own supposed class and sub-culture' (Razavi, 1992, p. 161).
5. See also, for example, Ladner (1971) and Foster (1994).
6. 'Act in such a way that you always treat humanity, whether in your own person or in the person of any other, never simply as a means, but always at the same time as an end' (Kant, 1964, p. 96).

# REFERENCES

Barone, T. (1992) Beyond theory and method: a case for critical story telling, *Theory into Practice*, 31.2, pp. 142–146.

Biddulph, M. (1996) *Can only Dorothy's friends speak for Dorothy? Exploring issues of biographical positioning in qualitative research with gay/bisexual men*, paper presented to BERA Researcher's Conference, Lancaster University, 11–12 September 1996.

Charlton, J. I. (1998) *Nothing About us Without us: disability power and oppression* (Berkeley, University of California Press).

Driedger, D. (1989) *The Last Civil Rights Movement: disabled people's international* (New York, St Martin's Press).

Ellen, R. (1984) *Ethnographic Research: a guide to general conduct* (London, Academic Press).

Fine, M. (1994) Negotiations of power inside feminist research, in: A. Gitlin (ed.) *Power and Method: political activism and educational research* (New York, Routledge).

Foster, M. (1994) The power to know one thing is never the power to know all things: methodological notes on two studies of black American teachers, in: A. Gitlin (ed.) *Power and Method: political activism and educational research* (New York, Routledge).

Gitlin, A. and Russell, R. (1994) Alternative methodologies and the research context, in: A. Gitlin (ed.) *Power and Method: political activism and educational research* (New York, Routledge).

Griffiths, M. (1998) *Educational Research For Social Justice: getting off the fence* (Buckingham, Open University Press).

Haraway, D. (1988) Situated knowledges: the science question in feminism and the privilege of partial perspective, *Feminist Studies*, 14.3, pp. 575–597.

Haw, K. F. (1996) Exploring the educational experience of Muslim girls: tales told to tourists—should the white researcher stay at home?, *British Educational Research Journal*, 22.3, pp. 319–330.

Haw, K. F. (1998) *Educating Muslim Girls: shifting discourses* (Buckingham, Open University Press).

Homan, R. (1992) *The Ethics of Research* (London, Longman).

Ingstad, B. and Reynolds Whyte, S. (eds) (1995) *Disability and Culture* (Berkeley, University of California Press).

Kant, I. (1964) *Groundwork of the Metaphysics of Morals*, translated by H. J. Paton (New York, Harper).

Kreiger, S. (1982) Lesbian identity and community: recent social science literature, *Signs*, 8.11, pp. 91–108.

Ladner, J. (1971) *Tomorrow's Tomorrow* (Garden City NY, Doubleday).

Noddings, N. (1986) *Caring: a feminine approach to ethics and moral education* (Berkeley, University of California Press).

Patai, D. (1994) When power becomes method, in: A. Gitlin (ed.) *Power and Method: political activism and educational research* (New York, Routledge).

Razavi, S. (1992) Fieldwork in a familiar setting: the role of politics at the national, community and household levels, in: S. Devereux and J. Hoddinott (eds) *Fieldwork in Developing Countries*, pp. 152–163 (Hemel Hempstead, Harvester Wheatsheaf).

Reinharz, S. (1988) The concept of voice. Paper presented at conference on 'Human diversity: perspectives on people context', June 8 1988, University of Maryland, College Park, MD.

Rhees, R. (1970) *Discussions of Wittgenstein* (London, Routledge & Kegan Paul).

Russell, B. (1912) *The Problems of Philosophy* (Oxford, Oxford University Press).

Smith, L. T. (1999) *Decolonising Methodologies: research and indigenous peoples* (London, Zed Books).

Sparkes, A. (1994) Life histories and the issue of voice: reflections on an emerging relationship, *Qualitative Studies in Education*, 7.2, pp. 165–183.

Stanfield, J. H. (1994) Empowering the culturally diversified sociological voice, in: A. Gitlin (ed.) *Power and Method: political activism and educational research* (New York, Routledge).

Stake, R. E. (1998) Case study, in: N. K. Denzin and Y. Lincoln (eds) *Strategies of Qualitative Inquiry* (London, Sage).

Tierney, W. G. (1993) Self identity in a postmodern world: a life story, in: D. Mclaughlin and W. G. Tierney (eds) *Naming Silenced Lives* (New York, Routledge).

Tierney, W. G. (1994) On method and hope, in: A. Gitlin (ed.) *Power and Method: political activism and educational research* (New York, Routledge).

Wilson, K. (1992) Thinking about ethics in fieldwork, in: S. Devereux and J. Hoddinott (eds) *Fieldwork in Developing Countries* (Hemel Hempstead, Harvester Wheatsheaf).

Wittgenstein, L. (1963) *Philosophical Investigations*, trans Anscombe, G. E. M. (Oxford, Blackwell).

# 6

# Codes are Not Enough: What Philosophy can Contribute to the Ethics of Educational Research

ROBIN SMALL

*Formal codes of ethics are not the best way of addressing
ethical issues arising in educational research. Philosophers
have often exaggerated the importance of such codes,
although philosophy has little to contribute to them. What
we need rather is a closer attention to the ways in which
ethical decisions about research are actually made. Moral
theory can contribute here by clarifying this process and
identifying helpful procedures and strategies, such as those
used by institutional review committees in arriving at good
judgements. New and unfamiliar situations require us to
extend our existing abilities, not to return to first
principles and set up formal codes.*

Educational research is commonly multi-disciplinary in nature.
Properly understood, this is a rather demanding concept, for it
implies that meeting a single set of standards is not enough: the good
researcher must address the expectations of scholars from various
backgrounds in the humanities and social sciences. A more recent
addition to this demand is an increasing awareness of and emphasis
on the ethical dimension of educational enquiry. Here too we see a
multi-disciplinary character, mirrored at the institutional level by
ethics committees that contain members from a broad range of
research disciplines. In facing the ethical challenges of research, we
clearly need all the assistance we can obtain. In this discussion,
however, I want to focus on some relatively theoretical issues, and
consider the role that philosophical reflection can play in dealing with
them.

One idea should, I think, be ruled out at the start: any notion that a training in philosophy brings with it some special authority where ethical judgements are concerned.[1] It is true that the design of research projects may benefit from philosophical analysis and methodology, especially given the development of post-positivist theories of knowledge which reject the foundationalism of traditional empiricism without abandoning its realism. Can something similar be suggested in relation to the ethical aspects of educational research? Of course, philosophy of education is itself an area of research which presents some ethical issues, even though its inquiries may not involve human beings as subjects or participants. While there are no problems of informed consent or confidentiality, questions may arise about the integrity of authorship and the ownership of knowledge. Moreover, these researchers commonly work alongside others for whom questions attaching to the involvement of other people and the effects of their work on those others cannot be avoided. Members of this wider research community share a common responsibility to ensure that proper attention is paid to the ethical qualities of the design and performance of research.

My main question is therefore: what part can philosophy play in ensuring that educational research will be ethical research? I want to consider two possibilities. One is that it can contribute to the formulation of a code of ethics established to govern the conduct of research. As we shall see, this is an idea that has been widely pursued, and for good reasons. The other is that it can help to clarify the process of making ethical decisions about research and point out the procedures and methods which are most likely to be successful. Such decisions may be made by the researchers themselves, either as individuals or as teams, but they may also be made by groups of people who sit on ethical review committees at research institutions. These two approaches do not exclude each other, and yet their relative importance is a remaining question. I will argue that the first approach has been favoured too much, and that it is time to consider its drawbacks and the advantages of the other approach: that is, to take seriously the idea that the contribution of philosophy to research ethics should be methodological rather than substantial.

My view is that philosophers have found codes of ethics too congenial for their own good. This has led them, on the one hand, into exaggerating the importance of such documents and, on the other, into according a privileged and authorised status to a particular moral theory. The outcome is not good philosophy, and I think it is not good ethics either. Codes of ethics present a temptation to institutionalise one philosophical approach to ethics, namely, a 'top-down' strategy. By this I mean one which follows the successful models of logic and geometry by starting with abstract and universal principles, and proceeding to derive particular judgements from them through a kind of logical reasoning. This approach has some obvious merits—for example, it seems to guarantee consistency, surely a very desirable outcome in morality. And it certainly has the standing of a long history of support in philosophy. But there are serious questions about its relation to the making of ethical decisions, and in particular about its relation to what we might call the best practice in this area.

With this in mind, my discussion will take a sceptical line, in two ways. First, I question whether a formal code of ethics is a useful way of addressing the ethical issues arising in educational research. Second, I question whether philosophy has much to contribute to such a code of ethics. It is only right to note that a number of respected colleagues think differently on both questions.[2] There are arguments in favour of the adoption of a code of ethics, and for entrusting much of the responsibility for its formulation to those with expertise in a philosophical approach to moral issues. However, I will show that there are also arguments against both of these propositions. A codified practice is of very limited usefulness in arriving at ethical decisions. Furthermore, the appeal of this approach is bound up with the availability of a more or less ready-made model which barely needs adaption for this use. The codes of ethics I will discuss here have a specific and readily identifiable, although not widely known, source in the work of a particular thinker: Sir David Ross (1877–1971). The adaption of Ross's ethical doctrine, and the changes made to it in the process, provides an interesting example of the use and misuse of a philosophical theory for practical purposes.

Having taken this sceptical view, I accept a responsibility to point to some different approach to what is acknowledged as a genuine problem, namely, the task of making good ethical judgements over the design and conduct of research. We should be widening the ethical agenda in educational research by drawing attention to other ways of making ethical decisions: for instance, by clarifying the procedures through which groups of people can arrive at good judgements about the ethical dimension of research. In my final section, I will try to outline the sorts of considerations that this approach brings to bear on the problem.

## WHAT IS THE USE OF A CODE OF ETHICS?

I think we should not confuse a code of ethics with rules designed to guard against deliberate misconduct in research—that is, against offences such as plagiarism or the falsification of data. While such behaviour is plainly unethical, it is important to realise that many (though not all) of the practices which a code of ethics is intended to guard against are not underhanded and dishonest devices, but the actions of people acting with good intentions, who at the worst can be charged with haste or insensitivity. This is why it is appropriate to speak of 'ethics' here, and to define the task as one of education rather than enforcement, and the means for achieving it as learning rather than deterrence. In contrast, what institutions need to deal with research misconduct is a disciplinary apparatus of the sort used for sexual harassment and similar forms of misbehaviour.

Yet it may be objected that the situation is more subtle, given that a code of ethics is located in that area where external and internal influences on the individual's behaviour are not always easy to separate. This is linked with one striking objection to codes of ethics: that they are misnamed, since ethics is by its nature bound up with individual decision, and so cannot be legislated. John Ladd has argued on these grounds that 'the whole notion of an organised professional ethics is an absurdity—intellectual and moral' (1980, p. 154). Ladd is discussing codes of ethics for professional practice rather than academic or scientific research, but most of his arguments apply here as well. He maintains that ethical principles can be established only by deliberation and argument, not 'by fiat, by agreement or by authority', and goes on to argue that 'Even if substantial agreement could be reached on ethical principles and they could be set out in a code, the attempt to impose such principles on others in the guise of ethics contradicts the notion of ethics itself, which presumes that persons are autonomous moral agents' (1980, p. 154).

The assumption here seems to be that ethics is an immediate relation between the individual person and moral values, without the mediation of a social group as a source of either understanding or motivation.[3] This goes well beyond Ladd's more cogent point that if ethical precepts have an apparatus of enforcement, they are simply laws, perhaps with no more moral significance than library rules or parking regulations. In fact, his assumption is open to some serious objections. Such a radical individualism leaves the public dimension of ethics in darkness. Yet it remains a reality, and research institutions are faced with ethical problems which they must address in an organised fashion, or not at all. (Whether relying on a code of ethics is the best approach is another matter.) More seriously, his bias renders any account of individual moral learning very difficult, since it discounts not only precept and instruction, but any kind of external influence, as inconsistent with absolute autonomy. Such a sharp distinction between moral learning and other kinds of learning runs contrary to what we know about human development. When one is considering a practical approach to ethics, as in the present discussion, it becomes evident that any adequate theory should help us to understand how both individuals and groups are able to learn, to develop their understanding and to improve their abilities to make sound ethical decisions. This criterion counts strongly in favour of some theories over others, as I shall emphasise later.

Another point made by Ladd is that there are no ethical principles specific to any occupation. Where the behaviour of the individual person towards others is concerned, he argues, the only issues are general ones. 'Therefore, it should not be necessary to devise a special code to tell professionals that they ought to refrain from cheating and lying, or to make them treat their clients (and patients) with respect, or to tell them that they ought to ask for informed consent for invasive actions'. Clearly, these rules also apply to researchers. Other problems occurring in educational enquiry (those of privacy and confidentiality, for instance) are often found in everyday life, and require no new moral principles. However, I think there is a misunderstanding here. What Ladd complains about is just a necessary feature of any approach to professional ethics: that it be at least consistent with ethics in general. We have all heard propositions such as 'Business is business' and 'war is war'. These are attempts to separate one area of human activity from others, and condone behaviour within those areas which would be condemned elsewhere as immoral. The rhetorical use of tautology suggests either a lack of candour or a bad conscience.[4] So there should be no question of a compartmentalised ethics: to this extent, we must agree with Ladd. On the other hand, not everyone is equally likely to encounter given kinds of moral dilemmas. Hence, it is not a question of a 'special code' in the sense he suggests, but simply a task of making judgements about some collection of more or less related situations. Our chances of success are much increased if we can deal with these together, drawing on the practical wisdom gained through past experience, and not have to keep on reinventing the moral wheel.

Finally, Ladd argues that a code of ethics may itself have harmful effects. Since it sets only a minimal standard of ethical conduct, people are likely to condone whatever is not expressly dealt with by its provisions.[5] And this might well include unethical conduct. A writer who voices a related objection is Roger Homan, who argues that while codes of professional ethics help to maintain the ethical standards of a professional group, as well as increasing public confidence, they also present a problem. By defining moral obligations in a formal fashion, they give the impression that these may be satisfied by a single procedure of compliance, rather than through a continuing process of considering the ethical aspects of one's actions. Both codes of ethics and committees of ethical review take over the moral responsibility that each researcher should have for his or her behaviour. As Homan puts it, 'Statements of ethics invite the individual to surrender the moral conscience to a professional consensus' (1992, p. 331). It may be added that this argument also applies to the establishment of institutional systems of ethical review. In fact, the transferring of ethical responsibility may be seen as even more likely in that case, since the committee's members are closer at hand. I agree that such a division of moral labour is unacceptable. It is not the job of an ethics committee to take over ethical responsibility. It will very often happen that in the course of an investigation situations arise which have not been foreseen: in fact, this may be a sign that the research is of the highly valued kind which opens up new territory. If the researcher is unable to cope with any ethical questions these pose, that suggests something has gone seriously wrong with the process of ethical consideration of the project.

In an ideal world, we would not need either codes of research ethics or ethical review committees. As it is, these devices are no substitute for moral education. To this extent, the critics are right. Defenders of codes of research ethics have responded by arguing that they contribute to ethical learning in researchers. Martin Bibby suggests that they help 'by drawing attention to features of proposed research which are morally relevant, but which the researcher may have also overlooked' (1993, pp. 50–51) According to Judith Lichtenberg, 'Codes of ethics can increase the likelihood that people will behave in certain ways, partly by bringing to consciousness the character of their actions, partly by attaching sanctions to non-compliance, and partly by increasing the value of, and decreasing the sacrifice involved in, an individual act' (1996, p. 27). Finally, Nicholas Burbules argues that 'thinking of the codes as principles may promote a closer, more careful deliberation in the endeavour to "get it right"—even if this endeavour is illusory' (1998, p. 122).

Nevertheless, defenders of codes allow that the manner of their actual use is not evident, and that claims for their educational function may be hard to substantiate. Since codes of ethics typically consist of general principles which must be applied to particular cases, several questions arise. What are these principles, where do they come from and what status do they have? Second, how do they figure in the process of making ethical decisions about research? Both of these issues have a philosophical content, as we shall see.

## THE ROLE OF PHILOSOPHY IN DEVELOPING A CODE OF ETHICS

It has become a common practice for research bodies to call in philosophers to assist in the task of drawing up a code of research ethics. It is natural for philosophers to be involved in such a task; not just as people involved in research themselves, but because they can reasonably claim to have some disciplinary knowledge relevant to the task in hand. Yet it seems to me that philosophy does not show at its best in this exercise, for two reasons.

The first is that a code is a finished product, whereas philosophy is an continuing process. At least, that is one plausible view. Although there may be disagreement on this point, the builders of metaphysical systems have never succeeded in bringing the ongoing conversation of philosophy to an end by providing the last word on any of its main themes. One might argue that philosophy does produce things: arguments, theories, lectures, articles and books. However, these are only relatively finished products, even for the individual thinker. While a code of ethics too is subject to revision, it is institutionalised at a given time, and there is a definite distinction between its status and that of any surrounding ethical discussion. If it is read by researchers, this does not provide a dialogue between equals. Rather, they are simply expected to do what it says, and sometimes there are penalties attached to failure to comply. Here we see conditions which are very different from philosophy's natural environment. 'There are no classical authors of philosophy', wrote Kant (Allison, 1973, p. 133). He did not, of course, mean that there are no philosophical writers from whom we can learn much—rather, that even the best of these does not provide ready-made solutions to our problems.

In the second place, a code of ethics usually represents a consensus. Arising out of the democratic process through which differences are accommodated rather than eliminated, it is something that people feel they can live with, whether or not they support each particular item. For that reason, intractable areas of disagreement will be left out, or perhaps papered over with the sort of deliberately vague language found in the world of diplomacy. In contrast, consensus in philosophy is seldom found, or even sought as a goal. Consensus may occur in the form of domination by one standpoint, as with the version of Marxism supported by state power in socialist countries for many years. Or it may arise as a theoretical eclecticism which, on closer examination, soon loses any semblance of coherence. Again, therefore, philosophy does not show its own integrity well in this exercise, even when it does make some contribution.

Let us pursue this idea further. Of all disciplines, philosophy is most marked by perennial differences, such as those between various schools of moral theory: utilitarian, deontological and so on. How is that diversity to be dealt with in a code of ethics? The puzzle seems insoluble. Either the standpoint of one of these competing theories is arbitrarily adopted, or else readers are offered an accurate but unhelpful survey. In the second case we end with the situation that arises in some approaches to the teaching of ethics. The student acquires some acquaintance with the 'perspectives' (as they are likely to be called) of utilitarianism, Kantianism, intuitionism and others, and upon completion of the course is able to give responses to particular moral dilemmas in the following form: 'In that situation, a utilitarian would do—, whereas a Kantian would do—', and so on. As an answer, this may be quite accurate. As an approach to moral problems, it is not only useless but mischievous. For it undermines whatever capacity the person already has to think directly and purposefully about a moral problem by redirecting attention to the 'meta' level, and leaving a range of options from which an apparently arbitrary choice is to be made. Moreover, it holds out the false promise that the adoption of some ethical 'perspective' will solve our problems once and for all by supplying judgements for all occasions.

In some codes of research ethics we can see both strategies at work in different places, or an attempt to combine 'perspectives' in an eclectic approach. At the same time, a code of ethics is by its nature geared to one kind of ethics: what I shall call a 'principled' ethics, meaning one that takes the form of general principles of conduct. Whether there is one principle or a hundred principles, their role is much the same. They are intended to enable one to arrive at particular decisions through processes of reasoning in which these abstract and universal formulations serve as basic premises. This is what is sometimes called a 'top-down' approach to morality. As that label suggests, it is not the only possible approach, and there are reasons for thinking it is not the best one. Its main problem is just the one which is most relevant to a code of ethics, namely, the task of making particular ethical judgements. The model of deducing conclusions from general propositions can appeal to the very successful example of formal logic, yet it is far less appropriate in dealing with the complexities of everyday life and educational enquiry. Attempts to construct models of practical reasoning on the analogy of logical deduction have been notably unconvincing and unproductive. Such principles seem far too abstract to match the complexity of actual situations even in everyday life, let alone in more unfamiliar circumstances.

Worse still, we soon find anomalous situations in which a general principle seems not to hold true. As J. H. Newman observed, there is no rule on earth without exceptions. The adoption of a rigorous consistency as our starting point (for example, an absolute ban on any deception of participants in research, even by omission rather than outright lying) leads immediately to a series of qualifications to account for those situations in which we are prepared to condone some lack of candour (for example, as to the real direction of an investigation). But these qualifications must be justified by some further moral principle, since one principle can be opposed only by another principle of similar standing. Just as the retrograde motion of the planets required the introduction of epicycles into the geocentric model of the universe, so too these exceptions to moral rules demand a proliferation of principles, each as 'basic' as the previous one. Before long, the credibility of the ethical code must come under suspicion, as its structure shows the increasing strain of incorporating ad hoc additions.

Where do the principles contained in a code of research ethics come from in the first place? The prototype for many recent codes of ethics is *The Belmont Report*, a set of guidelines issued by a National Commission for the Protection of Human Subjects of Biomedical and Behavioral Research established by the United States Congress (*The Belmont Report*, 1978). After widespread consultation and discussion, the commission delivered a document which has had a wide influence, not only in the United States of America but in countries such as Canada and Australia.[6] It provides guidelines for the protection of human subjects which cover most of the common ethical problems in empirical research, and also sets out a clear and coherent presentation of a general ethical position which it describes as corresponding to 'our cultural tradition'. This centres upon three basic ethical principles, or general prescriptive judgements. The report makes no claim that they are the only basic ethical principles in this tradition, but says that they are the most relevant to research involving human subjects. These principles are: respect for persons, beneficence (taken together with non-maleficence) and justice. Each has consequences for the conduct of research. Respect for persons is expressed in the need for informed consent, beneficence in protection from harm and the maximising of good outcomes, and justice in an equitable distribution of the benefits and costs of research. (For instance, it points to the wrongness of drawing on some restricted part of the population as suitable subjects in research, quite apart from their chances of benefiting from the outcomes.) The report acknowledges that these principles may come into conflict when applied to particular cases, and goes on to explore some cases in point.

The plainest evidence that the ethical principles found in *The Belmont Report* and in many later codes of ethics come from a common philosophical source lies in their terminology. The key principles of beneficence, non-maleficence and justice are found in the writings of Sir David Ross. I suspect that Ross himself is not much read these days, and for that reason I will give a brief outline of his moral theory. Ross is, so to speak, a moral philosopher of common sense, often referring with considerable respect to 'the plain man' as a moral authority. 'The main moral convictions of the plain man,' he writes, 'seem to me to be, not opinions which it is for philosophy to prove or disprove, but knowledge from the start' (1930, p. 21n). Should our present moral consciousness be accepted without criticism? Ross thinks it does at least contain some judgements whose truth is so self-evident that no moral theory will lead us to repudiate our actual apprehension of what is right:

> I would maintain, in fact, that what we are apt to describe as 'what we think' about moral questions contains a considerable amount that we do not think but know, and that this forms the standard by reference to which the truth of any moral theory has to be tested, instead of having itself to be tested by reference to any theory. (Ross, 1930, p. 40)

What are these moral convictions? In Ross's view, they are of two different kinds. His thesis is that the concepts 'right' and 'good' are separate from each other. Many philosophers have tried to define right acts as those which achieve, or are intended to achieve, some good outcome. Ross's objection is that an act is sometimes right or wrong quite apart from its consequences. For example, he agrees with 'the plain man' that it may be right (that is, a duty) to fulfil a promise, even when the consequences are not particularly good. The consequences of an action may provide a good standard or criterion of rightness, but they do not determine what makes an action right. In his treatment of duty, Ross is one of the least moralistic of moralists. He treats the rightness of acts as quite separate from their motivation. Hence, his use of the word 'beneficence' rather than 'benevolence': because we can choose to promote the good of others, but cannot choose to have a sentiment of good will towards them, since we lack the power to determine our feelings directly and immediately, although we can work to promote better ones in the longer term. His hard-headed approach is even more striking in its refusal to give credit for attempts to do what is right: 'Success and failure are the only test, and a sufficient test, of the performance of duty' (1930, p. 45).

Ross gives a list of six prima facie duties, although one includes two items, so that there are really seven in all. Four of these are very general in their scope. These are beneficence, non-maleficence, justice and self-improvement. The other three arise only under particular circumstances. We have a duty to keep promises we have made to others a duty to show gratitude for benefits we have received from others, and a duty to make amends for harm we have done. Ross does not claim that this list is a complete one, and at one point mentions some special obligations which arise from being a spouse, parent, friend or neighbour (1930, p. 19). On the other hand, he is willing to keep the number of items down by arguing that some familiar duties are derivable from one or other of those he has already acknowledged. One example is the duty to tell the truth, an obligation which, Ross says, arises whenever we communicate with other people, because doing so includes an implicit undertaking not to deceive them (1939, pp. 112–113).[7] Perhaps more plausible than this is his account of legal punishment, which argues that when the state enforces the penalty for breaking one of its laws, it is keeping a promise made to the members of society when the law was established (1930, pp. 63–64).

This list of prima facie duties is not very systematic, but Ross argues that it is soundly based on reflection on our moral convictions. It may be objected that one is left with no principle for determining our actual duty in particular circumstances. But any theory which recognises a number of values has the same problem: for example, the ideal utilitarianism that takes both knowledge and pleasure to be good, leaving us with dilemmas where we must choose between them. Only a very simplified account will make the process of coming to a moral decision easy, and it will do this at the cost of either discounting or ignoring the complexities which give rise to genuine moral dilemmas. Ross's duties are all prima facie duties, and the possibility that they will come into conflict with one another is essential to his approach. This is what gives it the character of being true to the situations one is likely to encounter. Ross recognises that almost any human action 'contains various elements in virtue of which it falls under various categories' (1930, p. 28). It might be (or as Ross prefers to say, 'tend to be') wrong in one respect and right in another. In that case we have to weigh up all the relevant considerations to make a decision by finding the outcome that deserves to be called 'duty' without qualification. When we do this, he observes, we are taking a moral risk: we can never be certain that our judgement has been right (1930, p. 30). But there is no escaping such dilemmas.

Of all the moral philosophies available to us, Ross's is surely the best suited to a code of ethics. It would be absurd to insist on an orthodox interpretation of Ross's ethical system: writers on research ethics have no obligation to follow the formulations of any one philosopher. But comparisons with Ross's theory are useful in attempting to assess the consistency of the ethical principles embodied in a code of ethics. A code of ethics is concerned with the right, not the good. This is however a contentious issue, since the distinction is a disputed one. Ross is aware that a moral theory which contains both categories is lacking in economy, but his reply is that 'it is more important that our theory fit the facts than that it be simple' (1930, p. 19). And he takes it that, as these ideas figure in our moral judgements, they cannot be reduced to a single kind of value. Ross starts by looking like an empiricist, given his respect for the moral judgements of the 'plain man'. But this respect is really a belief that the plain man has a relatively small number of moral intuitions which are expressed in general moral principles. And these are just what writers of codes of ethics are looking for and quick to seize upon for their own purposes.

The most remarkable feature of those later codes of ethics which draw upon Ross's theory of prima facie duties is their consistent omission (invariably passed over in silence) of the duty of self-improvement. It may be that this is left out because a code of ethics is usually concerned with only a limited area of human behaviour, that is, our treatment of others. On the other hand, the theme of self-improvement was already a slightly anomalous feature of Ross's account, at least from the standpoint of attitudes to morality in modern society. Nevertheless, this elimination of one of Ross's four prima facie duties and its replacement by something quite different shows how difficult it is to answer an accusation of arbitrariness levelled against the whole scheme. Could respect for persons be fitted into his scheme somehow, to account for moral judgements which most thoughtful people nowadays are prepared to make but which are not adequately accounted for by the obligations he describes? We need to look more closely at how codes of research ethics have invoked this principle to answer this question.

## CODES OF ETHICS AND 'RESPECT FOR PERSONS'

I have identified a dominant philosophical source of the code of ethics exemplified in *The Belmont Report* and its many successors. The main difference is the great emphasis placed by *The Belmont Report* on a principle of 'respect for persons'. This seems rather different in kind from the other principles. For one thing, it is not immediately obvious what counts as acting with respect or disrespect for persons. We all know what is meant by doing harm to others, concealing the truth or breaking a promise. But what is treating someone with lack of respect? Ordinarily we would understand by this a breach of social custom but, without wanting to set aside the value of courtesy, I think this is not what is meant. It is because 'respect for persons' is more open-textured that it has proven invaluable to writers of codes of ethics, and has been invoked in order to back up many rules, such as a prohibition on deception of subjects in research.

As cases in point I will consider two relatively recent codes of ethics, one adopted in Canada in 1997 and the other in Australia in 1999, which have been based on *The Belmont Report*, but which go into some areas in more detail, as well as in raising issues which were not as clearly on the agenda when *The Belmont Report* was prepared. I have chosen these codes for discussion not because they make easy targets for criticism but, on the contrary, because they are the most thoughtful and well-prepared of their kind. I will look briefly at each in turn, restricting my attention to their broadest principles.

A *Code of Ethical Conduct for Research Involving Humans* was issued jointly in May 1997 by three main Canadian research organisations: the Medical Research Council of Canada, the National Sciences and Engineering Research Council of Canada, and the Social Sciences and Humanities Research Council of Canada. This code is quite self-conscious about its ethical framework, making a clear distinction between 'basic principles', the rules of conduct that follow from them, and the procedures through which research institutions can do their best to ensure that those rules are being followed. It distinguishes between principles and rules in the following way:

> Rules definitively determine what is to be done and can often be mechanically applied. By contrast, a principle is a consideration that ought to be taken into account when making a decision but may itself not be decisive in the circumstances. As well, more than one principle may apply to a specific case, and principles may point to opposite actions: for example, the principle of beneficence may conflict with the principle of non-maleficence. (*Code of Ethical Conduct for Research Involving Humans*, 1997)

The principle of respect for persons is treated as synonymous with Kant's moral imperative: 'Act in such a way that you always treat humanity, whether in your own person or in the person of any other, never simply as a means but always at the same time as an end' (Kant, 1948, p. 96). The task which the *Code of Ethical Conduct* sets itself is to translate this maxim into policies and practices for research involving human beings. Having explained this, however, the code immediately makes an important qualification to its philosophical conception of persons:

> It must be emphasised that *respect for persons* is respect for real life individuals, socially and historically situated, and not the idealised, abstracted, and decontextualized rational beings posited in various theories (e.g., the ideally rational agent, the egoistic consumer or the compliant patient). This means that respect must be shown for people as they identify themselves both as individuals and as members of groups. Factors such as race and gender, membership in a collectivity, and personal and social relationships can all have implications for the ethics of research involving humans.

This passage is of considerable interest, in both its philosophical and rhetorical aspects, but it needs some unpacking. To start with, an appeal to 'real life' is a device common in everyday debate on all sorts of subjects. In so far as it means anything, the phrase probably signals a resistance to theorising, or at least to explicit theorising. In the present case, however, 'real life' is immediately provided with a theoretical interpretation: the concept of persons as objects of respect (if that is the right expression) is explicated by expressions such as 'context', 'situation' and 'relationships', which are in turn contrasted with the terms 'idealised', 'abstracted' and 'decontextualized'. Rather paradoxically, it is the abstract and idealised concept which is characterised by relatively concrete expressions, such as 'egoistic' and 'compliant'. These are fairly off-putting descriptions, of course. They accentuate the point of this passage: it expresses a commitment to one theory about human life over another theory about human life, and not a rejection of every theory in favour of immediate experience (itself a debatable concept, as recent epistemology has pointed out). No doubt many readers of the text quoted above will recognise its language straight away and perhaps be ready to accept its drift without much trouble, given that a number of current approaches share some similar ideas as common ground. For instance, a prominent theme in the philosophical writing identified with feminism is that persons should not be taken as individual subjects, as they typically are in traditional liberal thought, but identified with broader social settings.

Yet is it possible for the Kantian principle of respect for persons to undergo such a revision? Does it make any sense in a very different context? In Kant, respect for persons is respect for the autonomy of moral agents, including oneself, and this in turn is based on the doctrine that our essential being transcends the phenomenal world and provides access to an intelligible realm, thus giving every person an 'absolute inner worth' (1991, p. 230). Hence, its status as a moral ideal requiring the highest respect and admiration can hardly be questioned. It is very different with the theory that humanity is not an essence within each individual, but the totality of social relations, as the sixth of Marx's 'theses on Feuerbach' puts it (Marx and Engels, 1976, p. 4). Any ethics this leads towards will inevitably be in sharp contrast to the Kantian version. A celebration of differences and shifting identities implies another ethics again. Respect for an ideal of personality is one thing, and respect for an 'identity' which is a cultural product is quite another. Why should our behaviour be governed by reverence for a humanity which is a diversity of conflicting social constructions? Again, there may be an answer to this, but it will not be the Kantian answer.

The language of 'respect for persons' now appears to have been used by the *Code of Ethical Conduct* for reasons other than its meaning: to claim a legitimate continuity with the humanist tradition, or perhaps just to strike an elevated tone of voice. It is like the way architects sometimes preserve an old façade to adorn a modern building which has, in fact, completely replaced the original one. Whether this is an isolated phenomenon can be judged if we now turn to a second recent code of research ethics, which represents an Australian attempt to address many of the same ethical issues.

In 1999 a *National Statement on Ethical Conduct in Research Involving Humans* was issued with the endorsement of leading Australian research bodies (notably the National Health and Medical Research Council) as well as ministers of the Federal Government. It differs from the old code of ethics in containing a lengthy rationale which appeals to four 'principles of ethical conduct': integrity, respect for persons, beneficence (which, following *The Belmont Report*, is taken to include non-maleficence) and justice. Integrity is an interesting addition to the usual list, in that it is a virtue applicable to all researchers, whereas the other principles apply to research involving human beings. The statement explains that integrity is 'expressed in a commitment to the search for knowledge, to recognised principles of research conduct and in the honest and ethical conduct of research and dissemination and communication of results' (*National Statement on Ethical Conduct in Research Involving Humans*, 1999, p. 11). On respect for persons, it goes on to state:

When conducting research involving humans, the guiding ethical principle for researchers is respect for persons which is expressed as regard for the welfare, rights, beliefs, perceptions, customs and cultural heritage, both individual and collective, of persons involved in research.

Here again we see a modification in the earlier principle of respect for persons, away from a purely individual interpretation to a more social and collective version, in which communities (such as ethnic or religious groups) have rights which must be acknowledged and respected by researchers. If such rights are not simply reducible to those of their members, they could presumably include the authority of the group or its leaders over those individuals. Respect for persons, as explained here, thus differs considerably from the Kantian concept. At the same time, respect for persons now appears in a primary role, as 'the guiding ethical principle'. The *National Statement* does, however, discuss beneficence and non-maleficence, understood as 'the obligations to maximise possible benefits and minimise possible harms'. Finally, justice is defined as a fair balance of the benefits and burdens involved in a research project, and an absence of discrimination either in favour of or against any particular group.

One interesting aspect of the principle of respect for persons, as it is explained in these codes, is a recognition that not all subjects in research are in fact autonomous agents. That point is especially relevant to educational research, where the subjects are often children rather than adults and cannot therefore, according to the common view, give genuine consent to their participation (although it is sometimes said that they can give *assent*). Now, such cases can no doubt be interpreted in accordance with a principled ethics, presumably through a conception of personhood which is not tied to immediately observable qualities. (Again, the Kantian model comes to mind.) This would explain the duty of respect for persons whose ability to give informed consent is impaired or lacking altogether, but how would it tell us what to do? The standard practice of seeking the consent of a parent or guardian suggests a different line of thought. Here the most straightforward case is being extended through an ethical model that draws upon familiar social relationships, especially those which bring with them rights and responsibilities. Here is an instructive example of practical ethical thinking which has little in common with any principled model. It provides a clue which we will examine in further detail.

## AN ALTERNATIVE PHILOSOPHY OF RESEARCH ETHICS?

So far we have explored some developments from *The Belmont Report*, a code of research ethics embodying a principled approach derived largely from the moral theory of W. D. Ross. As we noted, this has been extended and modified by more recent codes of ethics which have moved towards a communitarian ethics or a constructivist conception of identity, or both at once.

That interpretation of *The Belmont Report* may be quite misleading, however. Two of the participants in the writing of the report have since provided a revealing commentary on its content. One was Albert R. Jonsen, a member of the eleven-person team, and another was Stephen Toulmin, who worked with the committee as a consultant. In their 1988 book *The Abuse of Casuistry*, Jonsen and Toulmin give an insight into the process through which the commission drew up its recommendations. As they explain, the members of the board came from different backgrounds and in many cases were strongly committed to a particular religious or moral standpoint. Nevertheless, their discussions of particular problems usually led to consensus, because they approached the issues in a concrete, case-by-case way, using the problem-solving approach for which these authors want to revive the old label 'casuistry':

> Members of the commission were largely in agreement about their specific practical recommendations; they agreed what it was they agreed about; but the one thing they could not agree on was *why* they agreed about it. So long as the

debate stayed on the level of particular judgements, the eleven commissioners saw things in much the same way. The moment it soared to the level of 'principles', they went their separate ways. Instead of securely established universal principles, in which they had unqualified confidence, giving them intellectual grounding for particular judgements about specific kinds of cases, it was the other way around. (Jonsen and Toulmin, 1988, p. 18)

In a footnote to this passage, Jonsen and Toulmin clarify the presence of 'basic principles' in *The Belmont Report*. They reveal that the opening section, within which these principles occur, was the last in order of preparation:

On a *completely* general level, it is true, the members of the commission were able to share certain agreements—for example, as to the principles of autonomy, justice, and beneficence. But these shared notions were too comprehensive and general to underwrite specific moral positions. The National Commission did issue a statement of general principle, but it was composed only after the commissioners had worked through their problematic cases casuistically. (*ibid.*, p. 356)

If this account is accurate, then the presentation of *The Belmont Report* lends itself to misunderstanding. By *beginning* with the basic principles of beneficence, non-maleficence, justice and respect for persons, it suggests that its approach is a 'Euclidean' strategy of starting with definitions, postulates and axioms, and proceeding to derive theorems from those. Instead, the general principles appear to have been abstracted from the collection of particular judgements contained in the report's detailed recommendations. For that reason, it is not surprising that the impression they give is not that of a unified theory. The comment of one later writer is understandable: 'The Protection of Human Subjects regulations are an example of the blend of the utilitarian and Kantian perspectives' (Sowder, 1998, p. 43). Yet it is quite possible that none of the participants was adopting either a utilitarian or a Kantian approach to the moral problems under consideration.

Just as this interpretation misrepresents the origins of a code of ethics such as *The Belmont Report*, so too it misrepresents the subsequent function of such a code. Ethical decisions have to be made about research projects, not just by the researchers themselves, but by groups of people who are entrusted with responsibility for monitoring projects on behalf of some research institution. One assumption often present (though not necessarily made explicit) in defences of codes of research ethics is that the task for both individuals and groups is to 'apply' the relevant portion of the code. But this is not at all an accurate description of how such decisions are made. The working of an ethical review committee is of particular interest, in that it displays the process on a larger scale, making many of its features more readily visible. Here it is evident that the practice of making moral decisions does not correspond to the model proposed by a principled ethics. Rather, it resembles Jonsen and Toulmin's picture of the deliberations of the National Commission that prepared *The Belmont Report*.

What sort of reasoning is involved here? Jonsen and Toulmin suggest a useful analogy between moral judgement and medical diagnosis (1988, pp. 36–46). Their claim is that working with 'paradigm cases' is a methodology which also works in morality. We have standard instances of deception, coercion, breaches of confidentiality and so on, and ethical judgements which have proven to be appropriate. We then identify relevant similarities and differences and make an assessment accordingly. One could call this a problem-solving approach to ethics, in contrast with a top-down application of ethical principles already at hand. Even if the latter were possible (and that is questionable) the objection that the hegemony of a particular standpoint had been assumed would be valid. In contrast, the problem-solving approach leaves many of these issues aside as irrelevant to its task. It recognises that we already have some ability to make ethical decisions, and that the task posed by new and unfamiliar situations is to extend our existing abilities, not to return to first principles.[8]

This procedural approach needs to be supplemented in two ways. Although the great majority of research proposals tend to belong to some more or less familiar pattern, there will be problematical cases which cannot be decided by precedents. Second, there will be a need to be able to review existing policies and to change them if necessary, for otherwise the procedural approach will be incapable of responding to the learning expressed in the changes which do occur in moral attitudes. Much of the recent concern for the ethics of empirical research has been prompted by the constant appearance of new ethical problems. A look at any recent code of ethics will confirm this. The Australian *National Statement on Ethical Conduct in Research Involving Humans* contains guidelines on reproductive technology, genetic research and the use of human tissue samples which were not needed a generation ago. It also indicates guidelines for research involving indigenous groups (in this case, Aboriginal and Torres Strait Islander peoples) which *were* needed, but had not been developed a generation ago. These examples illustrate the two sorts of need for continuing change that I have mentioned. It is necessary to revisit past decisions and either extend or revise them, rather than treating them as having some permanent validity.

It is possible that some of John Ladd's objections to codes of ethics, discussed earlier, might also be brought to bear against this alternative. But I think his accusation that calling a set of rules governing professional conduct a code of *ethics* is 'pretentious and sanctimonious' (1980, p. 156) cannot be levelled against what is, after all, merely an extension of the ways we make ethical decisions in everyday life. The presence of so-called 'basic principles' is not a feature of these forms of thinking. The insistence of many moral philosophies on basic principles is, in fact, a parallel to the epistemology which looked for secure foundations on which empirical knowledge could be based, and claimed to find them in special kinds of observations. The same objections apply to both approaches. Hence, just as a philosophical approach can contribute to research by pointing out the need to move beyond a positivist methodology, so too it can draw attention to the implausibility of the traditional intuitionism whose foundational apparatus seemed to provide a code of research ethics in ready-made form. In both cases the alternative is not scepticism or relativism but, on the contrary, a reaffirmation of objectivity in a form more adequate to meeting some strong challenges.

I have argued that an alternative to reliance on a code of ethics is to place more emphasis on procedures and strategies for making ethical decisions, especially by groups such as committees. Moral theory can contribute here by looking more closely at how ethical decisions are actually made, and develop models which provide guidance for moral learning. Its role would be much like the one mentioned at the beginning in relation to scientific knowledge: that of exploring methodology. While a code of ethics does not rule out further inquiry into the methodology of ethical decision-making, a simple inclusiveness over-looks the task of finding out more about the best ways of making ethical decisions about research, not just by individuals, but just as importantly, by groups of individuals—a neglected topic. In many ways, the problems here are the same as those surrounding other kinds of learning. If it is reasonable to say that learning can be done by groups or organisations, this would apply to morality as well as other kinds of knowledge. A sound theory of moral learning would be valuable in enhancing the ability of both individuals and collectivities to make sound ethical decisions, and thus making a contribution to the preparation and continuing education of researchers.

There are pitfalls in this educational task, however. Ethics is an everyday activity, and most of the dilemmas which researchers have to face are everyday ones. It is not helpful to take the criminal 'experiments' punished by the Nuremberg tribunal as a starting point, even though they were historically important in making people sensitive to ethical issues in research. As one writer puts it:

When only outstanding and scandalous cases are defined as matters for ethical concern, then the daily perplexities, interactions and decisions occurring in the

field may well be perceived as merely 'personal'. Ethics then becomes an
academic subject, consisting primarily of abstract concepts counterposed by
shocking violations. (Burgess, 1989, p. 61)[9]

This is, I think, an accurate description of the way research ethics is
sometimes taught to students in academic institutions. Introducing
the issues through stories about notorious instances of systematic
deception, disregard for privacy or emotional harm is likely to create
a mood of moral panic, expressing itself in anxious efforts to find
ethical faults in as many research projects as possible. It is far better
to start with what we already know about such problems and their
solutions. Ross was right in insisting that most people have some
understanding here, despite his belief that fallibility is located only in
the application of moral principles which by themselves are beyond
doubt. If that distinction is untenable, and the search for incorrigible
universal 'principles' is misguided, then the differences between more
and less abstract or general moral judgements are differences in
degree rather than kind. Thus, a recognition of moral knowledge as
not only possible but quite common is perfectly consistent with the
view that our ethical judgements are always fallible and subject to the
possibility of later revision.

Whether codes of ethics have a meaningful use in this educational
process remains an open question. Yet if they do not figure here,
what other point could they have? John Ladd rather grudgingly
concedes that a code might be of some use as an aspirational or
inspirational document or, as he puts it, 'something to frame and
hang in one's office' (1980, p. 157).[10] Even defenders of codes of ethics
allow that they play some role in reassuring the wider community
that acceptable ethical standards are being observed by researchers
and other professionals. However, any emphasis on this is highly
vulnerable to cynicism, especially when breaches are known to occur.
A defence of the educational function of codes of research ethics
would need to be a modest one. It could be argued that they serve as a
point of reference for procedures within which they normally do not
figure, and that they do so by acting as summaries of the general
patterns that these procedures have shown in their most successful
forms, that is, in producing decisions which have stood up to the test
of later experience.

Having conceded this much to the formal approach, I emphasise
again my earlier point: whatever codes of ethics, committees of
ethical review, and academic lectures or workshops on ethical
issues can do in support of educational research, there is no
substitute for the individual's development of the capacity to make
ethical decisions about the design and conduct of his or her project.
In the end, it is everyone's responsibility to ensure that educational

research is ethical research, and the better prepared we are to address this task, the better our research will be.

*Correspondence:* Robin Small, Department of Education, Monash University, Melbourne, Australia.
Email: robin.small@education.monash.edu.au

## NOTES

1. However, the idea of 'moral expertise' is not without its defenders: see for example Singer, 1972; Burch, 1974; Woods and Walton, 1975; and Miller, 1975.
2. See e.g. Bibby, 1993; Lichtenberg, 1996; and Bibby, 1997.
3. Presumably something similar would apply to, say, any religious denomination's attempt to define its beliefs in a formal statement, given the highly personal character of religious faith.
4. To be fair, one should note that even a philosopher as reputable as Ross resorts to the same device in defence of 'fidelity' as a special obligation, when he writes: 'After all, a promise is a promise' (1930, p. 35).
5. Similarly, Martin Bibby warns that some research procedure could be defended by pointing out that it is not forbidden by the relevant code of ethics. 'Such argument is of course that of a scoundrel', he comments (1993, p. 49).
6. Closely related to *The Belmont Report* is a text widely used in courses on professional ethics, Tom L. Beauchamp and James F. Childress's *Principles of Biomedical Ethics* (Beauchamp and Childress, 1994), which I will not discuss here.
7. Similarly, William Paley wrote: 'A lie is a breach of promise: for whoever seriously addresses his discourse to another, tacitly promises to speak the truth, because he knows that the truth is expected' (1825, p. 123). In contrast, Richard Price argued that the duty to keep a promise is derivable from a duty to tell the truth, since a promise is just a categorical assertion about future events. 'When a person declares he *will* do any action, he becomes obligated to do it, and cannot afterwards omit it, without incurring the imputation of declaring falsehood, as if he had declared what he knew to be a false past or present fact' (1948, pp. 155–156). These two arguments—both rather strained, it seems to me—illustrate the problem: for many attempts to derive one ethical principle from another, it seems just as possible to go in the other direction.
8. See Small, 1998, for a more detailed discussion.
9. I have not been able to locate the original source of this passage.
10. He notes with some satisfaction that the academic profession has no code of ethics to display in this fashion.

## REFERENCES

Allison, Henry E. (1973) *The Kant-Eberhard Controversy* (Baltimore, The Johns Hopkins University Press).

Beauchamp, Tom L. and Childress, James F. (1994) *Principles of Biomedical Ethics*, 4th edn (New York, Oxford University Press).

*The Belmont Report: Ethical Principles and Guidelines for the Protection of Human Subjects of Research* (1978) (Washington, Department of Health, Education and Welfare).

Bibby, Martin (1993) Using a Code of Research Ethics, *Educational Philosophy and Theory*, 15.1, pp. 49–64.

Bibby, Martin (1997) Introduction Education Research and Morality, in: R. M. Bibby (ed.) *Ethics and Educational Research* (Coldstream, Australian Association for Research in Education).

Burbules, Nicholas, C. (1998) Principle and Process in the Ethics of Educational Research: Reply to Robin Small, *Australian Journal of Education*, 42.1, pp. 116–23.

Burch, Robert W. (1974) Are There Moral Experts?, *The Monist*, 58.4, pp. 646–658

Burgess, Robert G. (1989) Grey Areas: Ethical Dilemmas in Educational Ethnography, in: Robert G. Burgess (ed.). *The Ethics of Educational Research* (Barcombe, The Falmer Press).

*Code of Ethical Conduct for Research Involving Humans* (1997) http://www.mrc.gc.ca/ethics/code/english/context.html.

Homan, Roger (1992) The Ethics of Open Methods, *British Journal of Sociology*, 43.3, pp. 321–332.

Jonsen, Albert R. and Toulmin, Stephen (1988) *The Abuse of Casuistry: A History of Moral Reasoning* (Berkeley, University of California Press).

Kant, Immanuel (1948) *The Moral Law (Groundwork of the Metaphysic of Morals)*, trans. H. J. Paton (London, Hutchinson).

Kant, Immanuel (1991) *Metaphysics of Morals*, trans. Mary McGregor (Cambridge, Cambridge University Press).

Ladd, John (1980) The Quest for a Code of Professional Ethics: An Intellectual and Moral Confusion, in: Rosemary Chalk, Mark S. Frankel and Sallie B. Chafer (eds) *AAAS Professional Ethics Project: Professional Ethics Activities in the Scientific and Engineering Societies* (Washington, American Association for the Advancement of Science).

Lichtenberg, Judith (1996) What are Codes of Ethics For?, in: Margaret Coady and Sid Bloch (eds) *Codes of Ethics and the Professions* (Melbourne, Melbourne University Press).

Marx, Karl and Engels, Friedrich (1976) *Collected Works*, vol. 5 (London, Lawrence and Wishart).

Miller, Peter (1975) Who Are the Moral Experts?, *Journal of Moral Education*, 5.1, pp. 3–12.

*National Statement on Ethical Conduct in Research Involving Humans* (1999) (Canberra, Commonwealth of Australia).

Paley, William (1825) Principles of Moral and Political Philosophy, in: E. Paley (ed.) *The Works of William Paley, D. D.*, vol. 4 (Oxford, C. & J. Rivington).

Price, Richard (1948) *A Review of the Principal Questions in Morals*, in: D. D. Raphael (ed.) (Oxford, Clarendon Press).

Ross, W. D. (1930) *The Right and the Good* (Oxford, Clarendon Press).

Ross, W. D. (1939) *Foundations of Ethics* (Oxford, Clarendon Press).

Singer, Peter (1972) Moral Experts, *Analysis*, 32.4, pp. 115–117.

Small, Robin (1998) Towards an Unprincipled Ethics of Educational Research, *Australian Journal of Education*, 42.1, pp. 103–116.

Sowder, Judith T. (1998) Ethics in Mathematics Education Research, in: A. Sierpinska and J. Kirkpatrick (eds) *Mathematics as a Research Domain: A Search for Identity* (Dordrecht, Kluwer Academic Publishers).

Woods, John and Walton, Douglas (1975) Moral Expertise, *Journal of Moral Education*, 5.1, pp. 13–18.

# 7

# The Virtues and Vices of an Educational Researcher

Richard Pring

*This essay explores the contentious relationship between codes of ethics in research and the range of virtues that characterise ethical researchers in the face of the temptations that they face. I argue that the politics of research transforms our ethical appraisals of character and context. Researchers' duties towards research sponsors, the research team, and university or school, all ought to be brought to bear in particular judgements of ethically sensitive issues where there is no single or undisputed currency. This re-appraisal foregrounds the need seriously to consider the question of the virtues of the educational researcher.*

## INTRODUCTION

Educational researchers are becoming increasingly conscious of the ethical dimension of their research. Unlike medical and nursing researchers, they do not yet universally have their 'ethical committees' to check the acceptability of research proposals. But the British Educational Research Association (BERA) and the American Educational Research Association (AERA) have drawn up codes of conduct—principles and rules which should guide the research from an ethical point of view. Furthermore, it is now usually expected that research theses will explain what the ethical issues are in the conduct of the research and how the researchers ensured that appropriate standards of conduct were maintained.

This paper examines this ethical dimension and questions whether it is sufficient to think in terms of principles, codes and rules. It may be more important, from an ethical point of view, to consider much more carefully the virtues of the researcher than the principles he or

111

she espouses. In so arguing, I first examine four examples and, in the light of these, reflect on the role of principles and virtues in the exercise of research.

## EXAMPLES

### *The undercover bouncer*

In his recent book, *Danger in the Field: Risk and Ethics in Social Research*, David Calvey described how, in his undercover research to explore the 'cultural practice, work culture and social organisation' of club bouncers, he secretly tape-recorded conversations and recorded assaults, drug-taking and other crimes. His role as a researcher had to be disguised—discovery might literally have been fatal. Therefore, what he learnt (and then reported) was gained from confidential conversations and by the concealment both of his identity and of the purposes of the research. His justification (the moral argument, if you like) was that, first, he was contributing to an understanding of violence in society; second, the deceptive method adopted was the only way in which he could attain that worthwhile objective.

### *The toilet ethnographer*

Consider a second case. Some years ago an established researcher investigated the classroom ethos of three middle schools. Entry to those schools required gaining the confidence of the relevant teachers and the headteachers. He described the steps he took to maintain secrecy and unobtrusiveness—for example, always writing up his observations behind the locked door of the toilet. But the publication of the book, though steps had been taken to anonymise the schools and the teachers, greatly upset one of the teachers who recognised herself in reading the book and took offence at the implicit criticism of her teaching. The headteacher told me that, in consequence, he would allow no more researchers into his school.

### *The democratic researcher*

A third example is that of a researcher who took seriously the feelings of those being researched and negotiated agreement of what was permissible data and what was a permissible analysis of that data, prior to publication, before they entered into the report. It was agreed that a significant portion of the data would not be made public (for example, what the teacher had said when interviewed) and therefore could not enter into the analysis. This meant, of course, gaps in the overall picture and distorted conclusions. But in one sense this did not matter, because the process of negotiating the evidence and the conclusions was so prolonged that no report was ever written. However, the researcher justified the procedure of lengthy negotiation by reference to the benefit received by the school in going through the process, even though that process never reached any conclusions. (The researcher resisted one moral temptation, namely, to draw conclusions which were correct in the light of the evidence but which the sensitivities of the teachers had prevented from becoming public.)

## The contract researcher

A fourth example is that of the researcher, desperate to win further major research contracts from the government sponsor. Here, as is often the case, short-term contract researchers depended on a successful proposal for their continuation in employment. As with most government-funded projects, there were no absolute criteria for evaluating the success of the overall project. Most major projects of this kind (Education Action Zones, Fast Track Teachers, etc.) have a mixture of outcomes. Nevertheless, the researcher knew that there was a limit to how much criticism would be acceptable to his sponsor and, in any case, there was a team of experienced spin doctors (called the Press Office) to gainsay the research if the need arose. Experienced contract researchers realise that, with regard to research into policy, they are operating within a political context with an ideologically driven programme. The researcher in this case, therefore, distinguished between private advice and public documentation—between that which would be private to the government and that which would be open to the public. The public document, therefore, blunted its criticisms and thereby failed to con-tribute to a truly balanced debate on the issues. But the researcher claimed that, first, he did influence policy (which could not have been the case had he been less pragmatic and subtle in presenting the conclusions); second, he did receive another large grant and his research officer continued to feed his young family.

## REFLECTING ON THE EXAMPLES

Moral dilemmas which arise in research are often dealt with by appeal to certain general principles. These are then translated into codes of conduct of research. BERA has developed its code, so has the American Educational Research Association. And this is to be highly commended. It is impossible to conceive of a moral life without implicit reference to a set of principles that are embodied within moral practice. But that does not mean that one can, as it were, read off from that code or those principles what exactly one should do on any one occasion. There is no escaping moral deliberations—the complex judgements required for seeing, first, the relevance of particular principles or codes to this or that situation; second, the priority to be given to this or that principle when it is conflicting with another.

The examples above reflect the relevance of such moral deliberations or complex moral judgements. The person researching the culture of club bouncers (example (i)) was intentionally, yet secretly (and thus deceitfully), gathering information from unsuspecting bouncers. Indeed, it is likely that he engineered situations to get these accounts (gained their confidence, found safe places to talk, etc.). To be deceitful is, one might argue, a prima facie wrong. To engage in conversation with unsuspecting persons for ulterior motives which one takes care to hide (those motives being to publish what one hears and sees) would seem to be clearly wrong. But, then, had he revealed his purposes, first, he would not have got the information; second, he might have been seriously harmed. Well? Should he then not have engaged on the research? His argument was that the research was so important for the public good and for the general welfare that such deception was justified.

That, indeed, sounds plausible. But there is another dimension to the moral picture. As a result of the secrecy, there is no way in which the veracity of the conclusions could be checked. Remember that one general principle of good research is that conclusions are supported by evidence and that the relation of conclusion to evidence, and the evidence on which those conclusions are drawn, should be open to scrutiny—and might be considered acceptable only if they have withstood public criticism. Otherwise educational research, to a much greater extent than, say, scientific research, would be dependent on the trustworthiness of the researchers. Are they the sort of person we can trust? (Do they pass the moral test?)

The second example (that of the 'toilet ethnographer') is again one where moral judgement is required. The researcher needs to weigh up the importance to his research of concealment and the likely effect that the results of the research would have on those researched into. Is this another case of deception? And if so, then is it exactly the same as the previous case? In one sense it is, in another it is not. It is not the same in the sense that the first case, but not the second, was revealing information of utmost importance for society. Moreover, secrecy (and deception) were crucial to the safety (indeed, continued existence) of the researcher. Same principles, but different context, requiring different deliberations about the application of principles. But could the second researcher have approached the research in a different way, recognising the vulnerability of the persons researched into—and possibly respecting *their* interpretation of events (their conclusions from the data) which may not have been the same as the researcher's? Indeed, how far can we understand what is going on in classrooms without respecting the understanding of the main agents within those classrooms? But this is hardly possible without the teachers' views being solicited.

The third example (that of the 'democratic researcher') takes these moral anxieties seriously. Judgements are made such that those being researched into must be brought to the centre of the picture. The *moral* ground for this is that any other course would show disrespect for them as persons. To research them through deceptive methods (as in examples one and two) would be to treat them as objects, things, not as persons worthy of respect. This 'respect for persons' (as in the sense of people not to be used for other people's ends) would seem to be the dominant principle. But more than that, the moral principle is also related to a view about the nature of knowledge—the tentativeness of any knowledge-claims, their openness to refinement and further criticism, the importance in reaching conclusions (even if temporary) that have withstood the widest range of possible criticism.

But there is a difficulty here. The importance of deliberation is recognised—indeed, espoused enthusiastically. And that deliberation takes place between the many people in the research—no longer divided between researcher and researched but united in a common partnership to discover the truth (which, of course, is often made elusive by the very complexity of the deliberations). A moral as well as a research bond is created, and the concept of negotiation (once intelligible in the world of business) takes on a moral force not recognised in examples one and two. But part of that moral force lies, too, in a view about the nature of knowledge—something which is seen to be constantly constructed and reconstructed.

The final example (that of the 'contract researcher') takes on yet a different dimension—different complexities in the moral debate. The researcher has two obligations which complicate the deliberation. The first obligation is to a long-term influencing of events in the light of research—which requires playing a political game abhorrent to the moral purist. But such would seem to be inescapable to those who walk the corridors of power. One is surrounded by the spinners and manipulators of knowledge. These are the lobbyists who carefully select one aspect of the research, ignoring the overall and balanced picture. There is the long-term aim, achievable through carefully explored short-term measures. Politics transforms the context of moral judgement.

But there is the second obligation—the obligation to the long-term well-being of the research team, ensuring contracts, enhancing its reputation, promoting its trustworthiness. There is a social, as well as a political, context of research which, in its detail, escapes the direct application of high level moral principles.

However, in all examples there seems an inescapable dependence on the trustworthiness of the researcher—to exercise judgement in as impartial a manner as is possible, to conclude only those things which can be justified in the light of the evidence, to be open to the critical scrutiny of others where that is possible (and, where impossible, to imagine what that criticism might be).

What should be clear from a cursory consideration of the four examples is the unavoidability of moral deliberation in considering the ethical dimension of research. Such deliberation does inevitably call upon or embody certain principles, but can by no means be simply the application of those principles. Different principles can be evoked. But there is *judgement* required in deciding upon the overriding principle and in deciding what element in one's practice relates to what principle. The context, for example, affects the amount of harm that might be considered tolerable and indeed what might be said to constitute harm. The context also affects the significance of the research to the wider public good. The context affects the extent to which secrecy might be equated with deceit. And the context affects the degree to which this piece of research should be seen as but part of a wider, more significant programme of research such that moral imperfections might be allowed for the greater good of the whole.

It is necessary, therefore, to look more closely at the meaning and consequences of these considerations—first, at the role of principles in moral deliberations, but, second, at the moral requirement of research once one realises that no set of principles (and thus no ethical code) can exhaustively shape the moral deliberation which inevitably researchers are caught in. The solution in my view lies in the return to 'moral virtue' appropriate to research—not an easy recommendation since the natural humility and modesty of most researchers would normally lead to their denial of having such virtues. Moreover, it is less easy to assess virtue than it is to assess research competence—or to pronounce a list of principles. Canon lawyers have to be clever, indeed subtle; they do not necessarily have to be virtuous.

## PRINCIPLES

Moral deliberation is often characterised as a response to the question 'What ought I to do?' For much of the time, we do not have moral worries—getting up in the morning, preparing breakfast, choosing what to wear, etc. Of course, one can see the *possibility* of moral conflict even in such everyday practices; my favourite but food-stained tie upsets my wife over the breakfast muesli, and no doubt this state of affairs could and should provoke some moral deliberations. But although any activity or practice can pose the question 'What ought I to do?' (where the 'ought' refers to an ethically significant situation rather than to a merely practical one), few (thank goodness) actually do.

But why is that the case? For most of our lives, our daily actions and relationships spring from the sort of people we are, the forms of life to which we belong with all its built-in norms and values. By being brought up in a particular society or social group, one absorbs the social rules and the feelings and dispositions which go with them, which are recognised by that group and which are appropriate to its particular form of life. It is not the case that the majority of people live in a constant state of existentialist angst. The question I want to ask is why the life of an educational researcher cannot be just like that? Why is there a need to spell out or make explicit codes of conduct, rules of procedure, principles of proper behaviour? Why can not we simply employ virtuous people—with, of course, research skills?

The main reason is that the unreflecting but virtuous life is not sufficiently helpful when conflicts emerge—when underlying norms and values (previously only implicit) are challenged or eroded in the very social foundations of one's practice. It is then that the principles implicit in one's practice need to be more explicit. One then asks the question 'What ought I to do?', seeking genuine reasons.

One sort of answer to the questions might be purely prudential or practical, namely, what particular action is most likely to achieve a particular end. But the question may be as much about the ends to be pursued as about the means of achieving those ends. The appropriate reasons for acting in one way rather than another, where those reasons focus on the values worth pursuing, are expressed in statements of principle. One appeals to principles in justifying an action. Moreover, principles by their nature reflect a universality of application. The *principle* of acting in this way rather than another does not depend upon my whims or wishes; anyone in like circumstances would be expected to act in a similar way. Thus, in asking the questions 'Why should I tell the interviewee the purpose of my research?' or 'Ought I to omit some of the more sensitive conclusions?', one would eventually appeal to some general principle such as 'One ought to act in this way because such people have a right to know' or 'One should always tell the truth' or 'One should so treat others as one would wish them to treat oneself'.

One needs to distinguish between 'principles' and 'rules'. 'Rules' are more specific and less open to interpretation. There are rules for driving safely such as 'Always drive on the left' or 'Never cross a double white line'. Thus, the government may lay down certain rules about the reporting of research which it has sponsored—let us say, the research should be sent confidentially to the Department of State and then, *only with the Department's permission*, might it be made accessible to the wider public. Such rules are of the kind 'In circumstances $x$, one must do $y$'. There is little ambiguity or openness to interpretation. But behind the rules for the conduct of research will be principles. Principles, related to the rules of safe driving, would be of the kind 'So drive as to minimise the chance of causing an accident'. The rules for the conduct of government-sponsored research might be justified by reference to prescriptions such as 'The research report ought to be treated as the property of the sponsor' or 'The research ought to take account of the possible harm it might do to those who are researched into', which is then translated into the rules for the actual conduct of the research.

Principles, then, have the logic of general rules, but they embody the values appealed to in the establishment of the rules or in the questioning of the appropriateness of the rules on this or that occasion. There is a temptation, in recognising the moral and political dilemmas over the conduct and the dissemination of research, to establish specific rules of conduct. But that would be a mistake. Here, as in any moral conflict, there is no way in which rules can legislate for every conceivable situation as, indeed, is shown in some of the examples given earlier. What specific rules could have anticipated the unique features of research into the criminal activity of club bouncers? Certainly is it necessary to clarify principles, but these then need to be reflected on in the particular situations—in the full knowledge that other principles might also be evoked which would lead to more complex moral deliberation.

Moreover, a moment's reflection shows how unclear are general principles when it comes to their application. Thus 'maintaining confidentiality' might be narrowed down to the formal agreement not to mention what was said without the prior consent of the interviewee. But what about the case of the researcher talking to the club bouncers? No such agreement was entered into, but there was a deliberate deception (namely, the pursuit of information for a specific purpose whilst preventing the source of that information from knowing those purposes). Does that constitute a breaking of confidence? And is the situation so very different where the researcher engages in conversation and only subsequently (in the light of these private revelations) decides to use them for purposes of research or scholarship?

One needs to distinguish between those principles which are concerned with the consequences of one's actions (consequentialist) and those which express some general rules of behaviour, irrespective of the consequences (deontological). So, acting as to make people happier would be of the former kind; telling the truth or keeping confidences would be of the latter. It requires no great reflection to see how these different sorts of principles often conflict. Telling the truth can bring harm to others. Respect for individuals might entail a watering-down of the research conclusions. The utilitarians wanted to judge the morality of all actions by reference to the extent to which those actions led to a greater sum of happiness than would otherwise be the case—even if that could be achieved only by the occasional lies or concealment of truth. Of course, it is not easy to calculate the total effect of any one action, and therefore the utilitarians would argue a prima facie case for truth-telling and fairness as principles which generally speaking lead to a happier state of affairs. But the clash of consequentialist and deontological ethical positions is clearly apparent in educational research. Calvey (2000) deceived his bouncers for the sake of the greater good to society, spelled out (no doubt) in terms of greater happiness as a result of lower levels of violence, drug trafficking, etc. The researcher into middle schools put telling the truth (as he saw it) above the happiness of the individual teachers.

Such a *possible* conflict of irreconcilable principles can be resolved in one of four ways. First, the researcher simply does not recognise this to be a problem and pursues the research in a kind of moral vacuum. Research is cut off from moral life generally—it is put into an insulated occupational, amoral slot. Second, the researcher declares him or herself to be a deontologist or a consequentialist— and is always led by such principles to the exclusion of others (for example, one tells the truth whatever the consequences). Third, the researcher looks in vain for higher level principles to resolve the conflict. Fourth, however, the researcher recognises that there is no solution other than, as in most moral situations, through deliberation in which the different principles are pondered over within the particular context of the research. One situation is relevantly different from the next. Nonetheless, the researcher should be aware of what the key principles are which enter into that deliberation, namely, first, principles concerned with the respect for other persons (maintaining confidentiality when promised, preserving their sense of dignity, treating them as having a valuable point of view); second, principles concerned with maximising the happiness not only of the people immediately involved but also of the wider community (balancing that happiness created against the unhappiness which might be caused); third, principles concerned with the proper conduct of affairs irrespective of consequences (acting justly, keeping of promises, telling of the truth).

Let us look at these principles in greater detail. The principle which directs research would seem to be that of 'pursuing and telling the truth'. The purpose of undertaking research is, generally speaking, the generation of knowledge. The reasons for needing to know the truth concerns improvement of practice, development of policy, accountability of those in public and professional positions, and of course the solution of problems raised by previous research. The production of knowledge requires access to data. Research, therefore, provides a prima facie case for the researchers having the right to such access. At the same time, there is a need for wider public access to that data and to the conclusions which researchers draw from them. One ought not to feel confident in the outcomes of research without this wider critical debate. Growth of knowledge comes through criticism.

The 'right to know' applies particularly where matters of public interest are concerned—for example, where there are large-scale interventions which purport to improve standards or deal with a social evil. One can see why those in positions of power may wish to resist research or its conclusions. Research seeks to get at the truth where the truth might hurt. Research exposes the secrecy which too often permeates the conduct of affairs by public institutions such as schools, local authorities, government departments and committees. And researchers need a certain amount of courage to resist such powerful influences. However, policy makers (unless they have absolute trust in their spin doctors) should be keen to ensure that their decisions are informed by the most up-to-date knowledge and understanding and that the institutions are properly accountable. There would seem to be, therefore, a prima facie case for claiming the 'right to know'. Such research should remain independent of those who might benefit from or be disadvantaged by it, lest the conclusions drawn reflect the interests of the sponsors rather than the pursuit of the truth wherever that leads. Such is the importance of this right and this principle (namely, the 'right to know' and the principle that one should pursue and tell the truth) that they might be considered to be overriding, even when the research and its revelations damage the people and the institutions enquired into.

The justification for the principle of the right to know is implicit in John Stuart Mill's argument in his essay *On Liberty* for preserving and extending freedom of discussion:

> the peculiar evil of silencing the expression of an opinion is, that it is robbing the human race; posterity as well as the present generation; those who dissent from the opinion, still more than those who hold it. If the opinion is right, they are deprived of the opportunity of exchanging error for truth; if wrong, they lose, what is almost as great a benefit, the clearer perception and livelier impression of truth, produced by its collision with error. (Mill, 1859, p. 142)

Accessibility of information is a precondition of a proper discussion of any opinion, policy or practice. Therefore, there is, on Mill's argument, a prima facie case for establishing the right to know as a basic one in any society, where the eradication of error or the greater clarity of the truth is valued, and thus the right, indeed, the obligation to support and encourage independent research. There are no absolute certainties, and thus, faced with the continual possibility of self deception or of mistaken conclusions, any government or authority should welcome rather than spurn the well-researched criticism or proposal.

Therefore, the case for the right to know and the principle of pursuing the truth openly and independently (the ethical right and principle which should override all others and which should be supported through thick and thin) seems overwhelming. But those who have been engaged in research might well harbour some doubts.

First, the principle of constantly pursuing the truth (and supporting the connected right to know) is a principle, paradoxically, partly based on the premise that there are few areas where we can claim certainty. The growth of knowledge and understanding has constantly been at the expense of so-called certainties—bodies of 'knowledge' which were regarded as unquestionable. And the errors could be discovered only by constant vigilance—constant questioning of accepted truths. But the moral consequence of that lies in the appropriateness of modesty in the arrival at and promotion of the conclusions from research. All research and scholarship is littered with the corpses of authorities, of 'the last word' articles, of the definitive text which proved not to be definitive after all. Even in being guided by principles, the rational person needs to have the exercise of those principles softened by the virtues of modesty. The researcher might be wrong. If no researchers can ever provide the definitive word, then they must weigh the important but tentative nature of their research against the consequences of publishing it. What if they were wrong, and the consequences of their error were to cause harm to others? What if, given the political climate (with respect, for example, to effective schooling), they believed that the tentativeness of research findings would escape the less subtle politicians who quite clearly seek any scrap of evidence to support their policies? The researchers can, of course, put health warnings on their packets of research, but these (as we know from smoking) have little effect.

Second, there is the obvious tension between telling the truth and estimating the consequences of so telling. The insight into the school might harm the young teacher embarking on his or her career, or it might destroy the credibility of the school, thereby exacerbating the very problem revealed in the research. How much respect should be accorded to those who are most vulnerable in the light of the research? The obvious reply is 'It all depends...'—on the seriousness to the public good of the truth being revealed, on the degree of vulnerability of the potential victims and on their positions in the pecking order of power (presumably the much bigger salaries of headteachers are partly due to their greater responsibilities and accountability).

My third reservation lies in the role of confidentiality in the obtaining of data and in the interpretation of that data. As in the first example of Calvey (2000), the crucial evidence for the research would not have been obtainable had he observed the principle of voluntary informed consent. A certain deception was required. But then the purposes of the research were significant for the general good—the exposure of serious criminal activity. But cannot a similar argument be made for the significance of much educational research—the exposure of poor teaching, say, or the revelation of managerial incompetence at national or local levels? Where confidentiality is formally agreed, then the moral position is easier to resolve, but many aspects of the relationship between researcher and research are based on trust, not upon formal agreement. Virtues of loyalty, frankness, honesty, justice would be appealed to by the wronged person who was the object of the research.

How far, then, can one establish a set of principles for the conduct of research, bearing in mind the difficulties in translating these into a set of rules, and bearing in mind, too, the unavoidability of moral deliberation in reconciling conflicting principles or in seeing the applicability of this or that principle to this context?

There is a prima facie case for the right of access to whatever evidence will enable the researcher to get at the truth. But such a right should only be conceded where there are good reasons for conducting the research—and where there are grounds for believing that the research will be conducted honourably. (That is, there needs to be a trust in the researcher which can never be reduced to the faithful adherence to agreed principles and rules.) Hence, there would seem to be some very *general* rules which follow from the above analysis.

First, the researcher should set out clearly the *kinds* of knowledge required. Those being researched would have a right to know beforehand what in general terms the researchers would be looking for and for what purpose (with, however, already the exception to this principle in that research which needs to be conducted for the public good but which would not be possible were anyone to know its purpose). There would be the continuing opportunity to renegotiate the terms of the research contract as the research revealed new avenues for enquiry.

Second, the researcher would give access both to the data and to the conclusions drawn from that data, such that both might be questioned in the light of other data or of other possible conclusions. That is, there is the general principle that all should be done to enable and encourage public criticism of the conduct and conclusions of the research.

Third, the research should provide opportunity for the right to reply from those who have participated in the research but who may believe that alternative conclusions could be supported by the data. The researcher, therefore, should be open to cross-examination by those at the receiving end of the research—the main purposes and objectives, the research methods, the political implications of the research, the data collected and the interpretations being put upon that data. Such obligations arise from the ill-conceived nature of some research, and from the fact that all knowledge is both tentative and selective. There may be other perspectives and other interpretations of the data which should be considered.

Fourth, in terms of 'consequential principles' the researcher should take into account the possible ways in which research findings may be used. Research often appears in highly-charged political contexts in which the findings are picked out selectively to support different sides of the political spectrum. Or the research may cause much harm and unhappiness to individuals or to the institution. One rule which is often derived from such a principle is that one should make the institutions or the individuals within them anonymous. But such a rule may be impossible to apply where the significance of the research may be related to the distinctive context.

The gap between high-level principles on the one hand and action on the other depends, as I have explained, on moral deliberation. But how one deliberates—what features of the situation one picks out as relevant, for example—depends on the general dispositions which incline one this way or that. A courageous person sees danger in a different way from the coward; the kind person will recognise redeeming features which the uncharitable fails to see; the loyal friend will focus on ways to help that mere companions will not detect. So, too, the ways in which researchers engage in moral deliberations depend on the sort of persons they are—the dispositions they have to act or respond in one way rather than another.

## VIRTUES

There has been a tendency in moral philosophy, as in the conduct of research, to address what should be the principles of right action rather than the dispositions of the actor. And yet, as I have indicated in the previous section, it is not possible to proceed far without reference to such dispositions. On the whole, we act from character or from our dispositions to see, value and act in a certain way. Moral education, it might be argued, should concentrate more upon the nurturing of the virtues than upon the development of moral reasoning. By 'virtue' I mean the *disposition* to act appropriately in a particular situation. There are moral virtues and intellectual virtues. Moral virtues are disposi-tions like courage, kindness, generosity of spirit, honesty, concern for justice.

Similarly with regard to the ethical dimension of research. Educational situations are too complex to fall easily under this principle or that, or to be anticipated in every detail. Moreover, not every detail of the researcher's work can be checked. There is a need for the researcher to be trusted—and thus to be trustworthy.

The moral virtues would be those concerned with the resistance to the blandishments or attractions which tempt one from the research, even where the intellectual virtues press one to go on: courage to proceed when the research is tough or unpopular; honesty when the consequences of telling the truth are uncomfortable; concern for the well-being of those who are being researched and who, if treated insensitively, might suffer harm; modesty about the merits of the research and its conclusions; humility in the face of justified criticism and the readiness to take such criticisms seriously.

This can be illustrated in the importance attached to 'trust'. Clear cases of betrayal of trust are where a promise is broken. There is, of course, something peculiar about the *obligation* to keep promises. Where that obligation is not recognised the very meaning of 'making a promise' disintegrates. Little value can be attached to promises where it is understood that the promises can be broken when convenient. Keeping promises would seem to be a *prima facie* duty or principle. However, the trust which is built up between researcher and researched, on the basis of which information is given and intelligence gained, is rarely made explicit in actual promises. It is more a matter of implicit trusting with information, putting oneself in a vulnerable position. This respect for others as vulnerable puts real constraints upon the sensitive evaluator or researcher, however much public importance he or she attaches to the information that has been obtained. It is not possible to say what should be done without examination of the particular case. But the virtuous researcher will be aware of difficulties that others would not be; such a researcher would bring factors into the deliberations which others would omit.

Intellectual virtues would refer to concern to search for the truth and not to cook the books, openness to criticism, an interest in clarity of communication, a concern for evidence. Truth is not always kind and the rewards for its pursuit may be small. Self-interest might suggest cutting corners or being economic with the truth. But genuine researchers would feel ill-at-ease with such behaviours. They would go against the deep-down *feeling* concerning how they ought to act.

The deliberations, therefore, which are inevitable in the complexity of practical situations and the clash of principles which I have spoken of, will be greatly determined by the dispositions or virtues of the researcher. Indeed, even 'telling the truth' might be twisted to a partisan cause if one has not the right virtues. Was it not William Blake who observed 'A truth that's told with bad intent is worth all the lies you can invent'? The point is that clever people, knowing the conclusions they want, can, if so disposed (i.e. in the absence of the appropriate virtues), find the data and the arguments to justify those conclusions—and yet, despite the fact that no untruth has been told, be dishonest. Research, therefore, as has been argued, requires very special sorts of virtue, both moral and intellectual.

## THE VIRTUOUS RESEARCH COMMUNITY

Virtues are fostered—and indeed related to—particular social contexts and without that social support personal virtues so often weaken. A military society will foster a sense of chivalry and honour, and thus the dispositions to act in particular ways. Humility is a distinctively Christian virtue (though too infrequently observed) requiring an institutional support. Kohlberg came to realise that, without 'just communities', the fostering of the capacity to reason about justice would not translate into dispositions to act justly (Kohlberg, 1982). Therefore, if we are wanting virtuous researchers, then we must have 'virtuous research communities', communities which embody the very virtues which one requires of the members of those communities.

What then are the virtues to be fostered of such communities, which can in turn nurture the virtues of their members? Research is primarily concerned with the search for knowledge and the elimination of error. That in turn requires the spirit of criticism. Given the tentativeness and provisional nature of most conclusions (for example, that literacy is best improved through the literacy hour or that standards are best improved through naming and shaming), then criticism should be welcomed rather than discouraged. But that goes against the grain. Our natural tendency is to defend rather than criticise our most cherished views. Knowledge might grow through criticism, but knowledge often remains fairly static because the acceptance of such criticism goes against one's natural inclination. Hence, the importance of nurturing in researchers the spirit of self-criticism and the openness to the criticism of others. A research community—in schools, in universities and elsewhere—would provide the forum or the context in which such criticism would be invited and welcomed and become part of the normal life of the institution. But such an invitation is risky. It could open up a range of criticism difficult to sustain. Therefore, the embodiment of such intellectual virtues within the life of a community requires the moral virtue of courage.

But more needs to be said about the community's values in relation to the nature of knowledge claims. The third example, which I gave at the beginning, pointed to the need for negotiation of the research procedures and indeed of its findings. This presupposes a particular respect for the teachers in the school—their distinctive perspective, their insights into the situation, their critical appraisal of the provisional findings. Such respect, reflected in the negotiation of procedures and outcomes, implies a more democratic approach to the conduct of research—an approach based on certain principles but requiring shared dispositions if it is to be carried out. And it is quite clear that few institutions have such 'dispositions', especially when educational programmes are increasingly directed to ends which are external to the deliberations of those communities and have not had to withstand scrutiny within them. By saying the institutions do not have such 'dispositions' I mean that they have not incorporated those norms which influence their members to behave in certain ways. Increasingly, for example, the management of universities excludes the corporate or collegial deliberations over academic aims and values; few schools provide the forum in which teachers might question the educational priorities so often determined by pressures from outside the school. Democratic values (and the social and personal virtues which are associated with them) are difficult to sustain where policy and practice are increasingly controlled by government.

## CONCLUSION

There has been much criticism recently of educational research. Such criticism focuses upon the fragmentation of that research, the irrelevance of that research to the questions which teachers and policy makers are asking, the tendentiousness of some research, the poor quality of the methods adopted. But these criticism do not address what are possibly the most important questions—namely, those concerned with the qualities (in particular, the virtues) of those carrying out the research. Is there a disposition to find out and to tell the truth as it is and not as one would like it to be? Is there respect for the schools and teachers who are the objects of the research? Have researchers the courage to resist the opposition of powerful persons when the conclusions are critical? Have they the modesty to recognise the tentativeness of their conclusions? Are they sufficiently trust-worthy for us to accept both data and conclusions drawn from those data? Furthermore, are they members of a community where such virtues are respected and fostered—are they allowed to fail?

In beginning to spell out the virtues, I come to recognise my own vices. But that is why I am not a researcher. But perhaps many others should not be either.

*Correspondence:* Richard Pring, Department of Educational Studies, 15 Norham Gardens, Oxford OX2 6PY, UK.
Email: richard.pring@educational-studies.ox.ac.uk

## REFERENCES

Calvey, D. (2000) in: G. Lee-Treweek and S. Linkogle (eds), *Danger in the Field: Risk and Ethics in Social Research* (London, Routledge).

Kohlberg, L. (1982) Recent Work in Moral Education, in: L. O. Ward, *The Ethical Dimension of the School Curriculum* (Swansea, Pineridge Press).

Mill, J. S. (1859) On Liberty, in: M. Warnock (ed.), (1972) *Utilitarianism* (London, Collins).

# 8

# The Guilt of Whistling-blowing: Conflicts in Action Research and Educational Ethnography

MIKE McNAMEE

*This chapter discusses the role conflict of the educational researcher who comes upon an unprofessional relationship between teacher and pupil. It is argued that the whistleblowing literature in related professions, with its focus on standard conditions and solutions framed as obligations, is inadequate. Reference is made to the idea of 'guilty knowledge': the feelings of guilt that attach when one comes to know of harm visited on innocent others, and has no unqualified sense of which way to act. Distinguishing moral from causal responsibility helps to show how blame need not necessarily attach to the guilt-ridden researcher, whichever option she chooses.*

## I ETHICS, POLITICS AND CONFLICT IN RESEARCH: SOME OPENING REMARKS

Those who are by temperament or motivation guided to the educational life are, like politicians, apt to need thick skin as much as wise judgement. Their many professional roles are often shot through with incompatible demands. Among those roles, and increasingly so, educators in schools, and teacher-educators in colleges and universities are exhorted to research within their professional domain. Nevertheless, many educational researchers find that their forays into the thicket of human relations threaten to compromise their integrity. Of course, such challenges are thought to be part and parcel of the practices of politics and war, where innocence and experience are apparently incompatible. It is in these contexts that the problem of 'dirty hands' is most clearly posted. In positions of military and political power it may well be a professional obligation to harm others in the name of a greater good. In this vein Stuart Hampshire has remarked that:

> The idea of experience is the idea of guilty knowledge, of the expectation of unavoidable squalor and imperfection, of necessary disappointments and mixed results, of half success and half failure. A person of experience has come to expect that his usual choice will be of the lesser of two or more evils. (Hampshire, 1983, pp.167–168)

Such conflict is, if not the norm, certainly a commonplace in educational ethnography. Having helped to develop policies and procedures to promote ethically responsible research cultures,[1] I am moved toward the conclusion that certain types of educational research ought to come with a professional health warning: 'Personal engagement into the life worlds of others to gain knowledge for research purposes can seriously damage your integrity'. Most of the 'community of educational researchers' regard themselves as striving for the good of the particular practices they interrogate and exemplify, even die-hard positivists who think that the acquisition and propagation of human knowledge is a morally neutral process. It is the self-consciousness of this avowed normativity, a disavowal of value-neutrality in research, as well as the more standard issues of access, consent, deception and ownership, that can itself cause or exacerbate problems for researchers.

There are, of course, books and articles in the general academic literature[2] on the standard ethical issues just as there are codes of conduct for educational researchers[3] and those working in a range of sub-disciplines in education.[4] None, however, address specifically the phenomenon of guilty knowledge and the aptness of the whistle-blowing literature in the context of education. These ideas have been subject to analysis in the literature of other 'people professions' such as social work (Banks, 1995), nursing (Fletcher and Sorrell, 2000), and community care (Wilmot, 1997) and most frequently in the field of business and corporate ethics.[5] In Britain, however, the recently established General Teaching Council has not so far published a Code of Professional Conduct. Moreover, leading bodies such as the Economic and Social Research Council are yet to take a strong lead on matters such as research ethics. It is against this uneven background that one can properly challenge the level of preparation given to researchers in the field of ethics and educational research, and question whether it can sensitise and guide them toward more acceptably professional conduct.

What I wish to do here is to unpack two apparent conflicts in the context of educational research and to consider the ways in which we might think about them philosophically. In particular I want to revisit what may be, for some educational researchers, the familiar terrain of subjective conflict. In Section II, I re-describe an actual conflict that gave rise to feelings of guilt where the researcher came into certain 'illicit information' and then realised he was inextricably linked to some minor wrongdoing in virtue of this unsought but inescapable knowledge. In Section III, I consider a hypothetical case where a researcher is torn between conflicting courses of action as she uncovers professional misconduct. In neither case has the researcher done anything of which she need feel morally ashamed. Yet she might find herself burdened with 'guilty knowledge'. 'Guilty knowledge' is a term of art. Although there is no received definition, the term may be taken to refer to the feeling of guilt that arises when one both comes to know of certain harms or wrongdoings and is torn between courses of action to remove the sense of guilt that attaches to the knowledge. One common way of relieving oneself of the burden of this awakening is to blow the whistle on the perpetrators of the wrongdoing. But the nature of that whistle-blowing, and the question whether it is sometimes obligatory rather than merely permissible, are themselves open to contestation. These and related issues are discussed in Section IV. Precisely how we are to think of this subjective guilt and whether the feeling is rational is the object of the discussion in Section V. In Section VI, I try to draw together the threads of the discussion. I observe how the same messy ethical situations that arise in research can profitably be (re)described with closer attention to the concepts in play and the range of theoretical considerations that might lie behind them.

## II  THE EDUCATIONAL RESEARCHER CAUGHT IN PROFESSIONAL CONFLICT

For a great many educators who engage in it, and not merely professional researchers in colleges and universities, research is a means to promote professional development within their own institution as much as career progression. In some cases a funding agency will support research bids only where access to the relevant institution has been secured prior to the bid. This requires educational researchers to draw upon their networks in an attempt to court a suitable site for their investigation, upon the promise that the research will be mutually advantageous. In many other cases, in-service teachers are required to engage in an in-depth study as part of master's or doctoral programmes. As most of this constituency are part-time students but full-time educators, issues of time and efficiency are paramount. Quite reasonably many choose to use their own institutions as the site of their investigation. Access to relevant data, familiarity with the key actors in the institution, and awareness of local policy and procedures all facilitate the smooth completion of the study. Nonetheless, insider status can also be a source of ethical difficulties for the researcher. Others choose to go outside of their own institution in order to avoid potential conflicts of interest. Nevertheless, whether as insider or guest, there is another common cause of research conflict that I want to flag up: the problem of ideological commitments as a source, or compounding element, of conflict.

In his discussion of role-conflict, Burgess (1988) describes how he sat in on interviews in 'Bishop McGregor' school in a follow-up to an earlier study. Burgess had carried out research at the same school as a post-graduate student and was a familiar and trusted co-professional within the school, but felt his initial research was diminished by its failure to investigate hiring practices. In his second spell at the school, the headteacher had granted him access to interviews, and after consultation with the National Union of Teachers representative it was agreed that the research was acceptable to them, on the grounds that teachers ought to know what happened in such situations. To secure their consent,[6] candidates were informed that he was a researcher and this explained his apparent minute-taking throughout the interviews. Burgess writes:

> I agreed that I would not take part in the proceedings nor would I divulge any information to teachers about what transpired in the interviews. (1988, p. 67)

It is not clear how Burgess squared his two commitments. I presume that when he referred to the benefits of teachers understanding interview practices, he was referring to the teaching community in a general way. If this were not the case, then he would clearly have found his obligations to the particular staff (and would-be staff) of the school in direct conflict with his promise to maintain confidentiality with respect to the particular candidates. On one particular occasion, Burgess notes how his commitment not to engage with the proceedings of interviewing was compromised. After an informal round of interviews in the morning for a new post, it was clear that the Head had decided that two of the six candidates were not suitable for the post, and yet would be interviewed in the same manner as all the others during the afternoon. No justification was given for maintaining their presence except to make it appear to the Governors that a full and proper procedure was being observed. The afternoon interviews were thus effectively redundant for these interviewees. Burgess decided in these interviews to give the appearance of taking notes as he had done in the morning and in the informal interviews. But the interviews themselves did not follow a 'normal' format: the nature of the questioning changed, and the manner and tone of the interviews changed as well. To Burgess's and others' embarrassment, one of the interviewees who had been dismissed after the morning session saw through the situation and made an ironic parting remark to make plain that he had understood what was going on. Burgess explains his unease at being present and therefore party to the decision and his situation is complicated by the ruse that he had adopted to mask the fact that he was aware of the deception of the candidates.

Burgess notes the guilt that he felt with regard to the deception he helped to maintain. To reassure himself that he did the right thing, he might well have reflected upon: (a) his apparent complicity in the deception of the interviewees that they were being equitably treated in the process; (b) his feeling that he ought to retain some sense of loyalty to the group who had invited him to attend and to appear at least to take some part in the proceedings in order to conduct his research; (c) the fact that such a minor wrongdoing ought not disrupt the research project which had potential to secure greater good in the future; and (d) the fact that he had in no way engineered the wrongdoing but, like the unsuccessful interviewees, had been involved in it against his will. A final point to be made here regards the intentions informing this project as a whole. Burgess's work had no specific action-research agenda.[7] Like most social scientists, one presumes, he hoped that his research might make a positive contribution in a number of spheres, but he was not thereby committed specifically to improving the lot of those involved in the interviews. Whatever obligations he incurred to the research subjects arising from the research, as I have said above, they were of a very general kind. While Burgess does not make explicit his reasoning in this case, it appears that he had been sensitive to this unintended complicity but was focused on the minimal harm to those directly involved (disutility) and the prospect of benefit (utility) to the wider teaching community in illuminating hiring practices in education and in promoting good practice by the dissemination of his findings.

It is a proper philosophical task to attempt to characterise the subjective state Burgess finds himself in: is it to be thought of as ambivalence, disquiet, guilt or regret? Each of these concepts shades into each other and they are not separable without careful attention to usage. I will therefore develop an account of the felt or subjective guilt in such cases in the hypothetical scenario below, but with respect to an example of more serious wrongdoing leading to feelings of guilt. Moreover, in what follows I shall complicate matters by fore-grounding a specific normative/ideological commitment. I want to show that it is not merely the connectedness of the researcher to the research context that is problematic, but also how commitments to improve the lot of research participants, which are characteristic of educational ethnography, can seriously increase conflict.

### III  THE EDUCATIONAL ETHNOGRAPHER AS ACTION RESEARCHER:  COMMITMENT AND CONFLICT

Educational ethnography commonly comprises a triangulation of observation, interview and questionnaire. Necessarily, though, the researcher as engages in an extended period of observation of a particular environment while trying to avoid the failure the anthropologist fears: going native (i.e. subscribing uncritically to the norms of the group under investigation). Consider, then, that such a researcher has stumbled across some unethical practice carried on deceptively by one of the group who comprise the context of the investigation.[8]

Imagine a female teacher in a co-educational high school. We will call her Jo. She is studying part-time for a PhD and hopes to move into higher education. As a feminist researcher she has a clear ideological commitment to eradicate such gender inequities as are within her compass. Of course, she is not Joan of Arc, but in her own way she does what she can to alert pupils, members of staff and management to issues of equality. Her research is related to the stereotyping of girls and boys into and/or away from particular school subjects. Fellow staff members have only a vague idea of the research project. Before she was accepted onto the Doctoral programme she had noted how arts and humanities subjects were more likely to be chosen by girls whereas the scientific options are more populated by boys and she wants to explore why this is the case and, if appropriate, make suggestions as to how this situation may be redressed.

Jo embarks on a range of interviews with a representative sample of 16–18 year-old pupils. She gets to know them well. Many of the older girls identify with her as a role model. Over the course of her interviews she notes that some of the reasons why the girls opt away from physics and chemistry are not solely due to the nature of the subject, but appear to have more to do with how it is taught. As she probes the issue, it is not so much the pedagogical style that appears to be the problem here but a particular teacher and his attitudes toward the girls of the group: the way he addresses them, the comments he makes, his body language, and so on. There is even the suggestion that he has made passes at girls to whom he has offered extra 'tutorials'.

Jo is, of course, enraged by this but makes no obvious signs to the girls that she believes them unquestioningly. She tries, delicately, to corroborate the stories with other pupils (both boys and girls) by asking questions about the teaching styles of different teachers. A pattern of behaviour becomes clear. Worse, it appears that one girl (though a consenting adult in legal terms) is dating the teacher.

Leaving aside the problem of what strategy to adopt, she forces herself to consider fully the interested parties. Her feminist commitments push her hard to blow the whistle on her colleague. Her first thought is that the practice of teachers dating sixth-form pupils (16–18 years old), though lawful, is not simply inappropriate but despicable. Given that the power relations are loaded so heavily in the teacher's favour, how could the relationship be anything other than exploitative? By talking to other receptive colleagues about unspecified staff-student relationships, she finds out that this has happened more than once in the recent past and the management team of the school had dealt with the matter privately and either swept matters under the carpet or assisted the teacher in getting a position at another school. She comes to the conclusion that not only will they fail to address the problem, but that their chauvinist complaisance is part of the bigger picture. She wonders whether it is her moral duty or professional responsibility to blow the whistle.

The naïve may well say that the simple answer to the problem is to blow the whistle on such unethical practice. (There is in fact a range of options between silence and whistle-blowing—see Section V below). How Jo is to weigh the pros and cons is not a simple matter. Ought she even to engage in this kind of calculation? And if she were to gauge costs and benefits, to whom should they attach? Who properly counts in such an equation: the teacher's wife, the girl, all such girls? On further reflection she perceives morally justifiable reasons for and against the act. Would the reputation of all the teaching staff be tarnished by such an exposure? Would this be fair to them? What might this do to the school's reputation, with a forthcoming school inspection looming large in the staff psyche? Is she certain the relationship is not consensual? What if the girl's parents are cognisant and approving? Might her whistle-blowing be disrespectful of the autonomy of the girl, the teacher and her parents? Does the pupil not have a 'right' to choose her own relations? Perhaps strongest in her mind is the potential harm that would befall the student if the whistle were blown. Would it be fair to endanger the student's realistic possibilities of achieving her potential grades and gaining a place at university? She comes to feel that whatever act is chosen now entails harms done to those who are innocent of wrongdoing. And then she comes to ask whether her own interests should count in her judgements. 'What will happen to me?' she might well ask. Might she be ostracised by her male colleagues? What will happen to the research? Surely this unfortunate discovery marks the end of it if she goes public. All this is properly troubling to Jo.

What the researcher desperately wants here is reassurance. She searches codes of conduct to no avail. She wants to share the information with colleagues, but in order to do so, she knows that she will have to reveal data that will alert staff to what is going on. If she confides in her feminist colleagues (or her fiercely committed political feminist supervisor) she may well be ostracised as uncommitted and weak, unprepared to take genuine action against an exploitative patriarchy. Her self-examination is endless. She clearly is in a quandary. She is weighed down by the knowledge of the relationship. She feels guilt at the thought of the ongoing professional misconduct yet also strong unease at the potential harm she will bring about by blowing the whistle.

What would it mean to say here (as I have often heard colleagues say) that she must simply 'do the right thing'? Both moral theorists and reflective practitioners have held to the view that there will always be a right outcome to such quandaries if one thinks hard enough and has sufficient resolve or will. I am not persuaded by this view. To enable us to appraise the situation meaningfully requires an excursion into area of conflict and cost before we can understand properly the felt guilt and judgement to remain silent or blow the whistle.

The conflict I have described is one of considerable complexity. Nevertheless, it is not clear that it presents a full-blown dilemma.[9] For a conflict to be considered a moral dilemma, there must be at the very least two courses of action which each have a claim to be obligatory, yet which cannot both be taken in the circumstances. Enough of the scenario has been presented to show that Jo is indeed held in the grip of value- and role-conflict when it comes to the decision whether to blow the whistle or not. Nonetheless, there is a range of options between blowing the whistle and remaining silent, which I have not yet explored fully. Moreover, we need not assume that all moral conflicts are conflicts in the realm of duty. Most of us would recognise conflicts of value that fall short of conflicts of duty. And besides, in a complex predicament such as Jo's, the distinction between moral and non-moral considerations may not be easy to draw.[10]

What may mark out a salient difference between our first and second educational scenario is the potential harm, in the second, to particular individuals. Where the researcher is not a committed feminist, the conflict might not weigh as heavily. Part of the conflict is the particularity of Jo's commitments and identity that are internal to and not detachable from the scenario. A more general point can be made here too. It is not uncommon for research by in-service professionals to investigate their own professional context. The option of ignoring the nexus of other roles is not possible; one cannot decide to disregard one's identity as a professional engaged in that context taking, as it were, the view from nowhere. Our researcher here cannot extricate her evaluation of the problem from its description; she herself needs to be included in a full description of the very quandary, and thus so too do her judgements. While the epistemological dimension of this inextricability is widely acknowledged in research design where the research participants and the researcher are intimately connected, it is clear that there is wide scope for ethical difficulties too. This is why the decision to blow the whistle is far from straightforward.

## IV WHISTLE WHILE YOU WORK?

What, specifically, is meant by whistle-blowing; what does it seek to achieve? More than one theory exists.[11] What can generally, and incontestably, be said is that whistle-blowing entails the revealing of information, to prevent or to bring about the cessation of a significant wrong within an organisation, by a person within that organisation.

Bok characterises the general aim thus:

> The alarm of the whistleblower is intended to disrupt the status quo: to pierce the background noise, perhaps the false harmony or the imposed silence of 'affairs as usual'. (1988, p. 332)

Bok then sets out three morally salient features of whistle-blowing: dissent, breach of loyalty and accusation of wrongdoing. It is clear that our example above incorporates a sense of felt loyalty and an accusation of wrongdoing, though the notion of dissent appear to be idling here. Let us hold that thought for a moment. If Jo has arrived at the conclusion that she will get nowhere satisfactorily by using internal mechanisms, then her whistle-blowing in part comprises a challenge to the authority and probity of the management team and school procedures. If we agree roughly upon these features, we must recognise the issue of salience[12] (and here I am going to focus upon the right of the girl not to be harmed or exploited and the conflict raised by the breach of loyalty to the school and her colleagues— there are many more complicating factors as I have noted) entering into justifications of whistle-blowing.

Davis (1996, pp. 6–7) argues that the received or standard theory[13] recognises that an act of whistle-blowing is *prima facie* an act of disloyalty that may be justified when conditions 1–3 apply:

1. The organization to which the would-be whistleblower belongs, through its product or policy, [does] serious harm to the public...

2. The would-be whistleblower has identified the threat of harm, reported it to her immediate superior, making clear both the threat itself and the objection to it, and concluded that the superior will do nothing effective
3. The would-be whistleblower has exhausted other internal procedures within the organization or at least made use of as many internal procedures as the danger to others and her own safety make reasonable.

If conditions 1–3 are satisfied, whistle-blowing is morally justifiable, according to what Davis calls the standard theory; though we should note his emphasis on the duties or obligations of the would-be whistle-blower to exhaust the internal mechanisms of the organisation first. This is an inherently conservative position. The very mechanisms and ethos of the institution may well display sexist, racist or other unethical dimensions which might lead a reasonable person to conclude that the internal mechanisms (or lack of them) are themselves part of the problem.

But arguably, a more serious issue is Davis' position that whistle-blowing is obligatory if the further conditions prevail:

4. The would-be whistleblower has (or has accessible) evidence that would convince a reasonable, impartial observer that her view of the threat is correct;
5. The would-be whistleblower has good reason to believe that revealing the threat will (probably) prevent the harm at reasonable cost (all things considered).

First, let us note here the deontological approach: framing a universalisable obligation in terms of principles. I have tried to suggest above (without yet arguing the position) that it is the matrix of factors particular to a case that help us to judge the moral salience of our felt emotions and ethical judgements. I have tried to show how the same configuration of events may well entail a different scheme of salience for a different researcher. How do such considerations alter our attitude to criterion 4? For instance, what sense can be made of an 'impartial observer'? As we have noted, the idea of a view from nowhere is a non-starter, a throw-back to a naïve view of science and a rationalist conception of ethics. Emotions and their corresponding judgements can only arise in the light of particular situations. Indeed the very idea of moral perception or moral salience presupposes a situated agent, one in a position to see the conflict. So imagine the new researcher is not a feminist, has no action research commitments; and still believes the management will sweep it under the carpet; should we call this new researcher more impartial? Or should we recognise him rather as someone with a different set of attitudes or commitments? If the latter, just what would a truly impartial observer look like?

The fifth criterion is even more problematic. What sense are we to make of the idea of an obligation (a moral duty upon the researcher) to blow a whistle upon the basis of a consequentialist calculation of costs and benefits? It is ordinarily thought that the very idea of duties is precisely to secure minimal moral standards that prevent people being treated disrespectfully, or harmed unreasonably. The idea that an obligation only arises when the benefits outweigh the costs runs counter to the very idea of obligation. This is simply to be a utilitarian: to ascertain the facts of pleasures and pains, utility and disutility and then consider whether to blow the whistle or not. I will return to this point below in Section V.

Now if all this seems less than satisfactory, it should be underlined that Davis argues for a revised version of the standard thesis. The details of Davis' critique need not detain us here (notwithstanding its prominence within the professional ethics literature) except for the specific moral relevance accords to the organisational context of the whistle-blower and her acts. He re-titles the theory upon this fact and depicts it as the 'complicity theory': the obligation to blow the whistle derives from the complicity of the whistle-blower rather than the mere ability or inclination to prevent harm.

Davis claims that the agent in such cases enters the situation voluntarily. No one has coerced them to work in this or that institution. But I am not convinced that he has got things right here. Rather, I think he is wrenching the right cause the wrong way. He recognises the fact that voluntariness is not a necessary condition for justifying whistle-blowing but argues that 'involuntary participants will not have the same obligation of loyalty as the typical whistleblower; hence any theory justifying their "going public" will have a somewhat different structure than the theory developed here' (1996, p. 18). Nevertheless, what drives our researcher here, however, may not be a deep felt sense of loyalty to the school *simpliciter* but additionally, and powerfully, attention to the harm that will be caused to innocent others (specifically the pupil and perhaps even the wife and family of the errant teacher—for her feminist commitments also draw her attention to their undeserved predicament in this scenario). In any event there needs to be some conception of a degree of detachment; working within the organisation should not be taken to imply complicity. Now in Burgess's case there was some complicity but it was not of his construction (he volunteered to be part of the interview process proper, not the sham; he found himself unwillingly in that situation). Moreover the degree of harm is scarcely significant given the facts as he presents them. Jo, however, does not feel complicity with the teacher even though the ethos of the teachers' commonroom may allow talk of the sexual attractiveness of certain schoolgirls.

Furthermore, there are other prudential reasons that weigh, and not insignificantly either. In attempting to make our judgement whether we are obliged to blow the whistle, we are forced seriously to ask what constitutes 'a reasonable cost' and who is to be included in the counting that delivers the calculation. Whistle-blowing is at odds with three significantly important institutional considerations: (i) conformity with organisational cultures;[14] (ii) adherence to professional standards (including collegiality); and (iii) the dynamics of institutional loyalty (Gadlin, 1998). Whistle-blowers therefore often end up paying a very heavy price.[15] Sieber notes the chilling advice of one whistle-blower from the Environmental Protection Agency, a fruit of bitter experience:

> Don't make the mistake of thinking that someone in authority, if he only knew what was going on, would straighten the whole thing out. If you have God, the law, the press, and the facts on your side, you have a fifty-fifty chance of defeating the bureaucracy. (Sieber, 1988, p. 25)

One could note the point that if one does not blow the whistle, the possibility still exists for 'controlled leakage' (Eraut, 1984) where the researcher who is about to publicly report the research allows those who are its subject to have knowledge of some portion or description of the it. This, however, does not alter with sufficient significance the emotional set of the researcher. One might further ask whether she could blow the whistle now or later, publicly or anonymously.

A final related point made frequently in the literature is that of the need for examination of one's motives. Whistle-blowers ought not to be seen to profit from their blowing of the whistle; they should do it for entirely moral reasons, or so it is generally thought.[16] This takes us back to the way that those with feminist commitments, more so than those without, will judge certain conduct more severely. The same conditions that may be seen as exploitative by one might appear merely inappropriate to another. If the whistle-blower is seen to be advancing her cause, having an axe to grind, her chances of arousing the relevant community, of shouting 'foul' loud and clear in a way that compels professional support, will greatly diminish. A careful examination of her motives, and of her perception of the facts, will be critical if the whistle-blowing is to succeed and she is to be sure she has done the right thing for the right reason at the right time.

## V  WHY IS THE DECISION SO DIFFICULT: GUILTY KNOWLEDGE?

Consider the last time you said either, 'I'm not telling you this' or 'you didn't hear this from me'. Conversely, consider when someone said to you 'I didn't want to know about that' or 'you didn't tell me that' or even 'I'm going to pretend I didn't hear that'. There are ranges of everyday circumstances in which we come to know things we surely wish we did not. The phrase, 'when wisdom wakens woe' is felicitous in precisely these circumstances. One thing is certain, though: our researcher cannot 'un-know' matters. There is a sense in which our researcher must wish she had not come to hold such knowledge. It weighs her down. But how to characterise the accompanying emotional state: that is a significant philosophical, and not merely psychological, challenge.[17]

There are writers such as Rawls (1972, pp. 472–465) who characterise Jo's kind of felt guilt in the absence of wrongdoing as merely irrational.[18] And many of her professional colleagues would, I fancy make a similar evaluation. It is clear that she would not be unequivocally guilty of wrongdoing whether she blew the whistle or not; she has transgressed no code or authority. She has merely been the unfortunate person who came upon such an event and no blame attaches to her. If she is not responsible, not blameworthy, they say, then she ought not to feel guilty. 'Get a grip' might be the rationalist response. I have said above that the conflict is not a genuine dilemma. This is not a situation where, as sometimes in war, one might argue that wrong must be done to an individual as the only means to prevent the mass slaughter of innocents. Such a situation might properly be called 'blameless wrongdoing'. This is often characterised as the problem of dirty hands.[19] But to describe our situation here as one of dirty hands would attribute an authority to Jo such as that attributed to the politician or colonel and entailing their accountability.[20] But in fact, under action or inaction, Jo will not have been engaged in any wrongdoing—though she may well cause harm to innocent others. I want to show that what Greenspan refers to as 'subjective guilt' best captures her sense of conflict and justifies the reasonableness of the feeling.

To understand why the term 'guilty knowledge' makes sense here, we must distinguish the concept of guilt from its close cousin shame—two concepts often run together in everyday discourse. Of course, both concepts feature heavily in the regulation of conduct by self and others. To illuminate some important features of the two concepts we may say very generally, after Taylor (1993), that shame may attach to us through actions outside of our control or responsibility (I may be ashamed of the low station of my birth, or of being a certain caste), where a feeling of status-deflation attaches to my whole self. There can be no washing or wishing it away, as it were.[21] By contrast, guilt entails a localised sense of wrongdoing for which reparation may be due and, when effected, negates or defuses the emotion and its potentially corrosive effects. As Greenspan remarks:

> the agent in a state of feeling guilty is typically motivated by that state to escape it—in a way that makes guilt provide a potentially powerful motive even after a moral lapse. (1995, p. 132)

And later:

> Shame involves lowering oneself, or taking a submissive posture, we may say-hanging one's head—whereas guilt involves a kind of emotional self-punishment. . . . The central point that distinguishes guilt from shame—to focus on its main competitor—seems to be self-alienation. Shame does not divide the self against itself in the way that guilt does. (1995, p. 133)

There are several points worth dwelling on here. First, it could be said that shame is only felt in the presence of, *before*, as we say, others. Our researcher's guilt, however, attaches to her quite privately. It is an internalised product of a cultivated conscience. The notion of being lowered, head-hung in front of the relevant community does not gain purchase here; she has nothing to be ashamed of. Whatever Jo does here, she appears to be doing it in good faith, having perceived the potential salience of all reasonable possibilities and the affected parties. Second, she feels the guilt as alienating. Her professional integrity, perhaps her personal integrity, appear under threat. The conflict between her ideological commitments, her friendship, her concern for the maintenance of the school's reputation in the face of *laissez faire* and chauvinist management, displays her loyalty to her colleagues, and her sense of the exploitation and wrongness visited upon the pupil. All these considerations pull her apart. So the sense of guilt is divisive in that way. It represents dis-integration and can be powerfully damaging because of this. Third, the notion that this negativity is a form of emotional punishment requires further examination, because punishment implies wrongdoing and I have thus far stressed the inappropriateness of that notion.[22] Yet she will be instrumental in visiting harm on apparently innocent persons either way she acts. Might the girl's parents later say of her failure to blow the whistle; 'it's her fault—if only she had gone public at the time'? Alternatively, might the teacher's wife or indeed the headteacher not say, 'it's her fault; if only she had told me'? Both might then hold her to blame. Is there a sense in which she is responsible for this harm, that she might

really be blameworthy? Again, attention to the conceptual boundaries is crucial. Gaita throws considerable light here by attending to
linguistic usage:

> Blame is a word with many connotations and it is sometimes used in a general
> way to mean no more than 'to hold responsible' . . . To hold someone
> responsible in this sense means to hold them, to fix them in a lucid response to
> the significance of what they did. It means that the moral significance of what
> they did must not be evaded either by them or by us, but it does not, thereby,
> mean that we find fault with them, that we can accuse them, or that we find
> them culpable. (1991, p. 44)

Now this seems just right here. They may indeed say that she is 'to
blame' but it is clear that this is to be understood in a weaker sense
than in relation to one who has directly done evil.

Whichever way our researcher acts she feels the weight of harm she
will visit on an innocent other. Her state will indeed be captured by
what Bernard Williams has called 'agent-regret',[23] a notion he claims
is not taken seriously either by duty- or utility-based ethical theories.
Williams' notion of 'moral cost' can helpfully illuminate the sense of
conflict. In situations where the best or least bad course of action,
and its implications for the researcher as a human agent, still entails
wrongdoing, we are left with what can be called a 'moral
remainder'.[24] Greenspan notes how a sense of 'moral cost' or
'moral remainder' can result where the interests of a single person are
traded-off against the common good. So we might think with Jo that
if she were to blow the whistle and the consequences were (for
example) that the pupil was distraught and failed her exams, left
school, and went to live with the errant teacher, that she may well
have done the right thing but only at a cost to the innocent student.
Under this, perhaps accurate, description of the scenario, there is a
conflict between a consequentialist calculation that drives decisions
toward the greatest good for the greatest number and a right to self-
determination. What we have here then is moral and theoretical as
well as practical conflict.

Jo's guilt remains while she holds this conflict in tension. At its
simplest, she wants to expose the teacher, but not to harm the
student. The two options appear irreconcilable. If she does either, she
feels grounds for regret. And such regret will be in order if and when
she acts. On one side of the equation, she feels guilty for not acting to
halt the relationship, in line with her projects and identity-
constituting feminist commitments. On the other, she does not
want to jeopardise the girl's future at this critical time. One way to
ease the path to a decision, and remove the feelings of guilt, may be to
delineate precisely the concept of responsibility that may exonerate
her from blame.

Here I think we need to distinguish, as Greenspan does, between causal and moral responsibility. If she blows the whistle it will be clear that she is causally responsible for the harms that befall the innocent wife and child, and those others I have tentatively suggested (other teachers in the school, their reputations and so on). Yet she appears not to be *morally* responsible: that lies with the errant teacher. On the other hand, if she fails to blow the whistle, if she overrides the ideological and professional obligation, she is, albeit to a limited degree, morally responsible for any potential ongoing exploitation, though not causally so. But there is a notion here that is of great interest: what is the relationship between a belief, a thought and an evaluation? Greenspan holds the rather vague, but important, notion of an unconscious thought of guilt without a corresponding belief. In certain cases, she writes:

> guilt does involve a thought of oneself as morally responsible but . . . it need not always involve the corresponding belief. The non-judgemental analysis will therefore allow guilt without cognitive delusion . . . in which the agent feels guilty just as a result of passive causal involvement (in the event of some harm) though he knows he lacks even causal responsibility for it. In effect, the analysis limits his disturbance to the level of detaching emotion from belief. It also has the advantage, as I shall argue, of allowing for guilt in some cases where one might be tempted to detach the emotion even from a thought of moral *or* causal responsibility. (1995, p. 159)

What we need, then, is to detach the strong sense of blame from the researcher who yet feels guilt. This will bring the subjective guilt into perspective and, once registered, allow it to dissipate thereafter. And asking what the guilt is doing in such situations can help us. Among the suggested functions of guilt is that it is a kind of punitive, self-cleansing mechanism. If we were to focus solely on the negative aspects of guilt and its relations to punishment we could easily miss this positive aspect. It is importantly related to seeing the whole picture: of enlarged moral perception. Were we to focus on one aspect of the picture, we would fail to see the salience of the many and related dimensions of the conflict. The felt guilt registers the researcher's sense of concern for the victims in the scenario. But Greenspan draws our attention to the fact that the guilt functions positively in another way: the researcher needs not merely does to register her standpoint but also to ameliorate the dis-integrating, self-alienating effects of that guilt. Her felt guilt has registered the harm that will be visited on innocent others. It ensures that she identifies, appropriately, with the potential victims. (It also highlights the inadequacy of those who try to comfort us in such moments with the phrase: 'don't worry about it—there was nothing you could have done' or 'don't worry about it—anyone would have done the same'.)

The guilt need not be objectively tied to moral culpability for us to feel it properly and appropriately. It is with this in mind that I do not wish to describe the feeling as 'irrational guilt' as Rawls does and certain psychoanalysts do too. Where we feel neither guilt nor regret in such a case, we display the moral callouses of indifference and insensitivity. I have argued that our researcher's feelings of guilt are not irrational but that she is morally blameless, whatever she now does, having attended to the particularities of this conflict. I have noted how her apparent passivity prior to her decision is not the product of a callous indifference but a reasonable estimation of what hangs in the balance.

Whether or not Jo blows the whistle is not so pressing a question for me to address here. I have tried rather to show that the formulae for justified and obligatory whistle-blowing are inadequate at the level of theory. The standard theory requires obligations and utility considerations to co-mingle in an incoherent way. The complicity theory does not capture all cases. And neither speaks to the experience of the researcher. I have attempted to show how the conflict necessarily entails harms but how the guilt which attaches to the knowledge, and the need to act upon it, may be set aside by a proper understanding of moral and causal responsibility. I have also suggested how regret is an entirely appropriate emotion for Jo to feel, even where she does the right thing and that her guilt at holding the knowledge (coiled to action as it is) is indicative of her moral maturity and not irrationality.

It is at this point that I want to note the sense in which the whistle-blowing literature here is inadequate. On the one hand there is a cadre of institutional bureaucrats who use such formulae uncritically in order to arrive at clear-cut answers at the cost of considering the many factors engaged in ethical and professional conflicts. In these circumstances an institutional code is a blunt instrument and the conception of research ethics merely technicist. On the other hand, however, I have tried to show, at a theoretical level what limitations attach to a deontological conception of whistleblowing.

## VI  SOME GENERAL REMARKS ABOUT ETHICS AND OUR RESEARCHER'S CONFLICT

Rather than dwell upon the phenomenological and logical aspects of our emotional attachments in research, professionals tend commonly to focus instead on the technical aspects. Some readers may still want to ask 'yes, but should or should she not have blown the whistle?'. I have described what I take to be some weaknesses in certain received ways of reading the problem Jo faces. The clash between our deeply-felt and committed relations to others and to our projects, seems light-years away from the traditional moral demands for impartial, objective, universalised principles. I have pointed to the moral ambiguity in the theory of whistle-blowing that is a problematic blend of deontology and consequentialism. By way of conclusion, I will review the contours of the conflict more generally in relation to traditional ways of conceiving the problem and generating solutions.

First, the matter cannot be resolved simply by working out general principles for ascribing obligation, nor role-related principles, for the roles occupied actually add complexity to the conflict rather than resolve it. Second, resorting to codes of conduct may help eliminate the worst excesses of professional conduct but they may do so, I fear, by focusing upon a limited set of moral features. Harm may well be visited upon innocent others in many cases. In the hypothetical scenario, I have tried to indicate the wider range of considerations that properly weigh with the researcher who is implicated in the context under investigation. The rules of such codes, however, as with all professional codes of conduct, will always require attention to the particularities and contexts of the cases.[25] Each regulation will allow latitude commensurate with the ranges of conduct it seeks to prescribe or proscribe. Third, it is not plausible to argue that the range of harms and benefits to the girl, the teacher and his family, the school or the profession now and in the future (if these are all the relevant communities—there may be more in the future if the action goes unchecked) are commensurable. But that would need to be the case in order to be able to make a utilitarian calculation on a single, coherent, scale. Moreover, even if such a calculation were possible it is not clear that its conclusion would indicate to Jo a course of action she could pursue with good faith; in our judgement of the situation we must not set aside the researcher's integrity, for this too is a proper part of the conflict.

Whatever is done here, it ought to be done with a heavy heart—even if the decision is to do nothing. Jo's sense of guilt registers this, as will her regret at whatever action she chooses. Unlike the politician, she is not in elected office; in a clear sense she makes her decision alone, although she may be answerable to the diverse communities in which her professional life is nested. The very idea of *a* calculation of the greater good is difficult for educators and educational researchers to sustain because of the range of obligations which may be entailed by the particulars of diversity I have set out above, which may not be compatible or even commensurable. Moreover, the appeal to public utility or interest over individuals' rights fails to gain a foothold. The scenario I have constructed is helpful in only very general ways. Insofar as educational researchers are committed to certain values and principles they must be prepared for them to clash. Educational researchers as action researchers or ethnographers do not have the option of leaving their values and commitments outside the classroom and assuming a mantle of objectivity. As far as action researchers go, they properly should eschew such a position as one not so much of innocence but of impotence.

It helps, rather than hinders us, to be aware of the complexity of our emotional investments in research, as elsewhere. Determining which emotions are, and are not, relevant in a moral appraisal is never easy. In complicated interpersonal contexts such as schools, where more or less deep personal relations are held together or kept separate by a welter of power-related considerations, our deliberation is best characterised as an non-theoretical, emotionally-laden negotiation between goods and harms. Rather than aiming at righteousness, perhaps the best we can hope for at times is the more modest aim of not bringing about further harm and misery in our research. Where awareness of the proper objects of guilt is cultivated, we are at least sensitive to the concerns of others. Where does this get us? Not very far I am afraid. Except perhaps for this: if you want to do educational ethnography and/or action research in educational contexts, you must first decide how you will cope with dirty hands. You may sometimes have to blow the whistle.[26]

*Correspondence:* Mike McNamee, Faculty of Environment and Leisure, University of Gloucestershire, Cheltenham, GL50 4AZ, UK. E-mail: mmcnamee@glos.ac.uk

## NOTES

1. See http://www.chelt.ac.uk/gradschool/forms.htm for an example of the institutionalisation of research ethics.
2. There is very little however in the education-related literature with the exception of Burgess, R. (1989). Prominent in the broader social scientific literature is Homan (1993) and Sieber, (1992)
3. See for example the British Educational Research Association and American Educational Research Association Codes.
4. See for example parent professional organisations' codes: British Psychological Society http://www.bps.org.uk/about/rules5.cfm, British Sociological Association: http://dspace. dial.pipex.com/britsoc.
5. Prominent in these literatures is Davis (1989, 1996) De George (1990).
6. Burgess honestly observes how the situation could scarcely be one of 'informed' consent. It will be evident form the power relations that are part of the interview situation, the power differential effectively coerces the candidate to consent or risk being labelled at the start of the process (1988, pp. 64–7).
7. I am grateful to Bob Burgess for clarifying this point for me in conversation.
8. Although the scenario is hypothetical, it developed as a partly-conscious consequence of reading two chapters in the Burgess volume: Riddell (1988, p. 77–99) and Kelly (1988, p. 100–113). I did not realise this until I was already re-working the paper from an earlier draft and went back to the Burgess volume. One might ask, then, whether it follows that the

failure to observe this much in an earlier version of the paper was a form of 'sub-conscious plagiarism'.

9.  Since the essay was first written, the law has changed to make it an offence in the UK for an adult to engage in sexual activity with a person under 18 who is in a position of trust over someone receiving full time education at such an institution. The legal alteration does not nullify, of course, the ethical issue at hand though it may alter its contours somewhat. I am grateful to Celia Brackenridge for alerting me to this new legislation and to Simon Hobbs for the detail.

10.  For a given conflict to be considered a dilemma (i) there must be a moral requirement for an agent to adopt each of two alternatives; (ii) neither moral requirement is overridden in any morally relevant way; (iii) the agent cannot adopt both alternatives together; (iv) the agent cannot adopt each alternative separately (Sinnot-Armstrong, W. (1988, p. 29).

11.  A classic sceptical account is to be found in Williams, B. A. O. (1985), pp. 174–96.

12.  Its derivation is also contested. Geoffrey Hunt asserts that it probably owes its genesis to referees or umpires who draws attention to a foul in a game by blowing a whistle. Conversely, it has been claimed 'Whistleblowing has been derived from the act of British constables after the commission of a crime to warn the public of any danger and to alert other law enforcement officers in the area. (Author not disclosed: reference http:// exodus.broward.cc.fl.us/pathfinders/whistleblowing.htm.

13.  I am using the term 'salience' here in a technical sense—one that is becoming, I think, established in the mainstream ethics literature. It refers to the ethical significance of certain features of a situation (others might say 'morally relevant features') that are perceived by an agent. See for example its use in the deontological writing of Herman (1993, pp. 73–93) and in the aristotelian writings of Sherman, N. (1989, pp. 44–50).

14.  Davis asserts that the standard theory is attributable to De George, R. T. (1990, pp. 200–14).

15.  Sieber (1998, pp. 16–17) discusses this point under the description of the prevailing ethnocentrism of organisational culture.

16.  Boisjoly (1998, pp. 71–72) lists an American 'Government Accountability Project' which lists standard organisational responses:

 (i)  make the whistle-blower, instead of the message, the issue;
 (ii)  isolate the whistle-blower from the mainstream organisation to a bureaucratic Siberia;
 (iii)  set the whistle-blower up for a visible fall—the more obvious the better;
 (iv)  destabilise the whistle-blower's support base;
 (v)  make outrageous charges against the whistle-blower;
 (vi)  eliminate the whistle-blower's job;
 (vii)  make the whistle-blower struggle for self-preservation or career, family, finance and sanity.

17.  See James (1988).

18.  The challenge, such as it is, has been articulated in ancient and modern literature. In his poem *Mycenae Lookout* Seamus Heaney talks of the shepherd's cross-purposed silence in withholding from the King his knowledge of the prince's concealed homosexuality. Heaney notes that his inspiration is drawn from Aeschylus' *Agamemnon*, whose own lookout declares: 'The ox is on my tongue'.

19.  I am grateful to Ellis Van Damme for drawing my attention to this point.

20.  See the classic essay by Walzer (1973).

21.  I take this to be a standard position. An account of conflict taking seriously the attendant emotions is Stocker, M. (1992, pp. 9–36) who argues for a loosening of the dirty hands view however, arguing that it need not be restricted to institutional and public immoralities. I simply take the standard line here, noting the lack of publicly vested authority in the role of the teacher in relation to the awareness of the relationship.

22. Taylor observes the sociological distinction between primary and secondary deviance where the former 'applies to those cases where a person accepts that he (sic) has done wrong but does not thing of this wrongdoing as affecting his overall standing as a person' while the latter is someone for whom 'what he has done is not alien to himself (sic) but expresses what he really is' (XX p. 60).

23. I am not, of course, suggesting that the emotional punishment of felt guilt is sufficient or that it replaces legal punishment.

24. See Williams (1973) and (1981 pp. 166–86).

25. The term is Greenspan's (1996, p. 183).

26. See McNamee, M. J. (1997).

27. Earlier versions of this paper were read at the World Congress of Philosophy, Boston 1988, and the Philosophy of Education Society of Great Britain, Oxford, 1999. I am grateful for the comments of those who attended those papers but most especially to Nigel Blake for his very helpful criticisms.

## REFERENCES

Banks, S. (1995) *Ethics and Values in Social Work* (London, Macmillan).

Boisjoly, R. M. (1998) Applications to the industrial sector: commentary on how to blow the whistle and still have a career afterwards, *Science and Engineering Ethics*, 4, pp. 71–74.

Bok, S. (1988) Whistleblowing and professional responsibilities, in: J. E. Callahan (ed.), *Ethical Issues and Professional Life* (Oxford, Oxford University Press), pp. 331–339.

Burgess, R. (1988) Grey areas: ethical dilemmas in educational ethnography, in: *The Ethics of Educational Research* (Falmer, Lewes), pp. 60–76.

Davis, M. (1996) Some paradoxes of whistleblowing, *Business and Professional Ethics Journal*, 15, 1, pp. 3–21.

De George, R. T. (1990) *Business Ethics*, 3rd edn (New York, Macmillan).

Eraut, M. (1984) Institution-based curriculum evaluation, cited in: H. Simons (1988) Ethics of case study evaluation, in: R. Burgess (ed.) 1988, pp. 114–38.

Fletcher, J. J., Sorrell, J. and Silva, C. J. (2000) Whistle-blowing as a failure of organisational ethics, http://www.nursingworld.org/oijn/topic8/topic8/htm.

Gadlin, H. (1998) Can you whistle while you work?: commentary on how to blow the whistle and still have a career afterwards, *Science and Engineering Ethics*, 4, pp. 65–69.

Gaita, R. (1991) *Good and Evil: an absolute conception* (London, Macmillan).

Greenspan, P. S. (1995) *Practical Guilt: Moral Dilemmas, Emotions and Social Norms* (Oxford, Oxford University Press).

Hampshire, S. (1983) *Morality and Conflict* (Oxford, Blackwell).

Herman, B. (1993) *The Practice of Moral Judgement* (London, Harvard University Press).

Homan, R. (1993) *The Ethics of Social Research* (London, Macmillan).

James, G. G. (1988) In defense of whistleblowing, in: J. Callahan (ed.) *Ethical Issues in Professional Life* (Oxford, Oxford University Press) pp. 315–322.

Kelly, A. (1988) Education or indoctrination: the ethics of school-based action research, in: R. Burgess (ed.) 1988, pp. 100–113.

McNamee, M. J. (1997) On professional codes and ethical conduct in education, *Pedagogische Tijdshrift*, 22, 6, 309–326.

Rawls, J. (1972) *A Theory of Justice* (Oxford, Oxford University Press).

Riddell, S. (1988) Exploiting the exploited: the ethics of feminist educational research, in: R. Burgess (ed.) 1988, pp. 77–99.

Sieber, J. E. (1998) The psychology of whistleblowing, *Science and Engineering Ethics*, 4, pp. 7–23.

Sieber, J. E. (1992) *Planning Ethically Responsible Research* (London, Sage).

Sinnott-Armstrong, W. (1988) *Moral Dilemmas* (Oxford, Blackwell).

Sherman, N. (1989) *The Fabric of Character* (Oxford, Oxford University Press).

Stocker, M. (1992) Dirty hands and ordinary life, in: *Plural and Conflicting Values* (Oxford, Clarendon Press).

Taylor, G. (1986) *Pride, Shame and Guilt* (Oxford, Clarendon Press).

Walzer, M (1973) Political action: the problem of dirty hands, *Philosophy and Public Affairs*, pp. 160–180.

Williams, B. A. O. (1973) *Problems of the Self* (Cambridge, Cambridge University Press).

Williams, B. A. O. (1981) *Moral Luck* (Cambridge, Cambridge University Press).

Williams, B. A. O. (1985) *Ethics and the Limits of Philosophy* (London, Fontana).

# 9

# Accountability and Relevance in Educational Research

## Christopher Winch

*Educational research has been criticised recently for being poorly conceived, self-indulgent and of little practical use. These allegations are discussed via an overview of the various functions of educational research: the production of knowledge about education, the formulation of educational policy, the promotion of improvements in educational practice, the promotion of radical change in society. The responsibilities of educational researchers are then discussed: proper attention to the functions of educational research, accountability for monies spent, recognition of responsibility for their activities. The pressures exerted by external funding bodies and the distorting effects of the research assessment exercise in the UK affect our sense of priorities here.*

## INTRODUCTION

Educational research has come under particular scrutiny in recent years. This is an aspect of the more general scrutiny to which Education and the public services have been subjected in the Western liberal democracies, but such scrutiny is particularly threatening to educational research, because critics have tended to question its very value. The critiques have taken the following, often connected, forms. First, it is maintained that educational research is intellectually second-rate, without proper rigour in the way it formulates research questions, devises methodologies, evaluates results and draws conclusions.[1] Second, it is thought to be self-indulgent, following obsessions that are not central to the concerns of educators. Finally, it is thought to have little or no practical import. It is not my aim to evaluate all these claims in detail, but I wish to question the responses made by some in the educational community, which, I feel, have been unduly defensive.

There are two good reasons why the quality of educational research is partly an ethical issue. The first is a general concern about the duties that those in receipt of resources intended for a particular purpose incur, namely to use those resources to the best of their abilities to carry out the activities for which they were intended. The second is more specifically related to a professional ethic in research. Naturally, accountability in the sense above is an important component of a professional ethic of research. Nevertheless, a professional ethic implies more. There are particular dispositions, and qualities of character, that should be cultivated if individual researchers are to meet the standards internal to their own activity, which broadly speaking is concerned with pursuit of the truth, enduring worth, clarity and enlightenment, however these are conceived. One does not have to agree with Carr (1999) that the professions have a particular moral salience in this respect, merely that occupations more generally have an ethical basis, which is connected with the primary aims of their activities.[2]

These ethical considerations become politicised when the accountability issue is raised, and also when we ask whether the internal professional virtues are themselves under threat. In the former case, there is a political issue for the wider society. In the latter there is a political issue within the educational research community itself. However, the two are connected in this sense. If confidence in the internal professional ethic is lost, both within and without the educational community, then doubts as to the accountability of educational researchers will inevitably arise as well. I suggest that we are facing a situation where the internal ethic is coming under vigorous critique and the wider political community appreciates the seriousness of that critique to the possible future detriment of educational research. It is only fair to point out, however, that the maintenance of a professional ethic with the attributes described above can come under threat from external, accountability-related sources. In particular, it will be argued, the Research Assessment Exercise (RAE) has the potential to undermine the concern of researchers with the enduring worth of their work.

Why should these internal critiques be taken seriously? It is not only against education that the charges of lack of rigour, self-indulgence and irrelevance can be directed. Indeed, it is a favourite tactic of critics from outside disciplines, who seek to expand the boundaries of their disciplines at the expense of those they attack, to launch such critiques. Radicals within a discipline often aim to shake it up by attacking some of its basic assumptions and ways of operating.[3]

The burgeoning of an internal critique and the existence of influential external critics, such as the former Chief Inspector of Schools, is not necessarily all the fault of educational researchers, but it suggests, at the very least, that there has been a failure of communication concerning the nature and purpose of educational research and, perhaps more fundamentally, a failure in self-understanding on the part of the educational research community. It is evident that educational research has powerful enemies, both within and without education, and that it can only defend itself if it develops a proper perspective on its own nature and purpose. The main aim of this paper is to advance such an understanding. This does not entail that there is a particular methodology to which educational research must conform, but merely that the object of the professional ethic be kept in mind, namely a concern with truth, enlightenment, clarity and worthwhileness, which can be approached through a variety of perfectly legitimate methods.

## WHAT ARE THE AIMS OF EDUCATIONAL RESEARCH?

In order to assess whether or not educational researchers are carrying out worthwhile activities, in the sense outlined above, it is necessary to look at the *aims* of educational research, be they implicit or explicit, or a mixture of both. If we find that there are problems with the aims or with the ways in which they are achieved, then we will come nearer to assessing the claims of the critics. We should not, of course, expect a complete consensus about aims, even amongst those within the educational research community. More likely, one will find different schools of thought within the research community concerning aims, with some groups placing more emphasis on some aims than other groups and some groups even suggesting aims that are contrary to those of others. The issues here are similar to those that concern the aims of education more generally, and, as with the aims of education, some will be more readily accepted than others by the non-educational community. The point of difficulty in the wider community concerning *aims* rather than their achievement is likely to come when radical aims, such as projects of social and personal liberation, are foregrounded. The issue here is similar to that concerning the tensions produced by radical progressive educators, particularly when they follow their aims with the assistance of public funding.

Within an overall concern to defend the four key elements of a professional educational research ethic, it is possible to identify four principal aims of educational research which exist in greater or lesser degrees of harmony with each other. Given the background aim of educational researchers to produce recommendations based on the truth rather than on false propositions, there are nevertheless four clearly identifiable aims of educational research, which will assume a different importance for different researchers.

### To produce knowledge about education

One might describe this as the liberal view of educational research. This is as true of empirical as it is of conceptual work. On this view, knowledge about education in its broadest sense is an intrinsic good, whatever its extrinsic value, and so is worth acquiring for its own sake. The analogy here is with the pursuit of liberal theoretical and practical knowledge in fields as diverse as philosophy, music and sociology. It is simply part of the human endeavour to achieve excellence in these areas and to pass on the concern for excellence to those who wish to strive for it. This liberal view is strengthened by a consideration about education as a discipline. Although the study of education has a specific subject matter, namely the ways in which human beings are prepared for life, the *methods* which are used to study this subject matter are eclectic and owe a great deal to other well-established disciplines, particularly although not exclusively: philosophy, history, anthropology, sociology, psychology and economics. There is no reason to suppose that a study of the way in which humans are prepared for life is of any less intrinsic interest than the study of the structure of human value or epistemic systems, or of social structure or the ways in which society organises its material life. And since the *methods* as well as the aims of the 'pure' subjects have intrinsic value (they constitute an essential part of intrinsically valuable activities), one can say that the study of education in a broad sense is as much entitled to an attribution of intrinsic worth as are any other of the well-established academic subjects.

### To help formulate educational policy

This is one of the well-established practical aims of educational research. In this sense, educational research is thought to assist in the direction of education at anything from the national to the local or community level. It is, perhaps, here that the accountability criterion assumes most importance. There is, however, an important ambiguity concealed by the formulation above, which needs to be teased out. 'Formulating educational policy' can, on the one hand, mean 'contributing to the formulation or the ordering of educational aims' or it can mean 'devising ways in which educational aims can be put into effect'. The first is a normative enterprise whose main methodological focus is philosophical and which inevitably involves a consideration of the values that a society should adopt and the ways in which those values should be ordered and implemented. It is, in this sense, also a political endeavour, to the extent that politics concerns the implementation of values held by different and sometimes conflicting groups.[4] Thus there are questions about *which* values a society should adopt and further questions about the *consistency* and *relative weighting* of these values. If, for example, a society wishes to emphasise *both* personal growth *and* socially responsible citizenship as major aims, as a result of normative discussion to which philosophers of education have contributed, then questions ought to arise about which of these aims is to take priority and the extent to which the full implementation of one is compatible with the full implementation of the other. Such an investigation will probably require further conceptual and normative analysis, together with more practical considerations of curriculum content, pedagogy and resource allocation.[5] The devising of curricula, pedagogical approaches, assessment methodologies and institutional types would fall into this category.

*To improve the workings of education*

On the other hand, if educational policy is to be concerned with the implementation of aims already agreed on and prioritised, then a shift occurs to a more empirical and practically-focused activity. This may involve issues of curriculum design and pedagogic practice, but it is also liable to involve evaluative studies of both current practice and of the implementation of new initiatives. Because there is a certain amount of discomfort about the explicit discussion of educational aims, the most favoured kind of policy research is that which takes aims for granted and seeks ways of putting these into effect. The most striking example of this kind of research in recent years is that into school effectiveness.

School Effectiveness Research (SER) is predicated on the idea that the effectiveness of a school makes a discernible difference to educational outcomes, irrespective or in spite of the social class of pupils. SER is interesting not just because of its enormous importance in the development of practical educational policy making, but also because it illustrates two of the ethical issues that affect educational research: normative debates about aims and the difficulties of maintaining academic independence. SER is the kind of research programme that, in a rational world, would be preceded by both the kinds of policy research described above, namely disinterested research into the nature of educational aims and policy-oriented discussion of the aims desirable in our society. Among other things, such a debate would contribute to judgements as to whether or not a certain mix of aims was achievable and whether the curricula, pedagogies, assessment methods and institutional arrangements in place were capable of achieving what they set out to achieve. In the real world, SER has tended to move forward on the basis that these questions have received a largely positive answer based on a non-professional 'common sense' agenda that numeracy and literacy are quite fundamental educational aims. The assumption then is that the main problems outstanding are those of identifying the managerial strategies that schools need to put in place in order to be most efficient in achieving those aims. Sometimes pedagogy becomes an issue, but questions about the appropriateness of different methods tend to revolve around 'getting the balance right', rather than engaging in fundamental re-appraisal. A minority of SER researchers believe that research into pedagogy is more or less an exact science and that this will, in due course, be demonstrated.[6] This is a legitimate view within the spectrum of acceptable approaches recognised within the research community, but like the adoption of other methods it needs to be argued for.

A key feature of educational research of this type is its implicitly hypothetical nature. The full logical form of research of this kind is 'If a society wishes to achieve $X$ as an educational aim, it must first adopt $Y$ as the best means'. Too often, the antecedent of the hypothetical is left implicit in order to avoid controversy about what the aim might be. But then the research makes little sense to many people, since it does not follow that one should adopt $Y$ as a means if one dislikes $X$ as an end. This suggests a primary responsibility of educational researchers in this mode, namely to clarify what it is that they are doing in this broader, policy-oriented sense. It can be argued that this is what SER has signally failed to do, for fear of arousing controversy through making explicit its implicit concern with maximising educational achievement in the academic subjects on the curriculum.[7] Needless to say, this is an issue for any kind of practical educational research of this kind and its authors do the community a disservice if they fail to make clear the assumptions on which they are basing their work.

*To contribute to radical changes in society*

The most strident critics of educational research often assume that this is the aim of most researchers. On this view, educational research is a Trojan Horse whose aim is to subvert the consensus on how education is to be conceived, organised and run. Radicalism in educational research is hardly new. It can be found for example, in Plato's *Republic* and Rousseau's *Emile* to name but two highly influential tracts, to which one can add *What is and What Might Be* by Edmond Holmes and the work of the 'soixante-huitard' gurus such as Ivan Illich and Neil Postman.[8] A recent example of this phenomenon is the work of Tooley and other neo-liberal thinkers, which is largely dedicated to the privatisation of state-run educational systems.[9] The examples used here illustrate that by 'radical' is meant 'uprooting' whether this be done from the political left or right, although it is worth noting that a 1960s 'radical' critique of conventional education has more in common with the neo-liberal agenda than its proponents might be happy to admit.

This style of educational research is often eclectic. It combines elements of the three mentioned above, but usually with little attempt to separate out their various components. Thus one finds a mixture of philosophical reflection or analysis, together with a persuasive rhetoric and curricular, institutional (or anti-institutional) and pedagogic proposals. These are combined with evidence, usually of a piecemeal kind.

Although it is often decried as 'irrelevant' or 'subversive', there are good reasons for allowing it space, even within the context of publicly-funded educational research. There are at least two good reasons for taking this attitude. The first is that this kind of work is not easily distinguished from research in the other modes, except, perhaps, by its relative emphasis on *radical* change. The second is that it is, arguably, healthy for a society to encourage a dissident view of the aims, nature and operation of its education system. Even if the views of dissidents are not adopted, they may well prove valuable in forcing the clarification of long-held assumptions and the evaluation of long-established practices. This does not mean that 'radical' educational researchers are free from their own responsibilities, both to their audiences and their funders, as we shall see below. They too have to pay attention to the truth. For them (as for all researchers) biased or selective presentation of evidence, careless empirical work or slipshod argumentation are violations of their professional ethic. If they are so radical as to see themselves outside the educational research community then they should say so and accept the consequences.

## WHAT ARE THE RESPONSIBILITIES OF EDUCATIONAL RESEARCHERS?

These can be formulated as follows: *first, to attend to the aims of educational research as they conceive them (subject to a qualification below). Second, to account for the money spent on educational research to those who provide it.* This seems to entail that the users of such monies justify their use in terms of the ends for which it was provided.[10] This involves recognising the needs and sensibilities of their audience, the effects on their own research community and the influence that their relatively authoritative pronouncements may have on their audience.

Let us look at the first responsibility. This breaks down into:

## The production of knowledge about education

Educational research in this sense is aimed at an intrinsic good, namely addition to the sum of non-applied human knowledge. Evidently, it cannot be a criterion of fulfilment of responsibility that such knowledge be useful in the sense of having an immediate and obvious application. This does not mean to say that 'pure' educational researchers do not, however, have responsibilities. Specifically, they are responsible for maintaining high standards of work. Where such systems as the UK Research Assessment Exercise (RAE) operate, the success with which they achieve this is monitored and rewarded accordingly by panels of peers.[11] But even at an individual level, educational researchers, as members of an educational research community and of a wider academic community, have responsibilities to those who nurture their own activities, namely to maintain and advance the reputation of educational research through the pursuit of high standards of achievement. This is merely a component of the professional ethic mentioned earlier.

## Help in the formulation of educational policy

I have already argued that this is not simply a pragmatic and applied activity, because consideration of the aims of education is an important part of the formulation of educational policy. In this respect, educational researchers have a responsibility for contributing to the well-being of their society through the well-being of its educational system. Of course, they may well have views as to what the well-being of their society consists in different to those of the government or even the majority of their fellow-citizens. This sort of case will be examined in more detail below. When, however, researchers are engaged in discussion about the *mix* of aims appropriate, their *relative weighting* and their *implementation*, they have a responsibility to do what they have been funded to do, to the best of their ability. This involves a responsibility to engage in reflection on these issues to the best of their ability without at the same time compromising their own values and beliefs. It is very often flattering to be asked to engage in this kind of high-level reflection by, for example, a government and there seem to be two temptations to avoid when doing so. The first is that of giving one's audience what one thinks it wants to hear, so as to maximise one's influence, prestige and the chances of being asked to engage in similar reflection in the future. Second, there is the opposite temptation of remaining 'excessively true to oneself' and failing to take a view of the matter which extends beyond one's own ideal of what should be the case.[12]

This is a difficult point to make, because it seems to contradict the idea that one should remain true to one's values. But remaining true to one's values certainly entails not negotiating them away. It does not, on the other hand, mean that one should never engage in compromises about their *implementation*. In other words, it seems that the difficult task that a researcher in this position has to carry out is to do with the difficulties of maintaining an imaginative appreciation of what the society as a whole, as it is presently constituted, can evolve towards and the need to preserve the personal integrity of one's own beliefs. This involves the imaginative taking into account of the needs and requirements of others whose values and priorities one does not necessarily share. This ability is one of the highly specialised virtues of applied educational research. Imaginative sympathy is not simply something that one can be trained into; it is however, more likely to be developed if one starts with an attitude of openness to possibilities, both of social change and of how others might view change. Indeed, openness is an important component of a concern with the truth; having a mind closed to possibilities is a poor disposition for the selection of methods most appropriate to the task in hand.

As an example, one could consider the position of liberal educators asked to reflect about the future of vocational education. A natural reaction at the level of personal values might lead them either to reject the invitation or to accept it and to advocate ways in which liberal education could be promoted at the expense of vocational education. However, to take the latter course would, in a sense, be to act in bad faith, since they had been invited, presumably, precisely so that they could be in a position to make some recommendations that would be positive rather than negative for the future of vocational education.

What, then, should their reaction be if they do accept the invitation? One would not expect such people to give up what they value most, merely because they had been given such an assignment. On the other hand, they would have a professional responsibility to consider the issue on its merits, which would, in turn, involve taking into account the views of other 'stakeholders' in the investigation, namely those paying for the research and those likely to be affected by its recommendations. This in turn would involve taking a more impartial view of their own beliefs, accepting that others had a valid point of view that needed to be taken account of in relation to their own. Such a stance would illustrate the characteristic of openness that is an important component of the professional virtues constitutive of educational research.

Naturally, such a response would be difficult for someone who found it difficult to take such a detached view to adopt, neither would a person unable to make compromises about the implementation of their beliefs be able to enter such a role. One might, however, suggest that such individuals were temperamentally ill-equipped to engage in policy-oriented educational research. There might, even for the committed liberal educator, be very good reasons for taking on such research sincerely and at the same time making a positive contribution to vocational education, if they were to approach the problems in a constructive spirit. An openness of approach to a problematic with which one has little sympathy can be fulfilling, not just of the professional commitments of a researcher, but can also lead to personal enlightenment and an enlarging of sympathies, which, in turn, are likely to enhance the professional abilities and dispositions of the researcher.

It might, for example, be the case that the researcher began to notice more affinities between liberal and vocational educational aims than he had previously been aware of. He might, on studying the matter more closely, come to realise the value of vocational education for society in general and for particular individuals, without at the same time giving up his beliefs in the value of liberal education. He might come to see the need to allow room for those who have different views to his own to develop their own ideas, and see his task as to influence them for the better with his own at the same time. What I am suggesting is that one can operate as a policy researcher making a useful contribution (and developing oneself) without, at the same time, giving up one's personal values. This might entail operating at a certain level of moral and social sophistication, but it is not unreasonable to expect an educational researcher, by virtue of his or her professional formation, to do so.

## The improvement of education

A researcher engaged in this kind of work is likely to be considering the practical implications of a policy proposal or the improvement of some existing practice. While some commitment to the nature of the enterprise might be expected of someone in this position, it is not necessarily the case that such a commitment is essential, rather than a more detached attitude of professional good will (see previous subsection). What is more important is the ability to work to high professional *technical* standards of evaluation, using approaches and particular methods that seem to be most suited to the understanding of the issue in hand.

This may not be as easy as it sounds. The example of school improvement (as opposed to school effectiveness) research will provide an example. First, school improvement strategies are predicated on school effectiveness research. That is, one cannot improve schools until one knows what makes for effective schools in the first place. This in itself is no straightforward matter, as the literature amply illustrates.[13] It does not follow, however, even if one had successfully identified those schools that were demonstrably effective in relation to certain educational aims, that it would follow that one could then, in any straightforward way, introduce those elements that were responsible for success in effective schools, into ineffective ones.

A researcher in this position is under some quite particular pressures. School improvement research is very much concerned with palpably 'making a difference' to the lives and futures of children. The expectations of the sponsors of research, of the subjects of the research and of society in general are, therefore, likely to be high. In this respect it is unlike action research in that it is undertaken not primarily for the personal development of the researcher, but on the behalf of financial sponsors, for a highly specific end, which, it is hoped, will have direct and beneficial effects on the pupils concerned. Unfortunately, it is very often in the nature of research into the behaviour of human beings that simple answers cannot be acquired in a short space of time. This is very often difficult to understand for those not directly involved in this kind of research. The situation of the school improvement researcher is more difficult than that of an anthropologist or a sociologist researching a complex social phenomenon, because the school improvement researcher, unlike them, is expected to provide a practical solution to a practical problem, and is very often being paid on the assumption that this is what he or she will do.

The pressures on researchers in such a position are, therefore, like the pressures on many researchers into interventions, great. An honest answer to the question of what is to make a particular school improve may or may not be unpalatable (when the improvement strategy is, for one reason or another, impractical). The position of the researcher is not improved by the fact that his future livelihood may depend on further contracts of a similar nature, which will themselves be contingent on a desired outcome in the current piece of research. A researcher may successfully resist the temptation to consciously look for a 'quick fix', but the unconscious temptation to be less than rigorous in relation to the drawing of conclusions for practical purposes may be less easy to resist.[14] Conducting such research may, then, both from the perspective of accountability and from that of the researcher's own professional ethic, be no easy matter.[15]

## Contributing to radical changes in society

As already argued, there is an important and valuable place for such research. Those who carry it out are, however, under obligations which are not always clearly recognised. It is easy enough to see that they will recognise obligations to those who share their views and, no doubt, to what they conceive to be good canons of research.[16] What, however, are their obligations to those for whom they are seeking to promote radical educational change?

Part of the answer to this is relatively easy. Radical researchers, of the right, as well as of the left, usually wish to articulate an alternative vision either of how the aims of education are to be conceived or of how they are to be achieved (or maybe both). Is it so easy, however, to explain with integrity just what the proposed radical change will mean in practice to those who will be affected by it? What, in particular, if it is likely to be so unpalatable to large sections of society that they would immediately reject it? Or, more subtly, how honest is the researcher with himself in thinking through the consequences of his proposals, including those that are likely to lead to unpalatable consequences for the recipients?[17]

While honesty with others is obviously enough a feature both of accountability and of professional ethics, honesty with oneself, like openness of attitude, is a particularly personal professional virtue, demanding of the researcher a certain degree of self-examination, and demanding of the radical researcher that he ask whether all the issues have been thought through in a careful and impartial way. The great temptation in this situation is to be over-optimistic, relying on ideological zeal to tide one over the more ambiguous pieces of evidence or the weaker sections of argumentation. While it is probably not necessary to expect impartiality of the radical researcher, this does not absolve the radical from a commitment to truth, worthwhileness, clarity and enlightenment.

The problem set out above is an example of a general one facing radical educational researchers. Since they wish to revise the terms on which society is organised and the criteria by which people are rewarded, it is almost inevitable that there will be significant losers as well as significant winners. This is the case whether the critique comes from the radical left or the radical right. The temptation is to adopt a particularly optimistic approach and to maintain that all will be gain, there will be no pain for anyone. Alternatively one might maintain that those who lose from the proposal are so privileged anyway that their losses will be easily bearable. A third approach is to be aggregatively utilitarian and to say that, although certain groups will have to bear heavy losses, the overall effect for society will make the sacrifice of the minority worthwhile. In this case, one is frankly acknowledging that the overall benefit to society justifies the losses of a certain group. This is difficult to say if one wishes to remain popular with everyone, and when one does make such a claim, one ought to be very confident that the gain overall really will justify the pain for some.

Most radical proposals show at least a plausible tendency to have strongly adverse consequences for some groups. An omelette is to be made: unfortunately some eggs have to be broken. Ethnic, sexual, social or financial privilege is to be attacked and eliminated for the greater good. There is an obligation on researchers to spell this out, not to conceal it. This is not difficult to see from the point of view of a professional ethic devoted to truth, enlightenment and clarity. Nor is it difficult to understand from the broader perspective of accountability, which requires conformance to externally acceptable professional standards of probity. Those who obscure or distort the implications of their research cannot reasonably complain if they are criticised for doing so.

Furthermore, they need to show that an omelette will actually be made and, if they are uncertain about this, they should say so and confine themselves initially to the advocacy of experiments, rather than the wholesale up-ending of established social arrangements. This might make radical policy research less exciting and more difficult to justify, but this is not a reason for not being honest with one's audience. To pretend that things will be otherwise than they are likely to be will also contribute to the lack of respect and trust that educational researchers suffer from.

The problems of public perception that face educational researchers cannot be entirely solved by the educational research community itself, but the research community can go a long way towards improving that perception. The responsibility to produce high-quality pure research lies with individuals and the journals and conferences that they run. If editors wish to have many issues of their journals each year and the quality suffers, then they must bear the consequences. If policy research fails to match conventional academic criteria for quality then again the research community feels the consequences, but they are ultimately responsible for such a failure. If researchers give in to personal temptation or to external pressure in order to produce findings that are superficially palatable, then that too is their responsibility.

The problem for individuals is that they are very often in competition with each other and thus tempted to take whatever is on offer in the way of funding. This kind of problem is best dealt with in a collegial manner, with the professional organisations involved in the research setting out criteria for what are minimum standards and for what one should do when subjected to pressures to alter findings or to present them in such a way that they will be acceptable to a funding body. This suggests a greater collective and conscious involvement in the development and maintenance of a professional ethic of research in education than has, perhaps, hitherto been the case.

## ETHICAL PROBLEMS EDUCATIONAL RESEARCHERS FACE AS A RESULT OF EXTERNAL PRESSURES

The UK Research Assessment Exercise has put pressure on UK researchers in education, as in other disciplines, to produce work that meets agreed standards of quality, particularly relating to international recognition. Since one's career and, possibly, the survival of one's department depend on meeting these criteria, it is hard to avoid carrying out research that is likely to appeal to the panel assessing the research. This involves producing material that satisfies the personal and disciplinary prejudices of the adjudicating panel and putting research in the most high-prestige journals and with the most high-prestige publishers.

These pressures need not, of themselves, be too onerous. Much depends on how educational researchers themselves manage to generate panels who can recognise academic worth in the field. In particular, Education, as a discipline, needs to be able to command the respect of the wider academic community, particularly those sections of it with whom it shares common concerns and methodologies. A clear danger for a discipline not thought to be amongst the most rigorous by some sections of the academic world is to be seen to have less demanding standards than those others. If educational research is considered as non-applied, then these difficulties are less pressing. On the other hand, if aims B and C above become increasingly important in assessing its worth (as seems more likely to happen), then the problem of maintaining standards is likely to become more acute, particularly in the case of contract research which, by its nature, is unlikely to lead to very innovative or profound conclusions.

There are two reasons for this: the first is that the criteria for assessment are bound, to some extent, to be in tension with one another. There is no *a priori* reason why research in education, judged against criteria of intrinsic worth, should be rated in the same way as research judged in terms of policy formation or implementation. This problem becomes more acute when the overall research worth of an education department is also judged in terms of the policy-relevant work that it carries out and the number and extent of the external research grants that it receives.

It may of course be quite reasonably replied that good research will naturally conform to standards of adequacy that will ensure both its intrinsic and its instrumental worth. While research being well-conceived and well-conducted is a necessary condition of its having quality in either sense, it is not sufficient in either sense. Relevance and usefulness do not always sit easily with a contribution to the subject that will withstand the scrutiny of scholars seeking to assess fundamental contributions to the subject in fifty or a hundred years time. At the very least there are tensions between the applied and less obviously applied areas of the subject that need to be resolved by the panels that sit in judgement on the quality of the work of researchers. The problem then, is that standards of quality may diverge in respect of the pure and applied areas of the discipline.

The second problem with standards relates to the fact that the RAE is, inevitably, a kind of game, which involves researchers second-guessing the criteria, prejudices and preoccupations of panel members. Indeed, the whole exercise was set up with partly such an outcome in mind. The focus of researchers is thus concentrated on what they think the panel sitting in a particular year will think of the contribution, not what future researchers fifty years hence will think. If the focus is increasingly on what is directly relevant in the here and now, especially in the judged view of panel members, then again, criteria of immediate and instrumental worth and criteria of long-term and intrinsic worth are in danger of diverging.

This issue is closely related to another one concerning funded research on policy formulation and implementation issues. There are good reasons for thinking that, given the high political stakes that often surround the outcome of educational research, there is often pressure by funders on researchers to produce results that support a policy favoured by the funding body.[18] There are then, pressures tending to compromise the quality of work that results from external pressures on the educational research community.


## PROBLEMS EDUCATIONAL RESEARCHERS HAVE CREATED FOR THEMSELVES

An account of the difficulties faced by the educational research community would be incomplete without a consideration of self-inflicted difficulties. These arise from two sources, both easily locatable in the dual ethical perspective on research outlined in the introduction to this chapter. First, insufficient attention has been paid to the development of considered responses to external demands for accountability. Second, not enough attention has been paid to the more explicit development and encouragement of an internal professional ethic. Both these failings can be seen as a form of parochialism or inward-lookingness. On the one hand, the wider community has not received sufficient concern; on the other, there has been too little desire to take a long-term view of the development of the educational research community, and to assess itself in relation to similar groups, particularly other research communities.

While there is a possibility of misunderstanding by those who do not accept certain research assumptions, this cannot be an excuse for not paying attention to what others outside the community might say about one's work. Even if research is considered to be non-applied, this does not absolve researchers from awareness of how their work might be seen, not only by the lay public, but also by academic peers in other disciplines, particularly the cognate ones, who may feel that they are able to provide a standards benchmark for the work done in education. This means that researchers need to be able to justify the importance of what they are doing and to defend the methods that they have used to arrive at their conclusions. There is a temptation to a form of methodological relativism here that should be avoided. If one disavows any attempt at a critique by those who do not share one's interests or philosophical or methodological assumptions, then it becomes difficult for any serious debate about the nature and purpose, let alone the practice, of educational research to take place. In addition, researchers cannot play the part of complete innocents in the political jungle, unaware of broader perceptions of what they do.

For better or for worse, educational research will always attract the interest of a wider community, because of the interest that any society has in education. Even if they do not feel that they ought to be accountable to this wider public in terms of producing practical research, it is hard to deny that there must be some standards for evaluating the intrinsic worth of what is being done, if it is being done with public money. When there is inevitably a degree of public interest, to ignore this requirement is not merely morally careless, it is also foolhardy.

This general complaint can be made more specific. Tooley and Darby's (1998) research looked at a random sample of papers published in four of the most prestigious refereed education journals between 1995 and 1998. They found that a significant number of these had serious methodological flaws according to some elementary canons of robustness. These are minimal and should be easily satisfied by any competent researcher.[19] Tooley and Darby's research can be criticised for a number of reasons, the most significant perhaps, being failure to ensure against researcher bias. It is significant however, that despite the furore that the publication of this research excited, there have been no detailed refutations of the methods or content of their work. A research community, sure of the importance of its preoccupations and the general standard of work within it, would have been able to refute this type of criticism without too much difficulty. The fact that this has not been done suggests that

Tooley and Darby were making a point that is worth taking seriously. This, in its turn, suggests that there is quite a lot more that the educational research community could itself do to ensure that such criticisms do not occur again.

Although a similar exercise conducted on other disciplines within the social sciences might yield a similar result, in a sense this is beside the point. The fact is that the public and political perception of education is that it is of some practical relevance and it will inevitably be judged on its ability to say something relevant to practical audiences. However unfairly, this in turn has an effect on how non-applied educational research is viewed and if it turns out that the standards used to judge the quality of such work appear dubious, then this threatens the future of education as an independent research discipline. Researchers have a responsibility to their discipline and to those who might enter or benefit from it in the future. A preparedness to ensure and maintain high standards, so as to sustain the future for educational research, however it is conceived, is a moral claim on the educational research community.

## CONCLUSION: HOW CAN THESE PROBLEMS BE AVOIDED?

The only plausible solution is through self-regulation. If journals were more prepared to exercise rigorous judgment concerning the quality of the material appearing in their pages then much of the problem concerning quality would disappear. It is up to editorial boards to ensure that articles accepted reach minimum standards of academic integrity. This is a basic requirement for the maintenance of a professional ethic of educational research. Material submitted can be sent back for revision and, in any case, the knowledge that standards are high and are going to be adhered to, will concentrate the minds of researchers. These considerations apply irrespective of the category into which the research falls. As already pointed out, there are problems concerning the way in which contemporary policy concerns impact on the long-term worthwhileness and relevance of certain kinds of research. For assessors on RAE panels, there is a need to ensure a balance between the different kinds of research that are assessed and to ensure that non-applied work gets due recognition. But in another sense, however real these concerns are, they are irrelevant to the serious and pressing problem, which is how to ensure *minimum* standards of academic integrity.

Second, the academic community needs to have a convention whereby funded research is only undertaken if the independence from direct interference, particularly from sponsors, in the data collection, analysis and presentation of the work of researchers in the conduct of their work and the dissemination of their results is respected. In this matter it is necessary that all act as one. If any institution or research group accepts funding that does not meet these criteria, then the world at large will be entitled to draw adverse conclusions about the integrity of the work. What are these standards to be and how are they to be determined? Well, that is a task for the educational research community to undertake. If the stakes are great then the debate cannot begin too soon.

*Correspondence:* Christopher Winch, University College of Northampton, Northants., UK. E-mail: Christopher.Winch@ northampton.ac.uk

## NOTES

1. James Tooley and Doug Darby (1998) *Educational Research: a Critique* (London, OFSTED).
2. David Carr (1999) Professional education and professional ethics, *Journal of Applied Philosophy*, 16.1, pp. 33–46.
3. Paul Ormerod (1994) *The Death of Economics* (London, Penguin).
4. John Gray (1995) *Enlightenment's Wake* (London, Routledge); Christopher Winch (1996) *Quality and Education* (London, Blackwell).
5. See, for example, S. Lawlor, *Common Core*, Centre for Policy Studies, 1988; Oliver Letwin, *Education: the importance of grounding*, Centre for Policy Studies, 1988.
6. E.g. David Reynolds (1998) Teacher effectiveness: better teachers, better schools, *Research Intelligence*, 66, pp. 26–29.
7. C. Winch (1997) Accountability, controversy and school effectiveness, in: J. White, M. Barber (eds) *Perspectives on School Effectiveness and School Improvement*, pp. 61–76, London, Bedford Way Papers, 1997.
8. Plato (1950) *The Republic*; I. Illich (1971) *Deschooling Society* (London, Penguin); J-J. Rousseau (1966) (1762) *Emile ou l'Education* (Paris, Editions Fammarion), English edition translated by Barbara Foxley (London, Dent, 1911); Edmond Holmes (1911), *What is and What Might Be* (London, Constable); Neil Postman (1970) The Politics of Reading, in: N. Keddie (ed.), *Tinker, Tailor . . . The Myth of Cultural Deprivation* (London, Penguin, 1973).
9. James Tooley (1995) *Disestablishing Education* (Aldershot, Avebury).
10. A. Davis (1998) *The Limits of Educational Assessment* (Oxford, Blackwell), suggests that educators should not be accountable for money which was intended to be spent on educational purposes that they deem to be immoral (p. 23). While this is a perfectly acceptable point, it can be replied to those who justify not spending money on the purpose for which it was intended on these grounds, that in good faith, they should not have accepted the money in the first place if they did not intend to spend it on the purposes for which it was allocated.
11. The position is now becoming more complex due to increasing emphasis on the practical value of educational research in the next RAE (in the year 2001).
12. The masculine pronoun is used here in a gender neutral fashion. For a justification of this practice, see C. Winch and K. Sharp, Equal opportunities and language: a critique of the new orthodoxy, 1994, *Studies in Higher Education*, 19.2, pp. 163–175.
13. G. Woodhouse and H. Goldstein (1988) Educational performance indicators and LEA league tables, *Oxford Review of Education*, 14.3, pp. 321–320.
14. See Stephen Jay Gould, *The Mismeasure of Man* (London, Penguin, 1984), for a compelling account of how this kind of unconscious bias may work on even well-intentioned researchers.

15. None of these observations should be taken to suggest that actual workers in the field carry out their work with anything less than complete integrity. They do, however, give us an insight into the pressures that they are likely to work under.

16. This may also cause problems if the radical researcher is not only committed to radical solutions but also to radical research methods not recognised by the main body of the research community.

17. The reader will readily appreciate that this difficulty is closely related to that of unconscious bias in empirical research. Overcoming both of these requires that the researcher possesses high levels of integrity.

18. That this is not just speculative paranoid fantasy can be seen from accounts such as that of U. Clark (1994) Bringing English to order: a personal account of the NCC English evaluation project, *English in Education*, 28.1, pp. 33–38.

19. Tooley and Darby, *op. cit.* p. 12.

# 10

# Educational Philosophy, Theory and Research: A Psychiatric Autobiography

## David Carr

*Interpretations of educational theory as essentially empirical conceive education and teaching as skill-based technologies which can be scientifically researched. Those in the educational research community who resist this picture nevertheless often regard good educational practice as empirically researchable by more 'particularistic' means (for example, action research). However, this chapter argues that such empiricist approaches neglect or distort what are essentially moral rather than scientific or technical questions. On this view, education is essentially a moral practice, ethical deliberation lies at the heart of principled educational enquiry and the expertise of teachers is better conceived in terms of virtues rather than skills.*

## I  A BRIEF TALE OF EXCESS THEORY

Not many years ago, my attention was drawn to a questionnaire designed for undergraduate students of teacher education who were invited to comment on the balance of theory and practice in their course of professional training. Amongst other things, they were asked to say whether: (a) the balance between theory and practice was just right; (b) there was too much practice and too little theory; or (c) there was too much theory and too little practice. Although I did not see the arresting conclusions of this investigation, I would nevertheless have put my shirt on the result—not least on the basis of some acquaintance with the particular constituency whose views were about to be polled. Indeed, in reasonable confidence that I would have kept my shirt, and assuming that it is reasonable to construe educational theory as (at least partly) a consequence of the sort of research which might embrace this sort of questioning, we may here foresee the mildly amusing prospect of educational research proving its own large professional irrelevance. Still, I believe that there are significant lessons to be learned regarding the vexed relationship of educational research to theory—and also about the consequences of both of these for professional practice—from some present reflection upon what is misguided, as well as naïve, about the general form and direction of any such educational enquiry. Moreover, it may be illuminating to approach these issues via a few autobiographical observations.

## II   FROM ISOLATION TO PARANOIA

Some three decades ago, I trained as a teacher in a fairly typical British College of Education. My college course consisted of a fairly loose mixture of school experience and academic study—including a 'Cook's tour' of past educational ideas (Plato, Rousseau, Dewey etc) and some exposure to more empirical (mainly psychological and sociological) theories of learning and schooling. Although I now recall little of the substance of such courses, I was nevertheless to acquire an interest—while employed as a young teacher in a variety of primary and secondary schools—in questions of psychology and human conduct. All the same, despite a brief flirtation with scientific psychological theory, I was more drawn to philosophical and literary insights into the questions which interested me, and in due course I left teaching to study philosophy in a northern English university. There I was soon persuaded that the analytical philosophy which formed the core of my university studies shed more light than any empirical social or other studies on those professional and other questions about education, learning, teaching and human nature which had interested me as a young teacher. It was armed with this conviction that I eventually found myself professionally involved, following a year of postgraduate study in educational philosophy at the London Institute, with the theoretical education of prospective teachers on (the then) new BEd courses of teacher training: in short, I became a professional educational theorist specialising in philosophy of education.

Thus, for most of my own professional life, I have been engaged in a seemingly up-hill struggle to persuade would-be teachers of the benefits of principled reflection upon the nature of educational practice. Moreover, I have for most of that time had to collaborate with non-philosophers in an essentially empirical social scientific orthodoxy or climate of educational research. Like others similarly situated, indeed, I have had to live with the sometimes peculiar failure of social science colleagues to understand the nature of philosophical argument and its contribution to educational theorising. On occasions, for example, I have listened to such colleagues advising students that any philosophical criticisms of their own social-scientific theories are merely alternative hypotheses or models which are neither right nor wrong, and between which students are at liberty to choose more or less according to taste—apparently unaware that a view might be objectionable, for example, on grounds of simple logical incoherence. (One psychologist colleague was also memorably fond of observing that he had often talked about life to old men in pubs 'who could knock your philosophy into a cocked hat'.) At the very least, such conceptual insensitivities have greatly served to reinforce my sense of isolation as a lone educational philosopher in a social scientific world (a feeling no doubt familiar to other educational philosophers also employed in professional support roles).

It is in turning from the academic climate in which I have been required to teach to the reception I have frequently met from those I have mostly been charged with teaching, however, that the sense of isolation collapses into downright paranoia. Indeed, having only relatively recently had much substantial involvement with the kind of self-selected groups of postgraduates with whom colleagues in older university education departments have more often been blessed, I am still trying to adjust to the contrast between the insatiable appetite for educational ideas of postgraduates and the often explicit hostility to any and all such ideas of the general run of pre-service student teachers with whom I have mostly dealt over the years. Driven by the conviction that much if not most poor education and teaching springs from failures to grasp the logical grammar (in the Wittgensteinian sense) of educational and pedagogical practice, I have laboured to show how policy proposals may be vitiated by simple ambiguities, or the actual teaching of particular subjects and activities can be compromised by failure to appreciate key distinctions. I have sought to construct lively and attractive practice-oriented lectures on teaching, learning and discipline, illustrating points by frequent reference to my own and other practical teaching experiences, or to observations of classroom practice drawn from a long career as a school placement supervisor. Sometimes, I have almost convinced myself that I am finally managing to communicate something of the urgency of principled, ordered or rigorous reflection upon practice for all educational professionals. Time and again, however, I have been brought down with a bump—in seminars in which trainee teachers exhibit marked disinclination towards intellectual engagement with any wider educational ideas, and in student course evaluations which continue to feature the familiar litany of complaints against 'irrelevant' theory.

On the other hand, in those precious moments of mood upswing—when my therapist assures me that I am having a good day—I can also recognise that this is all so much generalisation, and that it suffers from all the shortcomings of other statistical records of public opinion. First, there may well be some paranoia involved in taking an overall student estimate of theory in general as a measure of their regard for my (or anyone else's) lectures in particular, and it could be that the rather negative evaluations of general student questionnaires are more reflective of the crudity of the instruments by which their views are polled than of what they actually (especially individually) think: in this regard, since philosophy usually constitutes a fairly small proportion of the theoretical studies of professional teacher education in most institutions, there is no particular reason to take such work to be the prime target of general anti-theoretical sentiments. But, second, I have to concede that the generalisation is rather more plainly sweeping, and that not all student teachers are so vehemently anti-theoretical: indeed, a significant proportion—especially that fairly substantial percentage of mature students who are often drawn into pre-service BEd and PGCE courses—do often respond positively to the invitation to engage in principled reflection upon problems of educational theory, policy and practice. Moreover, combining these points, I have sometimes been pleasantly surprised to discover that the kind of philosophical explorations in which I have engaged with such students are actually compared favourably with other parts of their academic or theoretical studies.

Thus, more optimistically, one need not doubt that at least a section of pre-service students are able to appreciate the significance of critical philosophical analysis for a more coherent view of the teaching of this or that discipline or activity, or the importance of rigorous argumentation for effective educational policy making. Surely, moreover, only philosophical analysis could help them to see that any question of the sort which introduced this paper could not possibly yield valid results in advance of that elucidation of 'theory' and 'practice' needed to forestall the possibility of respondents answering quite different questions. For, after all, any general question about the balance of theory to practice is liable to diverse interpretations. For some students it may mean: (i) 'do we spend enough time learning to operate in classrooms as opposed to sitting in the lecture theatre?'. For others it might mean: (ii) 'do we spend too much time merely thinking about practice rather than getting on with it?'. For yet others, it can mean: (iii) 'do we spend enough time actually involved in reflection about issues and problems of direct relevance to classroom practice, rather than on wider issues of educational principle or policy?' (over which they may feel, with some justice, that they have no control). For others still, it may express: (iv) a deep (and not entirely ill-founded) scepticism about whether the rough generalisations or models of much social scientific theory can have much useful practical application to the experiential rough and tumble of classroom teaching. To whatever extent these doubts and complaints are consistent, they are certainly not identical: individuals may well hold some of these views without holding others, they are of different degrees of seriousness (not all of which can be dismissed as anti-intellectual or philistine) and they clearly call for very different sorts of responses from academic providers of educational 'theory'.

Question (i), of course, reflects a legitimate worry about the balance of the academic and experiential in professional course design which is of enduring concern to teacher educators—any response to which will also rather depend upon how one construes the proper character of professional reflection. On the other hand, (ii) (perhaps the most philistine) embodies a quite confused and untenable dualism about the relationship of thought to practice— which may or may not also be reflected in the rather more reasonable queries of (iii) and (iv). There can also be little doubt, however, that such misconstrual of the relationship of educational reflection to practice has itself been greatly reinforced by the already noted contemporary fashion for conceiving educational theorising as mostly a product of empirical social scientific research. The problem persists that students of teaching have been widely encouraged to subscribe to a (technicist) conception of principled educational practice as a matter of the external imposition on classroom conduct of prescriptions based upon empirical (scientific) generalisations concerning the efficient causes of learning or management. It is arguably the bitter discovery that such generalities may have little direct practical utility in the fires of initial contact with the untidy particularities of school placement which inclines many students to the non-sequitur that nothing in the way of principled reflection upon educational problems can be relevant to good practice.

## III THE INHERENT NORMATIVITY OF EDUCATIONAL DISCOURSE

All the same, while I have no great desire to add to the mountain of critical comment that has lately been heaped on this essentially inappropriate technicist conception of the relationship of educational theory or reflection to good practice, something needs to be said to clarify the difference between my own and what I take to be other critiques of applied science conceptions of educational deliberation. Principally, I want to distance myself from many currently fashionable 'particularist' criticisms of the sort of educational technicism apparently presupposed by (say) much school effectiveness research, which emphasise that only teacher action-research can properly reflect the 'situatedness' of authentic educational engagement.[1] While I would not wish to deny that real improvements in the technicalities of lesson presentation and classroom management can follow from exercises in action research, and that such research may therefore have its professional place, it has always troubled me that such research essentially misses—in its own potentially narrow or restrictive way—what is most deeply misguided about the applied theory approach. Indeed, in claiming largely that any really useful professional reflection on educational practice needs to be grounded in situated or contextualised empirical enquiry, it is not clear how action research departs significantly from the applied theory approach. Moreover, a related misunderstanding of the basic character of educational enquiry seems also to infect a currently fashionable characterisation of professional reflection as 'practical theory'.[2] What such conceptions may fail to question is whether learning to teach well is something which is first and foremost best approached via any sort of empirically or experimentally conceived research: it is a failure to appreciate this question which above all bedevils professional theorising about education and teaching.

In this regard, we might first ask whether the basic grammar of teaching is best expressed in the terms of skill, art or technology by which we might characterise the procedures of machine-operating, auto-repair or even the playing of musical scores. The latter are, to be sure, (very different types of) skills—for which there are (to a significant degree) set principles and procedures which require internalisation and reinforcement through practice. But it would be an obvious (category) mistake to suppose that all forms of human practical engagement are of such a practically codifiable kind: notwithstanding the suspect technicism of therapeutic culture, for example, it seems distinctly odd to suppose that one might learn love, friendship or caring via the grasp of experimentally grounded procedures or routines, or that failures of love or friendship are liable to be remedied by practising harder. To be sure, love, friendship and caring are more acquired than innate qualities and one can devote a lifetime to self-improvement with respect to them. However, it would be crass confusion to construe such improvement or development in terms of the acquisition of loving or caring skills: there is not the least contradiction, for example, in supposing that someone might learn whatever might be taught under the heading of such skills without actually becoming any more loving or caring—and it would be a rather rum sort of person who looked to psychological experiments (rather than, say, to poems, novels or religious tracts) as primary sources of inspiration in any conscious effort to understand love or care.[3]

Still, someone might say, however inappropriate it may be to speak of caring or friendship skills, do we not speak readily of teaching skills? I agree that we do habitually speak in this way, but since this may be a *façon de parler* itself foisted upon us by contemporary educational technicism, it rather begs the question whether it is proper so to speak. In the event, I suspect that there is something at least misleading about any talk of teaching skills—though this suspicion is susceptible of weaker and stronger formulation. The weaker version would concede that although teaching is significantly characterisable in terms of acquired skills, it is not exclusively so (so that people who had acquired all the prescribed skills might still be deemed poor teachers) and that even many of the skills that good teachers do acquire are not of a kind readily expressible in the causal generalisations of much empirical educational research. Thus, for example, it seems not just that communication is an important aspect of good teaching, but that we can speak reasonably enough of communication skills: but it does not follow that the best way to appreciate such skills is via scientific enquiry. Successful actors who need communication skills just as much if not more than teachers, learn these in the spirit of art rather than science or technology—by comparing and contrasting the different styles of other actors and by borrowing different elements of these to the purpose of forging distinctive voices expressive of individual personality. This is not to deny that there may be quite generalisable communicational techniques or strategies which all actors or teachers worth their salt would need to appreciate: thus, just as I may safely advise all actors not to speak with their backs to the audience, I can advise all teachers not to talk to the blackboard. But the skills which lie at the heart of any actor's or teacher's effective communication seem more products of complex and personally adapted expressive or 'aesthetic' influences than off-the-peg all-purpose techniques.

But the stronger position would be that teaching and learning are more logically akin to love and friendship than to auto-repair, bus-driving or even playing a musical instrument: in short, they exemplify primarily pre-theoretical, pre-scientific and pre-technical aspects of human social life. This, I suspect, is what accounts for the weirdness of the implication of much empirical educational research that one might discover 'new' modes of teaching and learning—rather in the way that natural scientific research discovers new sub-atomic particles. Teaching and learning, like making friends or caring for associates and dependants, are part of that general fabric of human association in which 'normal' human persons cannot but engage in order to acquire familiar capacities of personal agency: they are activities in which humans come to engage more or less successfully from infancy upwards in the regular course of personal development. Moreover, the qualifier 'normal' here is crucial in two significant respects. First, it signals that anyone denied experience of the sorts of association involved in caring, co-operating, learning and/or teaching is liable to be in a profound sense 'abnormal' or pathological: they will have precisely missed out, in humanly or personally disabling ways, on vital aspects of human development. But second, talk of normality also serves to alert us to the related 'normativity' or value-laden character of concepts of person and personal development. From this viewpoint, it is crucial to appreciate that while it is little more than a formal point about human personal development that those denied opportunities for the development of characteristically-human social forms of communication and co-operation court serious personal disablement, the essentially normative character of such social forms of communication and co-operation also authorises a diversity of competing cultural conceptions of 'normal' personhood and personality. There is no obviously empirically correct way of understanding human personhood and agency—and hence, by implication, no one scientifically objective conception of friendship, caring or (for that matter) teaching and learning.

The failure to appreciate the essentially normative character of concepts of education, learning and teaching and the corresponding large-scale attempt to turn education and teaching into a kind of science-based technology has, I believe, lain behind some of the deepest errors and confusions of contemporary educational philosophy and theory. It lies, for example, at the root of the failure of modern empirically-based educational research to solve or resolve those admittedly wearisome controversies between so-called educational traditionals and progressives or child-centred educationalists by the experimental testing of different teaching skills or the advocacy of 'mixed-economies' of teaching style.[4] As I have often argued, this will not dispose of the traditional–progressive dichotomy (indeed, to appreciate its tenacious hold over educational debate one has only to tune into any media discussion of education) because the traditional–progressive dispute is not primarily (if at all) a technical debate about the causal efficacy of different teaching skills, but an evaluative controversy about the (obviously) key role of education and teaching in the forging of positive human association. The dispute is essentially moral or ethical, and as such unsusceptible of any non question-begging resolution in the terms of allegedly value-neutral empirical data.[5] This is not, by the way, to endorse any wholesale postmodern rejection of scientific objectivity: I believe that there can be overarching meta-narratives, and that science is as good a candidate as any for one of them. It is simply to recognise that insofar as concepts of personhood and agency are normative concepts, they enshrine potentially variant visions of human flourishing, and therefore that any debates about those agencies and processes which are centrally implicated in the promotion of agency and personhood cannot be resolved by the conventional methods of natural or social science.

But this is also not to say that they cannot be resolved at all. Indeed, it is surely empiricist or postmodern folly to suppose that because we cannot test in a value neutral way between (say) particular traditional and progressive educational and pedagogical perspectives, we cannot therefore show—precisely by (moral) normative argument—that some are wiser, saner, more humane, more sensitive, or whatever, than others. Take, for example, the large postwar educational dispute in Britain about corporal punishment in schools. It is not obvious that corporal punishment was ultimately abolished in Britain (though it is still widely used in other countries) because it did not technically 'work' (by deterring misbehaviour), and even less obvious that even if it could have been shown to work we would have been right to retain it on those grounds. The cane and the strap were surely banned more because they were regarded as deeply at odds with the educational aims of any reasonably civilised liberal democracy. A key consideration here must be that if any such political and civic order is committed not just to the ideal of resolving problems and disputes by non-violent means, but also to promoting such commitment through education, it would appear practically (morally) inconsistent—and hence potentially self-defeating—to promote the sort of school climate in which violent coercion of miscreants was the perceived means of securing order and control: how can we preach non-violence on the one hand and practise violence on the other? But to point out that a physically violent response to misbehaviour is logically incompatible with the overall aims of a liberal education is to offer a moral or normative argument against corporal punishment—to which considerations of causal effectiveness may well be irrelevant: even if we admitted (what is anyway dubious) that corporal punishment does deter, we can nevertheless insist that it is wrong to practise it.

It should also be emphasised that this point about the inherent normativity or value-laden character of educational practice is quite general: it applies no less to those other aspects of teaching that we have been persuaded to regard as matters of generalisable technique than it does to matters of central and local government policy. It has been common of late, for example, for policy documents on teacher education to characterise discipline in terms of the mastery of 'management skills'[6]—and just as common for my students to suggest that I might teach them such techniques. But what, we might ask, are these? I was once told of a chemistry teacher in an English Grammar School for boys who would burst into tears and sob uncontrollably whenever his pupils misbehaved: at that point, so the story goes, the pupils would say to each other in a spirit of deep contrition: 'that's it lads, we've upset him—let's pack it in now'. I cannot see the least reason to doubt the veracity of this story—or, at any rate, to suppose that if it did not happen, it could not. But true or false, the tale may be considered instructive in at least two significant respects. First, this route to class control was or is clearly not a generalisable technique: whereas it might well work in some circumstances, one can imagine others in which it would be plain suicide. Second, it is not obviously a causally operative (and hence scientifically researchable) technique as such at all: insofar as the response 'worked', it was more probably because the teacher was expressing genuine distress at the misbehaviour and because the liking and respect in which the boys held him meant that they were sincerely moved by the hurt they had caused. Thus, while not wishing or needing to deny that class control can often go awry because teachers have not mastered certain readily teachable pedagogical or organisational strategies, the truth is that the heart of good discipline is more a matter of 'internal' moral association or ethos than of externally imposed organisational strategies. Disorganised dominies can be found in circumstances of high-class morale and motivation—and, on those occasions of placement supervision when I have witnessed total discipline breakdown, it has seemed more often to follow from loss of respect for a teacher who clearly did not care, than to be a direct consequence of poor organisation. Both are clearly important, but a climate of mutual respect—however generated or expressed—is clearly paramount.

## IV   PRACTICAL WISDOM, FACTS AND VALUES

However, the general normativity of education and teaching—the fact that pedagogy and discipline are liable to be informed by diverse moral and other values—should serve to remind us that respect and trust may be generated, and/or interest secured, in a wide variety of quite legitimate ways. Indeed, it is not just that approaches are apt to vary from teacher to teacher, but that particular (good) teachers invariably adapt their styles and strategies to the needs of diverse educational clienteles at different times. Like good parents, good teachers—so-called reflective practitioners—soon recognise that different pupils, like different offspring, respond to different modes of personal and pedagogical association. While there are, to be sure, some general and impartial rules of engagement to the extent that no good parent or teacher will want to disadvantage one progeny or pupil over another—it is common beyond this to find that one's (familial or other) relations with individual youngsters generate rather different chemistries. This is, of course, because—given the interpersonal sources of education and teaching— there is a not just legitimate but also unavoidable respect in which educational associations with pupils are as much social and affective as cognitive or technical. Indeed, it is precisely such aspects of educational engagement which have been well captured in the recent virtue-ethical preference for characterising teaching in terms of Aristotelian *phronēsis* rather than *technē*,[7] as well as in the rejection by ethicists of care of latter day characterisations of education and teaching mainly in terms of cognitive capacities or the observance of rules.[8] I suspect, however, that the full significance of *phronēsis* as a form of practical reason has not always been appreciated—especially by those mainly concerned to resist technicist ideas of educational or school improvement in the name of school-based or teacher action research. Hence, as already noticed, it seems to be a common line of argument against 'external' research into school improvement that good educational practice evades general statistical description because the judgements and deliberations of teachers are of a highly contextualised technical complexity, which cannot be thus codified: but the real lesson to be drawn from any recognition of the 'phronetic' character of teacher deliberation is surely that it is not primarily, if at all, technical—and hence not accountable to the experimental methods of conventional empirical educational research.

At all events, such observations find me in broad sympathy with other analytical educational philosophers who have generally taken a dim view of the value of statistical or quasi-natural scientific research into education and educational method—though it may be going a bit far to claim that because the conclusions of such research aspire to an unachievable generality or universality they can never be true.[9] I think that there can be true educational generalisations (e.g. avoid talking to the blackboard)—it is just that they are not usually of a kind for which we are likely to need statistical support. I believe that a more significant difficulty is that given the essentially normative character of educational discourse, there is a clear gulf between empirical observation and prescription: in short, it is difficult to see what in most cases would have to follow educationally from this or that set of empirical generalities. Thus, one may agree with some philosophers that one serious trouble with many research questions is that they often require disambiguation in a way that is liable to undermine their validity as general measures: for example, insofar as respondents may mean rather different things by any general statement to the effect that there is too much theory and too little practice in teacher education, the prospects of any valid universalisation here are likely to be dim. But suppose one could disambiguate such a question and it turned out that each and every student did unambiguously agree that there is too much theory and too little practice: what then? Should this result require us to remove all principled reflection from teacher education and to turn the education and training of students over to the schools? Might we not rather entertain the remote possibility that the students could be wrong: that, indeed, one reason they are still students is that they do not yet fully appreciate the need for certain kinds of principled reflection in their professional preparation? Again, it is a familiar problem with existing psychometric measures that they are not accurate predictors of attainment. But let us suppose we had one that was. Would this tell us how to school or educate children of different ability? Would it tell us whether to school them together or separately, or whether to give more help to the able than the less able— or vice versa? Or again, if we found that the average attention span of the typical class was such and such, would it tell us whether to work within that attention span or try to extend it? And so on and so forth.

Again, it is important to dismiss the spectre of 'anything goes' relativism here: evidence counts in educational policy as elsewhere, our values are related to the facts and it would be crazy to suppose that any one educational policy is as good as another. Wholesale relativism mainly follows, as I have argued elsewhere, from fatal confusion of the fact–value and is–ought distinctions.[10] Human agents generally value dental treatment because all find tooth decay painful: despite this agreement, however, they may disagree about methods of treatment—precisely at the level of moral and medical prescription. Notwithstanding this, the relative merits and demerits of extractions, general anaesthetics and mercury fillings can be debated, and there are sometimes overwhelming reasons for resolving such debates in a definite direction. To be sure, someone will say, this is only because despite the normative dimensions of many dental and medical debates, such controversies are still often addressed to scientifically or technically resolvable issues. If what I have claimed about the issues in which educational discourse is implicated is so— that all notions of pedagogy and/or discipline are intricated in questions of what is worth knowing, how human beings should associate and what is a good way to live—then they are more thoroughly normative, and few (if any) of such issues are likely to be resolved by received methods of empirical enquiry. However, there is no reason to believe that many normative questions cannot be settled via serious conceptual clarification and/or ethical argument—as, indeed, I have already indicated that the question of whether corporal punishment is consistent with the aims and principles of liberal democratic education can be so settled.

That said, I am also inclined to think that there are some normative questions about education which cannot be settled—if, that is, settling them implies securing substantial liberal-democratic agreement about them.The truth is that since educational controversies turn mostly upon different visions of human flourishing there will always be (indeed, in a society like ours, there must and should be) room for disagreement concerning what are clearly inherently evaluative, ethical and hence philosophical issues. This, however, is the crux. If some such educational questions are (consensually) irresolvable via ethical or philosophical argument, then they are not resolvable by scientific or technical means either. On the other hand, if some such educational questions are normatively resolvable, then their resolution will be primarily a matter for ethical or philosophical argument. But if some such educationally questions are not normatively resolvable then we · shall also need ethical and philosophical analysis to tell us which these are. In any event, ethical and philosophical analysis emerges as the key tool for understanding and clarifying educational questions, and for better understanding of the issues involved. However one views it, educational philosophical enquiry in general (namely, some systematic attempt to be clear about what we mean in talking about education) and ethical educational enquiry in particular (namely, some systematic attempt to arrive at a clearer articulation of what is educationally worth achieving and why) cannot but lie at the very core of any and all significant educational enquiry. In short, that branch of educational theory which so often seems dismissed as an airy-fairy chattering irrelevance to practical affairs by one's hard-headed social scientific colleagues precisely turns out to address those key questions in default of which so much empirical enquiry is just whistling down the wind. Throughout three decades of isolation and paranoia, I have never lost my faith that this is so, and that a philosophical education is the most powerful resource we have for enhancing teacher (or other) professionalism.

## V   PHILOSOPHY, PROFESSIONAL REFLECTION AND EDUCATIONAL ENQUIRY

All the same, in my concern to show that a kind of principled reflection, namely (analytical) philosophical and ethical enquiry, is indispensable to the professional education and training of teachers, I may seem to have greatly undermined the general project of upholding the value of educational theory *per se* for such education—precisely by calling into question the worth or credentials of much empirical or statistical work. Are we to dismiss all such work as worthless, and is there really no more to professional educational theory, reflection or deliberation than the development of analytical philosophical skills? Once again, there can be no straight answer to this wildly indiscriminate question. On the one hand, of course, insofar as more is required of any rational appreciation of education and teaching than is encompassed by any set of conceptual skills—since, indeed, when all is said and done philosophy needs something to philosophise *about*—there is obviously much that would-be professional practitioners will need in the way of theory and enquiry. For a start, they will require an appreciation of current educational policies which needs to be informed by an understanding of the intellectual, historical and political influences on such policies. This cannot but include, besides straightforward (albeit critical) acquaintance with contemporary and historical documentation, a knowledge of the important social scientific perspectives that have profoundly influenced the evolution of educational policy and practice. But, on the other hand, it is crucial for students to appreciate that insofar as such theories enshrine essentially norma-tive, often culturally specific, conceptions of human nature and flourishing—they are only dubiously treated as serious scientific descriptions of human development susceptible of technological application. To the (large) extent that the theories of development and learning of Thorndike or Kohlberg enshrine deeply philosophical or metaphysical assumptions, what have often paraded as descrip-tions of the human condition seem to be little more than covert prescriptions, and as such expressive of ethical more than scientific conceptions of human life and destiny.

Again, this does not render such theories worthless from the perspective of professional education: it serves rather to reinforce the important professional point that even if what is prescribed by such views could be effectively implemented—even if we could successfully condition or brainwash people into certain patterns of (from some perspective) desirable behaviour—the key professional questions would still embody normative concerns about whether we should do so. From this viewpoint, indeed, social scientific accounts of human mind and learning may be of neither more nor less professional interest than other time-honoured literary sources of insight into human personal and interpersonal life and experience. From this viewpoint, as I have also elsewhere argued,[11] there is no reason why explorations of education and teaching, or of human association generally, in wider imaginative and creative literature should not have equal standing in professional teacher education with social scientific analyses of teaching and learning. On a fair assumption that those intending to become educators of others ought to be reasonably well-educated people themselves, it has long been a concern to me that student teachers do not read enough—and often exhibit lamentable ignorance of their own rich cultural heritage. While there are many contemporary reasons for this, I think that competence and other practice-based models of professional education have often played their part in exalting the technical aspects of teaching over broader cultural and moral issues and considerations. Moreover, the main reason why some teacher educators may be inclined to look askance at the idea of using novels, plays and poems in professional education is because they are still held captive by a picture of teacher preparation as the acquisition of a kind of scientific research-based technical expertise. But if, as is being increasingly recognised, education and teaching are inherently normative practices, and the practical capacities which teachers need to acquire are the kind of morally attuned sensibilities to the nuances of human association expressed in the idea of *phronēsis*, then professionally-focused literary studies may well be appropriate means to the cultivation of such capacities. Moreover, as I have also argued on other occasions,[12] a major mistake here seems to be a confusion between technicality and difficulty—specifically to suppose that if a study is not technical it cannot be difficult. The truth is rather that many technicist or applied science conceptions of educational research often make teaching appear far less difficult than it is, and that attention to the moral and other evaluative issues raised in much great literature may well make professionally relevant intellectual demands on students which are hardly envisaged in many current models of training.

The principal upshot of these considerations, however, is that although the professional curriculum of prospective teachers will need to range quite widely over a variety of human, historical, social and political studies—indeed, I have suggested including even more of such studies than one is likely to find in many present day professional courses—the kinds of reflective and critical capacities which we should want teachers to acquire are at heart of an analytical philosophical and/or ethical character. At all events, insofar as we would wish teachers in schools to have acquired a principled and sensitive appreciation of the moral and personal as well as the cognitive needs of their pupils, an educated understanding of the intellectual, cultural and social influences on current educational policies and practices and some capacity for intelligent critical engagement with official or other educational proposals or media debates on education, more is needed for professional training than induction into officially sanctioned skills. But such professional requirements also seem to coincide quite remarkably with what were not so long ago conceived as the major tasks of philosophy of education in the postwar heyday of analytical educational philosophy. Indeed, at the risk of being thought to dwell in the past, it seems to me that three major works of educational philosophy published more or less simultaneously some twenty years ago—all written by distinguished mainstream philosophers—still serve between them to define effectively the three key theoretical and practical tasks for the teaching profession generally and educational philosophy in particular.

First, in *The Philosophy of Teaching*[13] John Passmore attempted (in the spirit of what we might call the 'analytical' task) an impressive extended conceptual analysis of the basic character of teaching as an activity—which might well have been described as pioneering, but for the fact that the ground broken by Passmore has hardly been seriously cultivated since. It may be that Passmore's work is today too much associated with a kind of analysis now widely dismissed as outdated—presumably on the grounds that no such analysis could be normatively or evaluatively neutral. But there is much simple confusion in this objection, Passmore's approach is still *de rigueur* in much if not most serious mainstream philosophy, and it is arguable that conceptual analysis has often been dismissed in educational philosophy before it has even been properly tried. From this viewpoint, though Passmore's work made a very promising start on the task of understanding the complexities of teaching as a task or activity, I believe that the absence of any real further attempt to provide a detailed philosophical psychology of teaching—despite much latter day interest in teacher reflection and deliberation—represents one of the most embarrassing gaps in contemporary educational philosophy.[14] Indeed, how could there be a more urgent task for educational professionals in general and educational philosophers in particular than the provision of an detailed account of the logical geography of pedagogical engagement which might help us move beyond those crude technicist accounts of teaching that have so prevailed in recent times? In this respect, we are in sore need of a much richer view of the very different qualities—moral and aesthetic, aretaic and technical, personal and interpersonal, innate and acquired, and so on—of flesh and blood teachers and teaching.

David Hamlyn's *Experience and the Growth of Understanding*,[15] however, clearly took us (in the direction of we might call the 'critical' task) into realms of professional concern which, whilst philosophical, cannot be addressed by conceptual analysis alone—at least in any narrow sense of this term. Still, teachers will always need to understand human learning and the nature of knowledge and understanding as such, and to appreciate—in a way that Hamlyn's work well served to show—that such notions are not scientifically neutral or value free and enshrine often deeply culturally biased philosophical anthropologies or epistemologies. Moreover, such understanding is not just professionally important for its own sake, but for a critical appreciation of the often contentious and sometimes dubious views of teaching, learning and/or discipline enshrined in contemporary official and other educational policies and initiatives. This, of course, takes us (in the direction of what we might call the 'normative' task) more squarely into the realms of explicitly evaluative educational enquiry into which David Cooper's highly controversial work *Illusions of Equality* did not fear to tread.[16] And, of course, to hold Cooper's work in the high regard which I believe it rightly merited, is not at all to say that one agrees with the general moral and political ground upon which it stood or with the policy conclusions which it drew: it is just to acknowledge the philosophically exemplary way in which this work addressed a crucial professional obligation to clarify one's moral, political and other educationally relevant loyalties and commitments in as honest and rationally consistent a way as possible.

At all events, while it is probably too much to hope that the chequered quality of much current teacher education might realistically aspire to produce reflective practitioners entirely equal to the intellectual demands of such modern classics of educational philosophy, I remain confident that even some degree of general insight into the issues such works have sought to raise—not least some appreciation of the rigorous and principled way in which they sought to address them—can yet be expected to make a real professional difference to the quality of educational practice of prospective teachers. Indeed, adapting from Plato on a different but not unrelated matter, one might say that there may be no good educational practice until all professional teachers become—rather than school effectiveness, action-researchers or other empirical researchers—educational *philosophers*.

*Correspondence*: David Carr, Department of Education, University of Edinburgh, Holyrood Road, Edinburgh EH8 8AQ, UK

## NOTES

1. A questionable combination of a particularist account of professional deliberation and action research seems characteristic of the work of John Elliott. See: John Elliott (1987) Educational theory, practical philosophy and action research, *British Journal of Educational Studies*, 35, pp. 149–169 and (1996), School effectiveness research and its critics, *Cambridge Journal of Education*, 26.2, pp. 199–224.

2. For the idea of 'practical theory' see: Paul H. Hirst: The theory and practice relationship in teacher training, in: M. Wilkin, V. J. Furlong and M. Booth (eds), (1990), *Partnership in Initial Teacher Training: The Way Forward* (London, Cassell); and The demands of professional practice and preparation of teachers, in John Furlong and Richard Smith (1996) *The Role of Higher Education in Initial Teacher Training* (London, Kogan Page). See also, more recently, John Furlong (2000), *Higher Education and the New Professionalism of Teachers: Realising the Potential of Partnership* (London, CVCP).

3. In a response to some criticisms of Terry Hyland's and my own of competence models of professional preparation, David Bridges has explicitly defended the dubious idea of moral skills. See David Bridges (1996), Competence-based education and training: progress or villainy? *Journal of the Philosophy of Education*, 30.3, pp. 361–375, 1996.

4. Such proposals to resolve the dualism of traditionalism and progressivism are characteristic of (respectively) Neville Bennett (1976), *Teaching Styles and Pupil Progress* (London, Open Books); and Robin Alexander, Jim Rose and Chris Woodhead (eds) (1992), *Curriculum Organization and Classroom Practice in Primary School* (London, DES).

5. On this issue generally see my Traditionalism and progressivism: a perennial problematic of educational theory and policy, *Westminster Studies in Education*, 21, 1998, pp. 47–55.

6. One prime source of thinking about school discipline in terms of 'management skills' is Department of Education and Science and the Welsh Office (1989), *Discipline in Schools* (London, HMSO) (The Elton Report). But such thinking is generally characteristic of competence models of professional teacher education and training.

7. For a classic treatment of Aristotle's idea of *phronēsis* in recent educational philosophy, see Joseph Dunne (1993), *Back to the Rough Ground: 'Phronēsis' and 'Technē' in Modern Philosophy and in Aristotle* (Notre Dame, University of Notre Dame Press).

8. For seminal works in the ethics of care, see Carol Gilligan (1982): *In a Different Voice: Psychological Theory and Women's Development* (Cambridge MA, Harvard University Press); and Nel Noddings (1984), *Caring: A Feminist Approach to Ethics* (Berkeley, University of California Press).

9. For general scepticism of this sort, see Robin Barrow, The poverty of research in moral education: beyond John Wilson, *Journal of Moral Education*, 29.3, 2000—though I am mostly sympathetic to Barrow's largely dim view of empirical educational research.

10. For an analysis of confusion of the fact–value and is–ought distinctions, see my paper, Is understanding the professional knowledge of teachers a theory–practice problem?, *Journal of Philosophy of Education*, 29, 1995, pp. 311–331; and The primacy of virtues in ethical theory: Part I, *Cogito*, 9, 1995, pp. 238–244.

11. On this, see my: The uses of literacy in teacher education, *British Journal of Educational Studies*, 45, 1997, pp. 53–68.

12. On this, see my: Is understanding the professional knowledge of teachers a theory–practice problem?, *op. cit.*

13. John Passmore (1980), *The Philosophy of Teaching* (London, Duckworth).

14. However, for some recent modest efforts in this direction, see my: Is teaching a skill?, in: Randall Curren (ed.) *Philosophy of Education 1999*, Urbana, Illinois: Philosophy of Education Society, 2000; also chapter 1 of my *Professionalism and Ethical Issues in Teaching*, Routledge Professional Ethics Series (London, Routledge) 2000.

15. David Hamlyn (1978) *Experience and the Growth of Understanding* (London, Routledge & Kegan Paul). For a recent fine attempt at further development of many of these issues, see Christopher Winch (1998) *The Philosophy of Human Learning* (London, Routledge).

16. David E. Cooper (1980) *Illusions of Equality* (London, Routledge). For an impressive recent alternative perspective on these issues, see Harry Brighouse (2000), *School Choice and Social Justice* (Oxford, Oxford University Press).

17. The idea that there can be no just government until kings become philosophers (and philosophers become kings) is a key theme of Plato in *The Republic*.

# 11

# Qualitative Versus Quantitative Research Design: A Plea for Paradigmatic Tolerance in Educational Research

Paul Smeyers

*The tension between the generality of approach in causally-driven quantitative educational research and the individuality of particular cases is exemplified in the types of reasoning employed. Unlike the scientific search for antecedents, still popular in some forms of educational research, investigating particular persons and policies necessarily requires a form of practical reasoning. In order to ease this tension between qualitative and quantitative research, this essay asks questions as to what is to be described and how this is to be done. Responding to these questions, it is argued, necessarily draws attention to a range of ethical issues often ignored.*

## INTRODUCTION

The need to apprehend the world one lives in is a fundamental part of the human condition. This apprehension includes understanding the meanings of various forms of expressions (concepts, symbols, art objects, rituals), of feelings and emotions, of actions in the world of human activity past and present (in terms of purposes, aims and more functional explanations), and last but not least, the understanding of natural phenomena. In the context of the physical world one may want to distinguish a unified style of explanation from a mechanical kind. The former explains in terms of basic comprehensive principles (for instance in biology: selection, mutation, heritability of traits), how in other words phenomena fit into an overall scheme; the latter answers questions of how things work (sometimes understood as

189

what they are made of), where what one is looking for is a causal kind of explanation. As will be argued later, these forms of explanations are by no means incompatible.

It is evident that one wants to understand how society at large functions, what other people do, and who one is. 'Understanding' here refers to knowing how things are, so that they can be taken into account in what one does later on. But in many circumstances, the concept of 'causality' seems to pervade our thinking about ourselves and others, our environment, even the entire universe we live in. Causal explanations are fundamental to the intellectual understanding of physical systems, living organisms, and to our practical deliberations in these contexts. They are involved in the use of technology (where we attempt to achieve particular effects while avoiding undesirable ones) and in our everyday practical planning and dealings. Not only physicists and engineers but social scientists too have since the Enlightenment been occupied with finding causes in order to be able to manipulate particular outcomes. Psychologists and educational researchers are no exception to this general tendency. Here, for many, to explain an event is to identify its antecedents, i.e. its causes.

There is of course a strand of criticism against the use of 'cause' in the sphere of human explanations. This is not to deny that human beings are exempted from causal interactions generally; no one seriously denies that, for instance, bodily functions are subjected to physical and biochemical laws and processes. Nevertheless, once it is suggested that our behaviour itself can be made clear either partly or exhaustively by these kind of processes, human scientists and philosophers generally protest. Philosophers of human action in the continental and analytical traditions such as Dilthey, Gadamer, Ricoeur, in addition to Wittgenstein, Winch and Taylor, have argued to the contrary that human beings *give* meaning to their lives. It behoves us to ask, then, whether causal explanations still have significance or not, and in what sense, and for which contexts? And is it correct that if one accepts causal explanations of human behaviour there looms the threat of the disappearance of ethical issues, thus inviting us to live 'beyond freedom and dignity'? Though these issues typically have been discussed within epistemological contexts, there is a dearth of them in the Anglo-Saxon philosophy of education literature. Nevertheless these matters are highly relevant for the area of education and for educational inquiries. Before dealing with these questions directly, a particular evolution within educational research itself demands our attention.

## EDUCATIONAL RESEARCH: THE NEW PARADIGM?

Mainstream educational research, dominated by the paradigm that might be labelled 'real research', has undergone an interesting evolution as is exemplified by disputes concerning the relative merits of quantitative and qualitative approaches. Although the latter are now regarded with greater respect (or perhaps less suspicion?) than ever before (besides journals particularly focused on this kind of research[1] there are several new or revised editions of methodological handbooks: since 1990 more[2] than 250 new titles have seen the light of day) significant debates still abound. There is time and time again the general suspicion that what is offered by social science research cannot adequately satisfy the demands of knowledge proper. The following may capture what looms behind this scepticism: the inability to understand everything is to be equated with the inability to understand anything. What is longed for is something similar to the law-like explanation and 'prediction' of the natural sciences. This desire parallels that of philosophers for whom philosophy has to amount to valid reasoning warranted by methods of conceptual analysis (necessary and sufficient conditions) and logical rules of induction and deduction, or those for whom it must offer an overarching metaphysical system. One author who vigorously attacked these stances was Ludwig Wittgenstein. So it is no wonder that some have found in his work ways of exposing the shortcomings of certain types of social scientific research.

According to Wittgenstein, in the *Geisteswissenschaften*, the human 'sciences', one must in attempting to understand human conduct comprehend an agent's reason for actions. This understanding must incorporate the descriptions of everyday language; it must always go back to the understanding of those engaged in everyday human practices. Wittgenstein also advises us to refrain from formulating 'theories' of conduct, because they are incapable of capturing the heterogeneity of cases and because they necessarily presuppose a homogeneity that does not exist. In suggesting that not everything is explainable or understandable, he draws our attention to different kinds of understanding. Examples of particular concerns are: 'What is important for a human being?' and 'What is relevant here without being useful for something else?' The important difference between understanding and explaining, according to him, can be indicated by the difference in the effects they have for those involved:

> Compared with the impression which the description makes on us, the explanation is too uncertain. Every explanation is an hypothesis. But an hypothetical explanation will be of little help to someone, say, who is upset because of love.—It will not calm him (Wittgenstein, 1979, p. 63).

There is, however, a more general concern in play here: instead of 'crystalline purity' we need first a better understanding of the nature of the problem we want to deal with before the proper method(s) for its research can be determined. Only if one understands what 'social' really means will it be possible to outline the contours of a social science. In the context of our present concerns this places upon educational researchers an obligation to clarify what is to be understood by 'education' and 'educational research' prior to embarking upon it—an issue which is of a philosophical nature and to be dealt with within philosophical educational research.

It is not only the particular inadequacy of quantitative research and the need for educational research of a philosophical kind that has to be taken into account. There is also a characteristic development within qualitative research that is particularly relevant here. If the question appears anachronistic, consider the distinction drawn by Polkinghorne (1995) between an 'analysis of narratives' and 'narrative analysis' in the research methods literature of social science. In an 'analysis of narratives' one looks for common features in different cases in order to define them as belonging to a broader category. By pointing at features that different experiences have in common, one can construct cognitive conceptual frameworks. The purpose of the paradigmatic analysis is not only to discover and to describe categories, but also to describe the relationships between categories. In narrative analysis, data are not commonly in narrative form. Rather the data come from different sources: the researcher arranges events and actions by showing how they contribute to the evolution of a plot. The plot is the thematic line of the narrative, the narrative structure that shows how different events contribute to a narrative. The writing of it involves an analytical development, a dialectic between the data and the plot. The resulting narrative must not only fit the data but also draw out an order and a significance that was not apparent in the data as such. The result is not so much an account of the actual occurrence of events from a detached point of view as the result of a series of constructions. In contrast then, in the 'analysis of narratives' the narratives are themselves the source of knowledge, whereas the narrative in 'narrative analysis' is the product of the research.

Researchers in the human sciences may find themselves bewildered by all of this. The tasks of research are to be found in interpretation, as Wittgenstein says: in placing 'things side by side'. One has to refrain from formulating theories, because they are not capable of bringing forward the heterogeneity of cases and always presuppose more homogeneity than in fact can be found.[3] It goes without saying that contemporary academic psychology, still very much operating along Popperian lines, finds it hard to come to terms with such a programme—just as it could not digest it half a century ago. But even among educational researchers who have come to accept the legitimacy of both quantitative and qualitative research designs, this will be found to be problematical. What is the point of these particular descriptions, it will be asked, if not to generate a theoretical approach that is useful for future cases? Is all theory superfluous, then? Though there are some differences between Wittgenstein scholars concerning the above, it is generally seen nevertheless as the inherited view of his stance and of its implications for research in social sciences.

In this paper I will not rely primarily on the criticisms of the philosophers of action I have mentioned, who are critical of causal explanation and whose criticisms[4] (at least in general) I fully endorse. I do not have any further thoughts on the nature or the necessity of description in contexts of educational research, nor on the nature of 'education' itself. I will take a different line. It is similar to the position Richard Pring (2000) argues for in a recent paper in the *Journal of Philosophy of Education* where he states that educational research is being subject to damaging criticism from both outside and within the research community. For government and policy makers educational research fails to provide the answers they are looking for. Worse, much research fails to enhance professional practice (cf. Tooley, 1998). Crucially, for the position developed here, it is also criticised for being fragmented into myriad incommensurable case studies which merely revel in their own uniqueness. On the one hand policy makers are looking for a science of education, on the other hand it is argued that such an aspiration is based on false beliefs about what research can deliver. Educational research should instead study the uniqueness of each situation, understand its transactions as constituted by the perception and interpretations of the participants—they can not be subjected to the general explanatory accounts required by those who manage the system. Pring interprets this debate as a return of the issue of Cartesian dualism. He convincingly argues that though there are no *a priori* limits to the number of ways in which we potentially conceptualise social life, it does not follow that there are *no* limits; the capacity for *indefinite* possibilities does not equate with *unlimited* possibilities. Moreover, just as the social construction of the physical world *depends* upon a real world, so the social construction of the personal and social world presupposes the independent existence of objects (persons). The very 'negotiation' of meaning, so passionately argued for by the 'interpretive camp', can be conducted only within a framework of shared meanings that are not open to negotiation.

I intend to move this debate on by a somewhat different strategy. I will attempt to take seriously the claim that we can look for causes in order to understand the reality we live (in). As a starting-point I will focus primarily on 'the natural world'. I will argue that even if we fully endorse the programme of looking for antecedents, a dominant driver for many educational researchers, this would still not solve the problems they commonly set out to address. I will argue that in as much as we are interested in an individual person or more generally in particular cases, what we need above all is practical (i.e. ethical) reasoning. In a Wittgensteinian manner I will try to sort out some of the confusions that surround the concepts we use in the language-game of educational research; the bewilderments that have kept us captive. I will use Elster's approach to exemplify another extreme position in the interpretation of human behaviour and of human beings (i.e. as 'intentional persons') and will finally draw some consequences for educational theory.[5] The apparent dichotomy between what is generally referred to as qualitative and quantitative research will thus be resolved.

## NATURAL PHENOMENA

*Necessary and sufficient conditions, determinism and indeterminism*

Perhaps the most obvious place to begin a discussion of the proposed regular nature of causation is Hume's *A Treatise of Human Nature*. Hume's example is of one billiard ball lying on the table and another rapidly moving toward it. His basic insight is that formal reasoning cannot reveal causation because we cannot deduce the nature of an effect from a description of the cause, or the nature of the cause from a description of an effect. One can imagine for instance that someone had screwed the second ball to the table. In this case the first ball is most likely to return to where it came from. As deductive logic cannot provide the answer, Hume turns to empirical investigations. On the basis of his observations he concludes that in situations where we believe that there is a causal relation, there is a temporal priority of the cause to the effect. There is furthermore a spatio-temporal contiguity of the cause to the effect and finally, on every occasion on which the cause occurs, the effect follows—there is constant conjunction. As there is, in his opinion, no physical connection between the cause and the effect (the connection does not exist outside of our own minds), the relation between cause and effect is to be found in custom and habit. As Hume could not find a necessary connection between cause and effect, either in formal reasoning or in the physical world, his argument answers the question whether and how we can explicate the concept of causality in terms that do not surreptitiously introduce any occult concepts of power or necessary connection, which is exactly what he wanted to do.

The form philosophical discussions of causality take is usually as follows: there are two facts (or types of) $C$ and $E$ or two events (or types of) $C$ and $E$ between which there is a relation $R$. Questions are raised whether $C$ and $E$ should be taken to refer to facts or events and, further, whether to individual facts or events or classes of them. Sometimes the logical structure of the relation is discussed in terms of necessary or sufficient conditions or a combination of both. Given the interaction of several conditions this leads to complex schemes to understand particular occurrences. Consider for instance the following example in which a cause is defined as a condition. If a barn burns down this might have been caused by a careless smoker, by embers from a nearby forest fire falling on it, by a stroke of lightning or even from spontaneous combustion engendered by fermentation of fresh hay. None of these is a necessary condition, but any of them might be sufficient. Moreover, no fire will occur unless some additional factors are present (for instance, in the case of the cigarette, that it falls on some flammable material and that it goes unnoticed). These other conditions, however, would not suffice to start a fire. Each of them is a condition that is an Insufficient but Non-redundant (necessary) part of a condition that is Unnecessary but Sufficient (an INUS-condition). The dropping of the burning cigarette is an example thereof. Such a clear example is helpful in order to make the particular points concerning causality. As matters of 'meaning' are always involved where examples from social sciences are concerned, an analogous case from that context cannot easily be given. We will continue further into the area of natural phenomena before refocusing on the human world.

After this brief sketch of 'causality' and the philosophical problems that go with it, a move to the general level will take the argument forward to the relevance of causality in scientific explanations. The success of the development of more sophisticated experimental and mathematical techniques has extended the application of Newton's laws to new phenomena. The nineteenth century deterministic worldview has in some ways been confirmed and extended by twentieth century science, for instance in the field of molecular biology, where the mechanisms of heredity are explained exclusively in chemical terms. Thus scientists find themselves just one step away from explaining learning, or feelings and emotions, in terms of specific chemical changes that occur in the brain. To the determinist, the fact that we are unable to make perfect predictions in all cases is the result of human ignorance and other limitations, not because nature is lacking in precise determination—clearly, prediction is irrelevant to determinism. There is, however, also another evolution that uses a different frame, i.e. one of indeterminism. The challenge of relativity theory is not simply that quantum mechanics is prima facie non-deterministic, but that under plausible constraints no deterministic completion of quantum theory is possible. In view of this it seems inadvisable to accept determinism as an a priori principle—and of course the truth or falsity of quantum mechanics is a matter of physical fact. Concerning this it would not make much sense to step, as Wittgenstein would call it, outside of our form of life, i.e. to allow that our concepts are no more than whimsical social constructions. Doubts about the possibility of finding causes for everything on the basic of either logical or empirical moves have thus moved us to indeterminism as the more rational choice for the overarching framework. What are the implications of this for our understanding of scientific explanation and consequently for educational research?

### Statistical and functional explanation, causal and pseudo-processes

There are, of course, different sorts of explanation. A popular kind is the one where specific conditions obtaining prior to the event are cited (initial conditions) together with general laws. Let me make this point clear. It is stated that the occurrence of the event to be explained follows logically from those premises. One can distinguish between deductive explanations that incorporate universal laws (which hold without exceptions) and inductive explanations that employ statistical laws (which hold for most or many cases). According to Hempel (1965) scientific explanation consists in deductive or inductive subsumption of that which is to be explained under one or more laws of nature. This is referred to as the deductive-nomological model (D-N). For him, however, inductive-statistical explanations are essentially relativised to knowledge situations—he suggested that the requirement of total evidence took the form of the requirement of maximal specificity, where all possibly relevant knowledge is available. If there were an inductive-statistical explanation whose law-like statistical premise involved a genuinely homogenous reference class then we would have an instance of an inductive-statistical explanation *simpliciter*, not merely an inductive-statistical explanation relative to a specific knowledge situation. However, as there are according to Hempel no inductive-statistical explanations *simpliciter*, ideally inductive-statistical explanation would have no place in his position. There is a striking similarity between this kind of explanation and Laplace's formulation of determinism. In view of this close relationship it is tempting to conclude that events that are causally determined can be explained, and those that can be explained are causally determined. And from this it is just one more step to say that when human actions and decisions can be explained, they are determined; this leads on to the conclusion that to explain human behaviour and choices is to show that they cannot be free (in which case moral responsibility disappears). However, it should be noted that in many cases *we do not have enough facts to be able to construct an explanation and we can never be sure that a new condition might not turn up* (one that in principle could not have been taken into account previously), that will jeopardise our D-N construction. Again, to put this in other words, one can never exclude whether a further relevant subdivision of a reference class might be necessary on the basis of additional knowledge. An important consequence is that this safeguards against a deterministic world-view, as it is not possible to spell out the necessary *and* sufficient causes to explain a particular event. Indeed, it is not possible to predict precise outcomes with absolute certainty. This in turn implies that prediction cannot be a solid criterion to test a scientific theory nor verify thus its truth—to say this is however different from saying that prediction is irrelevant in this context. I will return to this issue later, but there is also a further, even more worrying problem.

*The inferential conception suffers from the fact that it seriously misconstrues the nature of subsumption under laws.*

If determinism were true then, according to Hempel, every future event would be amenable to D-N explanation. However, the explanation of past events confronts us with a problem: as explanations are essentially inferences they demand an asymmetry, which is simply not present in inferences. Explanation requires a sufficient condition that is based on empirical evidence that something actually happened. Inference on the other hand refers to something in the future. To infer something that lies in the future not only presupposes determinism, but also relies on the fact that everything has been taken into account—a matter one can never logically be sure of. Indeed, inference (whether inductive or deductive) demands that all relevant evidence is mentioned in the premises. This requirement is automatically satisfied for deductive inferences. Explanation seems to demand further that only considerations relevant to the *explanandum* be contained in the *explanans*. As indicated, the *temporal asymmetry* reflected by inferences is precisely the opposite of that exhibited in explanation. Inference and explanation have opposing temporal direction. And when we relinquish the assumption of determinism the asymmetry becomes even more striking. Doubts about the fact that explanations are essentially arguments may follow from the impossibility of prediction as a consequence of the lack of all the facts and/or asymmetry of inferences—though this does not mean that we must give up the covering law conception, since subsumption under laws can take a different form.

Examples from the atomic and sub-atomic world show us that there is a limit to the joint precision with which two so-called complementary parameters can be known: there is an inescapable uncertainty if one attempts to ascertain the values of both the position and momentum of a particle, and similarly for energy and time. Ascertaining the position of an electron with great precision makes us unable to ascertain its momentum very exactly, and vice versa.[6] To offer an explanation here is something different: it comes down to the assembling of a total set of relevant conditions for the event to be explained, and the citing of the probability of that event in the presence of these conditions. The explanation is in this case not an argument (a logical structure with premises and conclusions governed by some rule of acceptance), but rather *a presentation of the conditions relevant to the occurrence of the event, and a statement of the degree of probability of the event given these conditions.* Evidently, a persistent statistical correlation—a genuine statistical-relevance relation—is strongly indicative of a causal relation of some sort, but one should not confuse statistical correlation with genuine causation. This would be to conflate symptoms with causes.

When two types of events, *A* and *B*, are positively related to each other, we hunt for a common cause *C* that is statistically relevant. The statistical-relevance relations must be explained in terms of two causal processes in which *C* is causally relevant to *A* and *C* is causally relevant to *B*. This is the heart of the matter where it is claimed that a statistical explanation is based on causality. Now the question is, why should we prefer for explanatory purposes the relevance of *C* to *A* and *C* to *B* over the relevance of *A* to *B* which we had in the first place? The answer is that we can trace a spatio-temporally continuous causal connection from *C* to *A* and from *C* to *B* (while the relation between *A* and *B* cannot be accounted for by any such direct continuous causal relation). Recall that causal explanations present us, according to Hume, with a problem. Nevertheless, his criticism needs to be qualified. Indeed, it seems that Hume overlooked an important aspect of causality, i.e. that causal processes are capable of transmitting information.[7] A proper understanding of this will make it possible to distinguish between causal processes and pseudo-processes. This distinction emerged from Einstein's special theory of relativity which claims that no signal (no process capable of transmitting information) can travel faster than light. The so-called 'at-at' theory of causal transmission is an attempt to remedy Hume's criticism. The basic thesis about mark transmission can be stated as follows: 'A mark that has been introduced into a process by means of a single intervention at point A is transmitted to point B if and only if it occurs at B and at all stages of the process between A and B without additional interventions' (Salmon, 1998, p. 197).

Thus, Zeno's paradox can be solved as follows: to move from $A$ to $B$ is simply to occupy the intervening points at the intervening moments. It consists in being at particular points at the corresponding instants. There is no question as to how the arrow gets from point $A$ to point $B$. (There is no zipping through the intermediate points at high speed.) The arrow is at the points between them at the corresponding moment. And there can be no question about how the arrow gets from one point to the next, for in a continuum there is no next point. 'Mark transmission' is the proposed foundation for the concept of propagation of influence. The ability to transmit a mark is the criterion of a causal process; pseudo-processes may also exhibit persistent structure, but this structure is transmitted not by means of the process itself but by some other agency. The basis is thus *the ability of the causal process to transmit a modification in its structure resulting from an interaction (a mark)* without appealing to any of Hume's secret powers.[8] Whether the result of the interaction will be transmitted is a question that can in principle readily be settled by experiment (thus one will investigate whether the resulting modifications in the process are preserved at other stages of the process). The patterns in which we fit events and facts that structure the world we wish to explain are statistical and causal relations. Causal processes play an important role for they are mechanisms that propagate structure and transmit causal influence. This together with the 'at-at' theory answers Hume's question about the nature of the connections between causes and effects. One can therefore conclude that causal processes exist *besides* probabilistic or statistical causality. In indeterministic settings it appears that necessary causes have at least some degree of explanatory force, but sufficient causes do not. According to the causal conception, we explain facts (general or particular) by exhibiting the physical processes and interactions that bring them about, but such mechanisms need not be deterministic to have explanatory force: they may be irreducibly statistical. Thus general laws and antecedent conditions do not rigidly determine a scientific explanation of a particular event.

To this different picture of causal processes and statistical explanation, finally another kind of explanation has to be added: *functional explanation*. An illustration of this is the following example from biology. Jackrabbits that inhabit hot regions in the southwestern part of the USA have extraordinarily large ears. These constitute an effective cooling mechanism. There are of course many devices that can fulfil this function. It can be shown therefore deductively (or at least with a high inductive probability) that such animals will have some mechanism or other that enables them to adapt to the extreme temperatures, but it does not follow that the jackrabbit must have developed large radiating ears (nor that it is probable that it would do so). Explaining this particular cooling device (as opposed to explaining why it has some mechanism or other that fulfils this function) demands therefore a different kind of explanation. That explanation is labelled 'functional'.

In the study of social institutions by sociologists, anthropologists and other social scientists, many of these kind of explanations may be found. Again, it might be claimed that functional explanations are always illegitimate, or at best incomplete. But it is not clear why they should be ruled out on logical grounds. They offer a particular *kind* of explanation that the received view of scientific explanation (deductive certainty or high inductive probability) cannot account for, without necessarily invoking teleological and anthropomorphical elements—criticisms that are usually brought against this position. In this approach, difficulties with Hempel's model (where there is always a demand for a sufficient condition) are overcome: the functional explanation provides a necessary condition. The epistemic value of such an explanation is measured by the gain in information provided by the probability distribution over the partition. Similarly, in the statistical-relevance model it is the amount of relevant information that counts; it consists of a probability distribution over a (maximum) homogeneous partition of an initial reference class. Thus a unified style of explanation (using basic comprehensive principles) can be accommodated with explanations of a mechanical kind (how things work). Both of them may be compatible for a particular problem. Because of their insistence on what is intelligible these kinds of explanation resemble understanding and description as used in the human sciences.

We have addressed only some of the seductive illusions and idle talk concerning scientific explanation of natural phenomena. But what follows from all this for our ruminations on paradigmatic claims to *superior* scientific explanation? Putting the question this way can bring to the foreground the 'normativity' of the debate. Clearly the paradigm of determinism of the material world has been shattered. For some, to explain an event is simply to identify its cause. Humean doubts about this possibility in terms of something more than contiguity, priority in time and constant conjunction were eased on the one hand by the so called 'at-at' theory, and on the other by differentiating pseudo-processes from genuine causal processes in terms of the ability to transmit a mark. Contrary to Hume it was argued that there is *real causality* in the world of natural phenomena. But the *fundamental indeterminacy of nature* requires that different kinds of explanation be used for different domains. There are several examples in which there is a necessary but not sufficient cause that invariably produces the event to be explained. Elsewhere there is a sufficient cause but no necessary cause without which the event to be explained could not occur. This was made clear by referring to the fact that inference and explanation both have a *preferred temporal direction* on the one hand and that in many cases we do not have enough facts to be able to construct an explanation. There is room for statistical and functional explanation without thus rendering scientific explanation impossible or unintelligible. The general conclusion must be that if indeterminism is a feature of the atomic and sub-atomic world (causal indeterminacy—the truth or falsity of (in)determinism is a matter of physical fact), and if it cannot be ruled out on logical or metaphysical grounds, there is no reason to use determinism as the paradigm *par excellence* (or the only paradigm) for other domains of understanding. Moreover, our everyday concept of human action implies freedom and the need for us to accept responsibility for what we do in normal circumstances.[9]

## IMPLICATIONS FOR THE HUMAN WORLD AND FOR EDUCATIONAL RESEARCH: ETHICS AND PARTICULARITY

What follows from this account of scientific explanation for the world we live in, give meaning to and investigate as educational researchers? Given that we cannot predict the future even in the presence of our best causal investigations does the mode of explanation really matter? Must indeterminism lead to indifference? Or is the conclusion that, though we may not live in a deterministic universe, the best we can aim for is the identification of necessary or sufficient conditions, for causal processes and statistical regularity?

In some sense the answer to the latter question must of course be positive, at least in as far as our investigations concern the question how things work—whether we are concerned with metals or with the functioning of our brains. Moreover, it is imperative that we consider the uses to which such research can be put in order to achieve particular policies or programmes. Given that precise outcomes cannot be predicted with absolute certainty, what we do will always invoke some kind of *practical reasoning*. To decide what to do in this or that particular situation based upon scientific knowledge alone is not enough. This holds not only for the indeterminacy felt by professional practitioners and policy makers who wish to formulate sound practice. It must be accepted more fundamentally by researchers: science alone cannot provide exclusively what is needed. Guidance for professionals in policy or practice requires scientists to enter the domain of practical wisdom. Of course, one must take as much relevant information into account as is available. But all kinds of ethical issues might be involved: such as those to do with the right to interfere, the 'cost' (financially, time-wise, in terms of effort) of the research, of possible interventions. One has to decide which issues to study, which aspects to consider as relevant, whether one will focus on local problems and thus perhaps jeopardise opportunities to publish in highly-regarded international journals, whether one follows fashion or instead explores new paths, whether one dares to confront given truths and question what is held as self-evident.

Moreover, human behaviour can be described in different ways: one may focus on its mechanistic side or on its intentional aspect, and these need not necessarily be seen as rivals. Though much more about this can surely be said, it may suffice to refer here to the fact that a particular mechanism (on the basis of which we are able to act) may not only be a necessary condition for particular actions, but will also characterise human activities more generally. It is only because we can get hungry or thirsty that it makes sense to invite someone for a meal or a drink. And because what people *generally* do in particular circumstances is not irrelevant either, quantitative research surely has its point. That this does not answer the question *why* people do what they do in terms of reasons, goes without saying—as that is a different question. How else other than by asking someone can we know what her reason for doing something is?[10] Understanding what something is, or rather 'what it is like' (which is typical of causal explanations) should not be confused with understanding what something is in the sense of 'what it means' or 'what it signifies' (typical for a teleological explanation). It is, as Von Wright (1971) argues, the intentional or non-intentional character of their objects that marks the difference between two types of understanding and of explanation. Indeed, people appreciate a particular situation from a teleological background in which norms and rules play a part—a functional kind of explanation may be able to spell this out. If we look at a case of punishment in an educational context it is crucial to appreciate what a particular punishment *means* for an individual, notwithstanding the particular *effect* it might or might not have, which is another way of looking at it, i.e. from a stimulus–response approach. The teacher has to make clear that certain behaviours are not appropriate in this or that context, which may refer among other things to customs or habits which might have been different. Though pupils may ignore the teacher (they could neglect what he says), they might also start thinking about his 'message' by themselves and with others. It is expected they will show in their behaviour 'some change' and again this will have to be appreciated within what is seen as 'normal'.

More must be said, however, than that on the one hand some kind of practical reasoning is always involved and on the other that there are mechanisms which tell us how things work and which characterise fundamentally the kind of beings we are. The intentional aspect too has its demands. Human action cannot fully be understood unless some kind of teleology, some kind of 'intentionality', is also taken into account. There is more to human action than statistical regularities. Many things people do cannot be correctly characterised under the heading 'well, these things just happened as they did', as if these outcomes bore only the mark of mutations or of atomic and subatomic structures. Elsewhere, I have dealt with what 'intention' may come down to in educational contexts (cf. Smeyers, 1998b).

Let me rehearse some basic Wittgensteinian ideas that illuminate the matter at hand. One speaks of intentions when one deals with descriptions of purposes or ends, of what one plans, and also when one indicates those things that are regarded as desirable by an agent. They can be found in the conscious thinking of agents as the result of ponderings, choices, felt obligations, roles in institutions or groups, emotions, moods and in character traits. An intention is embedded in the situation from which it arises. Intending is therefore not what some would call a private sensation or feeling, a mental act or activity one is engaged in. Neither is it merely a thought or an experience, nor a disposition nor mere accompaniment of action. Rather, to say that an action is intentional, is to characterise it as the exercise of a voluntary power, something done for reasons or out of inclination, and for which the agent can typically be held responsible. An action may be thought of as intentional even when it is apparently not done for a reason or 'not for a particular reason', as when one just feels like doing what one is doing (for a development of this cf. Winch, 1958). Nevertheless, of course, we typically have reasons for our intentional actions.

Some philosophers, however, have taken this concept to the extreme and have offered a radical interpretation of these points and a radical picture of human rationality. I want to focus on the problems we are led into if we do not resist the temptation to follow this particular way of focusing on the intentional aspect of human behaviour. In doing so, I will make clear how this, analogous to the discussion of causality offered above, may generate a distorted picture of human agency whose nature is at the core of most educational research. Jon Elster's methodological individualism and his rational choice theory (1989, 1999) is a typical example of this conceptualisation. His point of departure is that the elementary unit of social life is individual human action. Individuals are in a basic sense unitary, homogeneous entities, with one (real) will (and set of preferences) and one single consistent set of purposes, not characterised by contradictions or inner conflicts and tensions. It is in virtue of this unity and consistency that an individual may be said to act. The 'real' person who is capable of action (the 'intentional person'), is seen as the one who confronts causal forces within himself (the autonomous individual). Given this, there will typically be for individuals in any situation one and only one action that is best. If the individual does not choose this best action, we are obliged to say that she does something that she does not really want to do. And this in turn would seem to necessitate that the individual does not really choose but is moved by causal forces that appear to work from outside this real, monolithic consistency. It does not matter to what extent the real, monolithic, consistent apparatus may be placed inside the ordinary empirical person. For logical reasons, this account of human action is according to Elster superior.

The idea, however, that there is a single set of wishes, interests, and needs seems untenable. It appears problematic, as Sandven (1995) argues, to give any reasonable meaning to the idea that a person who likes cream cake and wants cream cake does not act intentionally if she takes a piece of cream cake, no matter how ambivalent she may be toward doing it (even if she may have thought that all things considered it would have been best if she had refrained from doing it). Though there certainly may be limiting cases, generally it is not plausible to claim that agents do not have freedom to do otherwise if they act in ways that do not correspond to what they think would be the best thing to do. A different picture in which wishes, desires, values and other motivations are connected in complex (often incompatible or even contradictory ways) seems nearer to the truth. A considerable set of our actions will in various ways be embedded in habits, routines and practices, which themselves may have complex, manifold determinations in which, among other things, social norms play an important role. This inherent complexity in the motivation of human action is incompatible with the idea that human action consists of maximising on the basis of a unique, consistent, complete preference structure in which all possible alternative courses of action open to the individual are ranked in one single, consistent order. Again, it is important to recall that for Elster, though empirically things may look different, logically they must be of a certain kind.

For Elster causality in the determination of human action and social processes is mainly restricted to two areas: preferences and other mental states, such as beliefs, emotions etc. on the one hand and the explanation of the consequences of individual actions on the other. In between is the action itself whose intentionality is to be understood on the basis of underlying beliefs and desires. He explicitly excludes reference to functional explanation. Nevertheless, it is clear by now that intentional and causal explanation cannot fully do justice to human action. There is of course a proper place for intentionality in human action and explanation. But human behaviour is neither causally determined nor exclusively intentional, if the latter merely means the characterising of agents with a consistent and optimising preference structure.

What follows from this for educational research and for the theory of education? Well, first, note the parallel that can be drawn between the development of philosophy of education and its counterpart, i.e. educational research. On the one hand philosophy of education is getting more and more empirical. It has rejected a timeless conception of rationality and has embraced a picture of rationality as embedded in particular historical periods, i.e. in particular discourses. The shift in many branches of applied philosophy or philosophy of given cultural practices bears witness to this. On the other hand, empirical educational research has become more and more 'philosophical': there is less and less a strict distinction between the a priori and the a posteriori and between what 'is the case' (facts) and what 'ought to be the case' (values). Thus concepts are as much discussed as factual statements about data; as previously mentioned this is exemplified in the growing number of qualitative studies and their insistence for instance on the relevance of narrative inquiry. As in philosophy, where these distinctions are no longer used to differentiate between different schools or methods or movements, so in empirical research the idea that the different aspects of a particular case have to be considered at the same time and in relation to each other has gained influence. This *rapprochement* between philosophical and empirical research sets a different task for the future.

Educational theory can I think confidently rely on four kinds of educational research: philosophical, interpretive (which includes historical and qualitative research), quantitative (statistical) and causal. At the one extreme one may find common ground with literature (fiction), and at the other with bio-chemical research. These different kinds of investigations make it possible to do justice to the full array of educational questions and the various functions research has to fulfil. As will be clear from what has been outlined, none of them can justifiably claim superiority over the other. Educational research will naturally reflect—as philosophy in general does—the spirit of its time. That means it nowadays may focus on the one hand on *phronēsis* (or *praxis* dealing among other things with 'ends') and on the other with means-end reasoning (taking into account the demands of performativity). This implies that 'skills' and 'outcomes' are as much part of education as the consideration of ultimate ends and 'what is worthwhile' that philosophers of education have traditionally focused on. Neither philosophers nor non-philosophical educational researchers can ignore this spectrum with impunity. They may therefore want to expose the hidden social mechanisms and manipulations that presupposes the gathering of relevant data and to study the influence of the constraints in which we live and operate. They may want to point to the dangers of manipulative forces in the context of education or investigate what is culturally worthwhile to cherish and pass on. Neither is it astonishing that philosophers go in for a certain amount of descriptive writing. For philosophical and empirical research alike a proper focus is on *what* is to be described, how this should be done, the *kind of things* one wants to draw attention to in this description, and finally on the *way* in which the description is offered.

None of this implies that quantitative research, whether statistical or causal, has no point whatsoever. What is clear though is that causal mechanisms neither threaten human freedom nor generally take away our responsibility. Complete determinism thus reveals itself as just another version of the transparency claimed by the project of modernity on societal, intersubjective or personal levels. In this sense what is presented here takes Pring's analysis a step further: the methodological tolerance that has been argued for does not focus exclusively at the level of cultural groups but applies also to the individual, not only to the general but also to particular cases. Therefore, practical reasoning has been highlighted together with the possibility of idiosyncratic choice (which rules out the necessity of the conclusion of an exclusive deductive application of a general law for a particular case). Within the scope of this paper it is regrettably not possible to develop these ideas further.

The result of our investigation is not spectacular: we are familiar with the idea that conceptual inquiries as well as empirical ones are both constitutive of understanding. Causality of course exists. Regularities in human action can be informative. The kinds of research that spring from these notions explain what people do; that agents usually have particular intentions when they do what they do; that sometimes they act out of habit or are just irrational; and even that people may remain a mystery for others and for themselves. None of this should surprise educational researchers. And all of it explains human behaviour. What follows of course is that educational researchers should take all of this into account, and should not turn their head and pretend they do not see the full spectrum of explanations.

The analysis of the proper place of causality in an indeterministic universe has made it clear that there are areas where it makes sense to look for it. Statistical regularities however do also inform us of 'how things are'. This parallels Wittgenstein's insistence on the relevance of 'following a rule' to understand what people say and do. Both point to the insufficiency of a strict rational model, either concerning the application of deductive rules to predict outcomes concerning natural phenomena, or to understand why it is that people do what they do.

The human mind does not seem to function as a calculus, either in its physiological or in its meaning-giving aspect. Certain social scientists have opted for a rationalistic and deterministic model to understand society and individuals. They have taken a wrong-headed picture of nature for their pre-eminent example. Nature has taught us a lesson: to give up this idle talk, to search again for 'friction' (cf. Wittgenstein, 1953, § 107), to abandon the metaphysical castle of air, and to take instead into account the multiplicity of reality and the various kinds of explanations we need to understand its complexity. This is the ultimate reason why responsibility is at the heart of research. It is why, in whatever we do or say, and in our research into what others do and say, deeply held commitments are at stake. Thus the ethical presses itself upon us in a way that is not limited to the domain of the strictly moral, but rather embraces normativity more widely. 'Good' educational research, be it empirical or conceptual, should reflect these insights in its search for an educational theory that speaks of education to its practitioners and is therefore necessarily occupied with values and the nature of 'the good life'.

Things are as they are; we have come to bedrock. Adopting a conception of educational research that springs from the nature of agency and action also puts us in a position where we can stop asking the wrong questions, where we are capable of overcoming a particular philosophical problem, of stopping doing philosophy. And so it should be: philosophy leaves everything as it is, but it is its student who might be changed. It should be no different in educational contexts.[11]

*Correspondence*: Prof Paul Smeyers, Centre for Philosophy of Education, KU Leuven, Tiensestraat 102, 3000 Leuven, Belgium. Email: paul.smeyers@psy.kuleuven.ac.be

## NOTES

1. For example, the *Journal for Qualitative Studies in Education* and *Educational Action Research*.
2. As recent discussions at AERA meetings illustrate; cf. also Denzin and Lincoln, 1994; Pring, 2000.
3. For a more detailed discussion of this, cf. Smeyers, 1998a.
4. As I have argued elsewhere, see for instance Smeyers, 1998a.
5. I propose to use this older label as an overall term to refer to educational sciences as well as to philosophy of education. Of course, in doing this I do not want to revive the older connotations (for instance, that the relation between 'theory' and 'practice' is one of application of theoretical insights). I think however that the distinction between philosophical (for instance conceptual) research and empirical (say quantitative research) is artificial and not fruitful. As both the conceptual and the empirical are part of any situation, a discipline which focuses on educational situations and their problems, and which

is in this sense a theoretical enterprise resulting in some sort of 'theory', should take both into account.

6. More precisely: when a photon strikes an electron, the direction in which the electron will go is not determined. There is a probability distribution over all possible directions. Furthermore, in this collision the amount by which the frequency of the photon will change is not determined. A probability distribution over all possible amounts exists. Because of the conservation of energy and of momentum, there is a perfect correlation between the direction of the electron and the change in frequency of the photon. The pair of values is however not determined. Incidentally, it is important in this context also to refer to problems with our instruments of measurement as well. The click that results from a genuine photon detection is utterly indistinguishable from the click that results from a spurious count. And finally, there is of course the presumption that conditions surrounding this particular occurrence can be specified in enough detail to establish the existence of a unique necessary and sufficient cause. (This example is discussed in Salmon, 1998.)

7. The development as before is mainly based on the position of Salmon (cf. Salmon, 1998).

8. The following example may illustrate this. Consider a rotating spotlight, mounted in the centre of a circular room, that casts a spot of light on the wall. A light ray travelling *from* the spotlight *to* the wall is a causal process: the spot of light moving around the walls constitutes a pseudo-process. The former process occurs at the speed of light; the latter 'process' can go on at arbitrarily high velocities, depending on the size of the room and the rate of rotation of the light source. The speed of light places no restrictions on the velocity of the pseudo-process. The fact that the beam of light travelling from the light source to the wall is a causal process can be revealed by a simple experiment. If a red filter is interposed in the beam near its source, the colour of the spot of the wall will be red. This 'mark' is transmitted along the beam. It is obvious how the transmission of such marks could be employed to send a message:

> Red if by land and blue if by sea.
> And I on the opposite shore will be
> Ready to ride and spread the alarm
> To every Middlesex village and farm.

It is equally evident, I believe, that no information can be sent via the moving spot on the wall. If you are standing near the wall at one side of the room, and someone else is stationed at a diametrically opposite point, there is nothing you can do to the passing spot of light that will convey any information—e.g., 'The British are coming!'—to the other person. Interposing a red filter may make the spot red in your vicinity, but the 'mark' will not be retained as the spot moves on (Salmon, 1998, pp. 194–195).

9. The concept of 'paradigm' is used here in a non-technical, general sense. One could also speak of the dominant belief in a certain world-view or *Weltanschauung* which sets the limits (or determines the framework) for paradigmatic approaches within a particular discipline.

10. Incidentally, this is a logical observation, and it has *nothing* to do with the matter whether it is possible for someone to give a genuine reason for what she is doing. 'Nothing' is not an overstatement, as in the limit case, where it is claimed that people can under no circumstances give reasons for what they are doing, the question itself does not make sense anymore (as there are no circumstances which may fulfil the requirements set for the answer).

11. For suggestions on a previous version of this paper and for his help with the correct English wording, I am very grateful to Mike McNamee.

## REFERENCES

Blake, N., Smeyers, P., Smith, R. and Standish, P. (2000) *Education in an Age of Nihilism* (London, Falmer Press).

Denzin, N. K. and Lincoln, Y. S. (eds) (1994) *Handbook of Qualitative Research* (Thousand Oaks, CA, Sage).

Elster, J. (1989) *Nuts and Bolts for the Social Sciences* (Cambridge, Cambridge University Press).

Elster, J. (1999) *Alchemies of the Mind. Rationality and the Emotions* (Cambridge, Cambridge University Press).

Hempel, C. (1965) *Aspects of Scientific Explanation* (New York, Free Press).

Polkinghorne, D. (1995) Narrative Configuration In Qualitative Analysis, *International Journal of Qualitative Studies in Education*, 8, pp. 5–23.

Pring, R. (2000) The 'false dualism' of educational research, *Journal of Philosophy of Education*, 34, pp. 247–260.

Salmon, W. C. (1998) *Causality and Explanation* (New York, Oxford University Press).

Sandven, T. (1995) Intentional action and pure causality: a critical discussion of some central conceptual distinctions in the work of J. Elster, *Philosophy of the Social Sciences*, 25, pp. 286–317.

Smeyers, P. (1998a) Assembling reminders for educational research. Wittgenstein on philosophy, *Educational Theory*, 48, pp. 287–308.

Smeyers, P. (1998b) Child-rearing and parental 'intentions' in postmodernity, *Educational Philosophy and Theory*, 30, pp. 193–214.

Tooley, J. (1998) *Educational Research. An Ofsted critique* (London, OFSTED).

Von Wright, G. H. (1971) *Explanation and Understanding* (London, Routledge & Kegan Paul).

Winch, P. (1958) *The Idea of a Social Science* (London, Routledge & Kegan Paul).

Wittgenstein, L. (1953) *Philosophical Investigations*, transl. G. E. M. Anscombe (Oxford, Blackwell).

Wittgenstein, L. (1979) Remarks on Frazer's Golden Bough, in: C. Luckhardt (ed.), *Wittgenstein: Sources and Perspectives* (pp. 61–81), (Hassocks, Sussex, The Harvester Press).

# 12

# Data Return: The Sense of the Given in Educational Research

## PAUL STANDISH

*Educational research is dominated by a particular model: data is gathered and analysed. Much literature on methods concerns either ways of processing data, or ethical issues regarding its collection and handling. The present paper looks beyond these matters to the taken-for-granted idea of data itself. What can be meant by 'data'? How does this connect with ideas of the given? What is the place of giving in education—in teaching and learning, in research itself? These issues are explored in the light of information technology's impact on research, uncovering ethical dimensions that the seeming naturalness of data otherwise obscures.*

'It is in the very act of *taking* that he speaks of the *given*.'
Wilfred Sellars

Research in education is dominated by a particular model: data is gathered and analysed. Of course, there is no data without research design, no data without conceptualisation, but it is this amassing of data that needs to be considered here. There is no shortage of literature on research methodology, especially concerning ways of processing and analysing data. There is also a growing body of work that addresses ethical issues to do with the way data is collected, stored and handled, to which the present collection is in part a contribution. But there is a background problem that the very assiduousness of these endeavours can mask. This concerns the ways in which the ethical has been reconceived in the modern world. The ethical comes in, as it were, at points of conflict—where there is a question over confidentiality, where there are competing interests, where a research finding is sensitive in some way... The ethical is

211

confined to what is sometimes (equally restrictively) called 'social morality'. What is left out is that broader conception in which it is recognised that values permeate our lives and that the ethical is in some sense prior. For, in this light, the ethical is there at the start in our actions and projects, and hence inevitably there at the start in research in education. It is there not only in the manner in which it is conducted, but in its aims and orientation. Education is itself an intrinsically ethical engagement, and research in education is implicated in that engagement.

To attribute this marginalisation or compartmentalisation of the ethical to the instrumentalism that characterises so much of the modern world scarcely does justice to the problem: a whole metaphysical picture is in question here, one in which we are, it is imagined, individual subjects confronted with a world of 'medium-sized objects' upon which we confer meaning, in which we understand ourselves in more or less naturalistic terms—as beings with needs and desires the satisfaction of which is, other things being equal, to be understood as our good.[1]

The present chapter considers the taken-for-granted idea of data, this apparently innocuous aspect of educational research, as it emerges within that broader metaphysics. What can be meant by 'data'? Data are what is given. But what is it to take something as given? From where does this given, or this gift, come? The question of the nature of data seems especially important in the light of the rise of information technology with its accumulating databanks, and with the audits and planning that they make possible. There are ethical dimensions to these matters that the seeming naturalness of data—its apparent givenness, one might say—is apt otherwise to obscure.

## WHAT WORKS

To bring the problem better into view let me begin by presenting a series of vignettes, with a brief critical comment on each to indicate the kinds of concerns that they raise.

### 'Framing the question'

A research student is engaged in a study of learning styles in under-graduates. Having read around the topic, she identifies the research question, works out her methodology and embarks on the literature review. In writing this up she details the findings of the different studies she reads—in fact, the different books and articles she reads. The data she eventually gathers will be matched against these findings. *The concern here is with the way that her uncritical commitment to a clear and explicit methodology determines in advance the way she is able to understand things. The characteristics of her methodology shape the framing of the question she asks and the terms of her analysis; but more significantly they also provide parameters for the way she reads literature in the field. Some of the literature consulted may not be empirical in kind. There is then a further problem where such writings are read as if they delivered 'findings'. It is the nature of this reading that is very much at the heart of the problem. It will be absurd to record Aristotle's or Derrida's 'findings', and if she does not see this she will scarcely have "read" that literature at all. Students schooled in what has become orthodox educational research methodology may find it difficult to read in any other way, and hence innumerable paths of thought will be closed off to them. What is taken as given determines the data the research student collects and her manner of interpretation.*

### 'Boxes of data'

An eminent research professor runs a team of assistants engaged in funded research. Projects are completed on time and results disseminated effectively, with maximal transparency to end-users. 'I don't know why people in this department don't do any research,' she is heard to say. 'There are boxes and boxes of data in the store-room just waiting to be taken away and analysed.' *The problem here is that the evidence that has been gathered is conceived as in some way inert, as raw material to be processed by the right research methods. And worse, the busyness and efficiency of the research centre in collecting and analysing the data is taken to be clear evidence of a vibrant research culture and to provide a paradigm for what research in education should be.*

### 'The examiner's dismay'

A research thesis of a discursive kind is examined by someone who is a recognised expert in the field but with a background predominantly in empirical work. The examiner finds that the work fails to observe the established procedures and strictures of research (as she sees it). She looks near the beginning of the thesis for a section entitled 'Methodology' that explains how the research was carried out and written up, but she finds none. When she eventually identifies the point in the text where the research question is expressed, it strikes her as vague and speculative, and oddly detached from the practical exigencies of education. Perhaps the approach seems complex and interesting, perhaps to have no point at all. Or perhaps, more likely, she finds it indisciplined and lax, and rejects it as lacking rigour. *The problem is that the research "was" the writing (and there was no 'writing up'—that is, no empirical investigation "first", subsequently to be written up), and the literature review was not so much a preamble to study as an on-going engagement, part of the conversation of the writing itself. There was no clear separation of ends and means. Of course, the candidate's supervisor may well be at fault here in having failed to find an appropriate examiner. But this should remind us of the extent to which the term 'educational research' can cover over the diversity of ways in which educational practice can fruitfully be studied, how it can cause us to forget the extent to which Education is not a single discipline or even a unified field.*

### 'Research methods for all'

The 1997 Dearing Report (a major report into higher education in the UK), following what has become standard policy and practice, emphasised the importance of training in research methods for all research students. There is a new emphasis on the completion of research degrees without delay. *There are three dangers here. First, there may be the presumption that there are general research methods, context-free skills, that apply across disciplines. The effect of this may be that difference is covered over and the distinctive challenge of the subject matter of a research topic fails to come into view. Second, training in educational research methods tends to be based on the assumption that these methods are social scientific, and these are understood along predominantly empiricist lines. Third, the assumption is made that a successful research institution will provide 'railway tracks' to enable its students to complete efficiently and without delay. But it is often research that comes with difficulty and with time that achieves greater depth. Failure to allow for this may drive standards down.*

### 'The latest research findings'

A friend of a friend tells me of a busy headteacher who had enrolled for a taught doctorate in Education. The headteacher had heard no doubt that policy makers expect research to provide answers to the questions that they pose. It would then simply be a question of applying that research. At the opening meeting of the course he said, with bullet-pointed emphasis: 'What I want is the latest research: bang, bang, bang.' *But why, for a start, should the latest be the best, as if time inevitably devalued and truth reached its expiry date? Why should the latest necessarily be appropriate to our concerns? Perhaps what is more distant is precisely what we most need, to gain perspective on our problems and to resist their parochial preoccupations. The general problem here, however, is that whatever can count as research remains within the circle of what is known already. The questions determine too much the kind of thing that can be found out. For all that this may be 'the latest' research, such questions restrict the possibility of our being confronted with something new, with being provoked to think in new ways.*[2]

### 'Technological and proud'

I quote David Reynolds: 'School effectiveness is about—indeed, celebrates and is proud of—a "technological" orientation to education, and is simply concerned to deliver "more" education to more children' (Reynolds, 1997b). Data-rich environments help us to develop highly controlled organisations with fail-safe operating procedures. Just as computers can provide the data-rich environment upon which efficient operating systems in schools depend, so too we should devote more research to the development of a science of teaching. Indeed school improvement 'eschews the values debate about goals that has been seen as an important part of educational enquiry by those who have obtained status and held power within the educational research establishment of the last twenty years' (ibid., p. 99). Teachers in Taiwan, in contrast, are 'proud to be applied technologists, not philosophers' (Reynolds, 1997a, p. 21). Reynolds sees the problem as a peculiarly British one, linked to the preoccupation with 'ends' and not 'means', in a culture that gives more status to the pure than the applied, to the educational philosopher than to the educational engineer (1997b, p. 99). *The problem is that the assumption that teaching is a technology, which is of a piece with the growing concern with effectiveness, with 'what works', rules out in advance certain ways of thinking about education. It is instrumentalist before it starts, the ends of the process being taken to be uncontroversial. It sets limits on what research concerning education can be. In the market place of educational research the honest practicality of 'effectiveness' and 'improvement' acquires a mystique, even a fetish value. Reynolds expounds the virtues of technological effectiveness in florid prose, the irony of which perhaps escapes him.*[3]

It is not, I think, just that these examples of research demonstrate certain kinds of confusion or failure. It is that our means for analysing this failure—the ones that I have offered in italics above—themselves founder: either the criticism is acknowledged and 'taken on board', which really lays the way for business-as-usual, or else the philosopher-critic is simply told to go away, and funds and jobs go elsewhere. Is there then a deeper pathology at work? In what follows I do not question or dwell on the cogency of the criticisms expressed above but try to draw out something further from the background to the ways of thinking that they attack, to explore the possibility of breaking out of the circle of research question and data returned in response.

What *are* the givens of educational research? The generality of such a question might well discourage further enquiry, but there are some preliminary responses that can be made. An initial distinction can be drawn between logical and prescriptive givenness. It is logically given that in any research there must be a starting point where some things are taken for granted, taken as understood; this applies to any research, indeed to any statement or question. While in some research, say in mathematics, the given may appear in the form of certain specific propositions, these in turn only mean what they do in the light of the calculus as a whole, and this 'as a whole' could not be made explicit. The given in educational research is incomparably more messy, and any starting point presupposes a wealth of detail about the practice of education, the ethical complexity of which resists easy analysis. The sheer weight of this difficulty can cause us to shy away from the fact of the matter: we fine-tune our research instruments, and the substance of that background fades all the more from view.

The prescriptive givens of educational research are the stuff of everyday life for contract researchers. The political and ethical dimensions here should be self-evident, but these tend to become naturalised as common-sense. (Of course, standards must be raised! Of course, children should learn to read more effectively! Researchers are employed to find out what works.) Here again there is the tendency to cover over the ethical or to reduce it to questions of method. The pressures of short-term contracts and the increasing reliance of university departments on external funding exacerbate the tendency to rush ahead uncritically. Moreover, this whole context of academic day-labouring is coming increasingly to be understood, and supposedly to be legitimated, in the light of the advent of the knowledge economy. While its inevitability and universal reach seems hard to deny, its idiom is increasingly difficult to resist.

## THE KNOWLEDGE ECONOMY

That the world economy is increasingly affected by both the practices and the products of information and communication technology seems clear enough; capital is fickle, future employment uncertain; we are witnessing, we are surely tired of hearing, the beginning of a knowledge explosion. But it is now a familiar enough criticism that the knowledge economy has brought with it a mutation in these very terms. 'Knowledge' has become synonymous with 'information', which itself has become a technical expression. To inform was to pass on the truth about something; in contrast, the data of information technology carry no such commitment. Similarly, there is a reductivism in the notion of economy here. It is construed in quasi-monetary terms: just as money functions as a surrogate for goods in a kind of idealisation of capital, so too knowledge itself—what is to be taught and learned—is reconceived in terms available for circulation and exchange; so too morality is conceived as an economy of give and take.

One feature of the knowledge economy is the surreptitious reinforcement of the tendency to think of the communication of information as the epitome of language, and, disastrously for education, to conceive of information as the substance upon which thinking skills are exercised. Heidegger's famous reversal of the autonomy of man in relation to language ('Language speaks man')[4] makes all the more serious the significance of 'ICT' (information and communication technology): the language that now speaks is in part driven by a technology itself conceived in terms of an exploitative relation to the earth and to what is beyond this planet (Heidegger, 1991, p. 124). In such an exploitative relation, Heidegger claims, there is no harvest that can be received as given. We cannon let things be or allow them simply to come into view. And this, Heidegger says, is symptomatic of our running away from danger. (Does not much research aim at a kind of playing safe, with the emphasis on calculable returns and the reduction of risk?) We need to be goaded to prevent us from subsiding into a way of thinking that 'carries an air of harmlessness and ease, which causes us to pass lightly over what really deserves to be questioned' (Heidegger, 1968, p. 154).

Moroever, the frenetic activity that ICT generates has surely increased the kind of tranquillised acceptance that helps us to pass so lightly over these problems. As Albert Borgmann has pointed out, the databases and spreadsheets of contemporary enterprises and institutions take on the form of a kind of idealisation of the operation—of a new surrogate reality (Borgmann, 1992, p. 68). Beyond all questions of its usefulness, what is most beguiling about that surrogate is the way that it hints at an ideal realm of forms of which the enterprise is but a shadow. The database and the spreadsheet have their own imperatives, which are then extended to the operation of the institution. And this may partly explain what seems to have become a fetishism with *data*: this technical word muffles any deeper sense of what *the given* might mean. The surrogate of the formal system entices us away from the stubborn messiness of everyday life in an ideal extension of the epistemology of 'what works'.

How much this picture depends on a particular unself-conscious orientation to what is given, where data are naturalised! The given returns in the shape of a metaphysical framework that in turn determines what is to come into view. We need to disturb this framework by considering how the question of the given is repressed and how its nature is perverted. We are not without resources for proceeding with this problem, though to a mind too concerned with quick process these may seem otiose or off the point. We need to proceed *indirectly*. Let us allow ourselves to be provoked: by considering our relation to the background in terms of a kind of observance of the given; by imagining the more or less inspirational possibilities (where inspiration involves a kind of receptiveness to something given) of, on the one hand, intensification and, on the other, opening; and by acknowledging the paradoxical nature of the ways of proceeding that we need.

## PROVOCATIONS

Any research presupposes a background incorporating a range of understandings and behaviour that is tacit or taken for granted. What is clear is that the background is not in general a matter of our decision; rather it is that in the light of which our decisions make sense and gain purchase. The background is what we mostly unwittingly conform with; it is what gives the possibility of making sense. Wittgenstein captures the force of this conformity and the sense in which so much is given: 'What has to be accepted, the given, is—so one could say—*forms of life*' (Wittgenstein, 1958, p. 226e). And the reason that this requires something of *us* is that 'Culture itself is an observance. Or at least it presupposes an observance' (Wittgenstein, 1980, p. 83e). It involves attention to, and conformity with, what is done, its development presupposing a large measure of prior acceptance. These remarks defy the desire for a fully understandable beginning to things, for a rational foundation for what we do. Foundationalist modes of thinking, such as positivistic empiricism, fail on this view to recognise the background. We need to appreciate the way circumstances *have us*: the background enables us as human beings *to be*. And with this recognition there may be a different, perhaps more reverential focusing of our contemporary cultural practices (see Dreyfus, 1980, p. 23). As something given in this way, it has the kind of reality to which a religious attitude might be directed. Such an attitude would be a resistance to the nihilism engendered where the objectifying tendencies of modernity eclipse or disperse these practices. That there is a background must be acknowledged, as must its particular (fragile and contingent) forms. In this sense the background is given to us, inexplicit as it must remain. It is that to which we owe our being. What does such an indebtedness require of us?

There is something inspirational about the way that concentration on a problem can become a kind of receptiveness that allows something new to come into view. Habituation becomes virtue, reinforcing patterns of attention, involving feeling, imagination and judgement. As against active pursuit and planning, Simone Weil sees this in terms of a waiting on truth:

> There is a way of giving attention to the data of a problem in geometry without trying to find the solution, or to the words of a Latin or Greek text without trying to arrive at the meaning, a way of waiting, when we are writing, for the right word to come of itself at the end of our pen, when we must reject all inadequate words. (Weil, 1977, p. 73)

In geometry we work with the given, towards truths that are analytic unfoldings of the given. This is not a matter of the application of a test instrument: it is the dawning of truth through patient attention. So too sometimes in the intensity of our writing, we do not choose our words: they come to us. It is passivity of a kind that is required here.

While the intensity in such cases is achieved through a narrowing of focus, a concentration, inspiration can also come where we turn outwards from a problem and make ourselves open to free and passing thoughts.[5] In a rather different context (though with these implications), Kierkegaard gives a young pastor advice on the preparing of sermons:

> When you go for a walk you must let your thoughts flutter randomly, letting them have a go now here, now there. That is how to arrange one's housekeeping. Themata are the accidents that the week should deliver to you in abundance. But the more you see to it that the dividends are uncertain, the freer, better, richer they will become, and the more striking, surprising, penetrating. (Kierkegaard, 1996, p. 454)

The management and focusing of research activity is not insignificant in determining how it is undertaken and towards what it is directed. With its careful evaluation of research proposals and allocation of funds, with its requirements of the careful specification of research in advance of the work being done, it encourages an aggressive searching, a supposed hard-headed realism, as opposed to a patient waiting for things to come into view: it is the latter that enables us to have fresh thoughts and to think in new ways, especially where we are not wholly sure what we are looking for. There is nothing mysterious about the rationale for that 'realism', but the question is what kind of research is thereby ruled out. The language of research methods develops a life of its own.[6]

But this language is always doing more than it seems. The researcher finds herself in the grip of the language of her research methodology, which seems self-authenticating and self-legitimating. The safe move for her is to accept its terms. What is suggested here, in contrast, is that the challenge of her research, the kind of research she might undertake, requires the risk of a different kind of attention. How she should attend, how she should proceed, will need to be indicated in more negative terms. In T. S. Eliot's poem 'Little Gidding' the paradoxical possibility of that more indirect way of proceeding is suggested:

> In order to arrive at what you do not know
>   You must go by a way which is the way of ignorance.
> In order to possess what you do not possess
>   You must go by the way of dispossession.
> In order to arrive at what you are not
>   You must go through the way in which you are not.
>
> (Eliot, 1968, p. 29)

To understand better, it seems, you must hold in abeyance what you already know because there are preconceptions here that will otherwise stand in your way. The skills of enquiry, the methods of approach that you possess, are in some respects like technical instruments with their characteristic tendency to amplify certain aspects of your perception at the expense of others. Fine-tune these skills, develop them further, and you will aggravate this disparity of attention: more will be hidden. And perhaps that larger view that might be available requires you in some degree to give up something of the way you have come to see yourself as a researcher in education, to give up something of what you are.

But is this asking too much? The empiricist can very reasonably retort at this point that there is much important research that needs to be done that manifestly does not require the greater wisdom that is here implied. Up to a point this is surely true. Undoubtedly there is in some cases straightforward information that we need. But the theorisation and practice of educational research rarely stays within such modest bounds. It is that more amplified empiricist conception of research that is here at issue.

These are as yet little more than suggestive remarks; it may be, by the lights of Eliot's words, that they cannot be otherwise. Let us emphasise, however, that one of the central problems with empiricist methodology is its misconception of the nature of language. There are, I think, two ways in which understanding here can be deepened. The idea of the given can be made strange by examining more rigorously—to return to the questions with which we began—what it is to take something as given, and from where the given or the gift comes. But first, the idea of the background can be further pursued, especially as this emerges within logical positivism. In logical positivism, which in some respects looks like an extreme case of the methodology in question, the problem of the given arises in stark form. To examine this let us consider what has become known as the Myth of the Given.

## THE MYTH OF THE GIVEN

'The phrase "the given" as a piece of professional—epistemological—shoptalk carries a substantial theoretical commitment, and one *can deny* there are "data" or that anything is, in this sense, "given" without flying in the face of reason' (Sellars, 1963, 127, emphasis added). With this denial Wilfred Sellars embarks on a general critique of what he calls the Myth of the Given in a way that extends beyond other, more local attacks to address the entire framework of givenness. While the attack on the given takes multiple forms, it is sense-datum theory that is its most common target, and it is the characteristic idiom of that theory that figures prominently in ensuing debate. In some ways, it must be obvious, sense-datum theory is far removed from the theory of educational research, indeed from social science in general, and it would be wrong to make too much of the connection here. What is significant is the symmetry or contiguity between the idiom of sense-datum theory and that of empiricist educational research (and indeed that of evidence-based policy and practice). Of course, not all empirically-based educational research is committed theoretically to empiricism, but this is the dominant strain. Of course, the data that the educational researcher gathers and analyses will be understood to be vastly different in complexity from sense data: in empiricism's own terms there can be no suggestion that such complex data as are considered by the researcher in education are primary and irreducible. But there is an impetus, as we shall see, towards a reification of data in such a way as to naturalise, if not to occlude, the ethical background within which they are embedded. This is in part the allure of foundations and of the belief that 'there is, indeed *must be*, a structure of particular matter of fact' such that each fact can be directly and independently known; it is this that constitutes 'the ultimate known court of appeal for all factual claims—particular and general—about the world' (ibid., p. 164). The idea that empirical facts can be analysed without remainder, writes Sellars, is a radical mistake 'of a piece with the so-called "naturalistic fallacy"' (ibid., p. 131). It is some such mistake, my contention is, that enables educational researchers to talk unselfconsciously about effectiveness and about 'what works'. Ideas of effectiveness or of improvement or of 'what works' are predicated on assumptions contestation of which is ruled out of court on the grounds either that these are so obvious as to be not worth discussing by people of good will[7] or that they are matters of personal point of view.

Sellars expresses concern that the emergence of a field of study known as 'philosophy of science' might hasten a tendency to demarcate the subject in such a way as to discourage broader philosophical thought. Classificatory schemes, as he puts it, have practical consequences: nominal causes have real effects. Once philosophy of science has nominal as well as real existence, there arises 'the temptation to leave it to the specialists, and to confuse the sound idea that philosophy is not science with the mistaken idea that philosophy is independent of science' (ibid., p. 171). So also, it might be held, the professionalisation of empirical educational research has led to the development of its own specialised language and methodology in such a way as to demarcate it from broader enquiry into education. The tenor of current theorisations of the relation of qualititative to quantitative research reveals an understandable uncertainty about the nature of the content of educational research—its object of study—that is not found in the same degree in the physical sciences, and this is a symptom of the larger problem that is here addressed.

The danger of demarcation, Sellars argues, is that any specialised field comes to be understood as if it were operating on an adjacent map, or as a peninsular to the mainland, and hence to be legitimately segregated from other kinds of discourse. By approaching the way in which empirical facts are ordinarily understood and explained with the presupposition of *givenness*, positivistic science (as, especially, in sense-datum theory) is led to a 'resolution' that is superficial and indeed mistaken. There is 'a misunderstanding of the ostensive element in learning, and a reification of the *methodological* distinction between theoretical and non-theoretical discourse into a *substantive* distinction between theoretical and non-theoretical existence' (ibid., p. 174). The mistake is to construe the particulars that the positivist scientist has come to be able to observe—which are then taken to be antecedent objects of knowledge that have somehow been in the framework from the beginning—as *data*. It is 'in the very act of *taking* that the positivist speaks of the *given*' (ibid., p. 195).

While Sellars' account claims to reveal problems not only in sense-datum theory but in the entire framework of givenness, to pursue these matters further it is necessary to look elsewhere. Of course, it may be objected that this is to turn to what is quite simply a different sense of the term, and hence to run the risk of confusion. But this looks too much like a convenient move to side-step a difficulty the nature of which has already been partially uncovered in Sellars' analysis. The idea of the given has come to masquerade as straightforward, and this is something that has serious reverberations in educational research. For there it is often what is given as the starting point of enquiry that needs most to be examined. The ethical presuppositions in such givens are presented in such a way as to foreclose enquiry. It is then through a different kind of approach to the idea of the given that we may be able to examine these implications.

## WHAT GIVES

The enquiry so far has served an important purpose if it has begun to make strange the idea of data. The strangeness is not just in the naturalisation of this Latin term, in its frictionless absorption into everyday speech: it goes to the heart of giving itself, and to see this we need to turn to giving in its everyday sense. For giving has this strange irony: where giving takes place reciprocally, it undoes itself by reverting to the circle of a kind of balanced exchange (and is then giving only in a compromised sense). There *can* be a giving that is free from such remuneration, in the gift without return. But even giving without exchange can find a kind of return in the gratitude of the receiver. A giving that is uncompromised then requires that the receiver be unaware who the giver is, even unaware ideally that a good from which she benefits is the result of a gift. This would be what Zygmunt Bauman identifies as the liminal concept of the 'pure gift': 'Judged by the ordinary standards of ownership and exchange, the pure gift is a pure loss; it is a gain solely in moral terms, the very terms that the logic of gain does not recognise. Its moral value actually rises as the loss deepens' (Bauman, 1990, p. 91). But this supposed purity may still not escape the currency of hubris. The paradox is that, in this best kind of giving, what is given must not be recognised as a gift because recognition returns us to the circle of reciprocity. As Jacques Derrida puts this, the implications of this go beyond giving to cause the institution of morality to tremble: 'The link between morality and the arithmetic, economy, or calculation of pleasures imprints an equivocation on any praise of good intentions. In giving the reasons for giving, in saying the reason of the gift, it signs the end of the gift' (Derrida, 1992, p. 148). It signs therefore the end of ethics; or, to put the matter less provocatively (and in a way that will better serve the argument below), it makes apparent a distinction between ethics understood in terms of mutuality and reciprocity in a balanced and totalisable circulation of goods, and ethics understood in terms of infinite and unconditional responsibility, beyond any circle of exchange and recognition. We can draw a distinction between two kinds of giving, one that finds its place comfortably in a circle of exchange, in a self-stabilising economy, and the other alien to exchange, in an *aneconomy* that preserves the pure gift as a giving without return or recompense or recognition. It is the difference between these structures that needs to be explored.[8]

But before this we should note a further resonance in the idea of giving, which Heidegger connects with being itself.[9] The idiomatic American expression 'what gives' (what's happening?) renders something of, is cognate with, the German *es gibt*. And the flickering mystery of this giving is akin to that of the 'there' in 'there is', in *il y a*. This 'there' that so much exceeds any sense of spatial location, derives from something beyond the indexical; it is not what is pointed at (here . . . there) so much as what makes pointing, indication, demonstration possible. The unconcealing of being is a giving, but it is the giving of a gift where the giver withdraws and hides itself. It is that stage back from what is given, that stage back from presence but to which presence is indebted, that will need to be pursued below.

## GIVEN SENSE

In his 1957 essay 'Philosophy and the Idea of Infinity' Emmanuel Levinas identifies two directions the philosophical spirit can take—directions that, a fortiori, can be seen to run through philosophical and other enquiries into education. In the first, the thinker maintains a relation with a reality distinct from him, with what is, in Jankélévitch's words, 'absolutely other'. It involves a movement that must lead us beyond the nature that surrounds us: it goes towards the stranger and extends towards the divine. This is heteronomy itself. In the second, the thinker freely assents to propositions that are then incorporated in such a way that his nature is preserved: it thereby brings into the same what was other. It moves towards a kind of autonomy in which nothing irreducible would limit thought. Disparate and diverse events are incorporated into a history; this might be seen as 'the conquest of being by man over the course of history' (Levinas, 1998a, p. 48).

In the latter, the other (*l'autre*)[10] encountered as different is understood against an array of different items, in categories of what is known. The other's difference is recorded in terms of predicates to be applied. It is incorporated into a totality and understood within structures of the same. Totality implies an ontology in which there is a circulation or exchange of what is given. Ultimately this is a return to the same. Its characteristic ethics is understood in the terms of circulation and exchange, and it readily supports social moralities of equality and reciprocity in the light of a kind of ideal equilibrium. A life can be lived autonomously and towards an ideal of full self-possession. In principle at least, ideas can be stated clearly and distinctly. The language of totality has a univocity in the sense that there is nothing that cannot in principle be translated into its common terms. The possibility of an encounter with the Other (*l'Autrui*) is denied. Philosophy, on this view, has the itinerary of Ulysses, 'whose adventure in the world was only a return to his native island—a complacency in the Same, and unrecognition of the Other' (Levinas, 1996, p. 48).

In the former, in contrast, it is infinity that undercuts totality's starting point, that takes the very ground of our being vertiginously from under our feet. And infinity begins with ethics, not ontology.[11] It begins in the concrete abstraction of the face: there it is, flesh and blood, but not to be analysed, not reducible to its parts; an enigma primordial to experience and primordial to the world. Unlike the cultural others arranged as it were horizontally in the world, this Other is absolutely foreign, beyond integration; it is the originary disturbance of this world. Never then just something else that I can 'take on board', the Other affects me in the manner of a visitation that overwhelms my tendency to convert it into a content of consciousness. Yet far from being a rarefied aspect of my life, this relation is something I live in the most ordinary experience. It is, Levinas says:

> the fundamental movement, a pure transport, and absolute orientation, sense . . . I find myself facing the Other (*Autrui*). He is neither a cultural signification nor a simple given. He is *sense* primordially, for he gives sense to expression itself, for it is only by him that a phenomenon as a meaning is, of itself, introduced into being. (ibid., p. 52)

My finding myself is not something that contingently happens to me: it is how I come to *be*, through the Other that I find myself to be. My relation to the Other, prior to my being, is a response and responsibility, impetus to this finding. It is my animation, 'pneuma of the psyche, alterity in identity,' where 'becoming "for the other"' constitutes the possibility of giving (Levinas, 1998b, p. 69). Hence it must be at the heart and at the start of education, and of any theorisation of education.

These preliminary remarks raise questions that I want to trace through Levinas' 1964 essay entitled 'Meaning and Sense'. Its guiding thought picks up the idea adumbrated in the indented quotation above: a sense (*sens*) is a way.

While Sellars shows the limitations of empiricist foundationalism, Levinas sees the error extending through the whole of what he calls intellectualism and leading to the phenomenological reduction. He considers the ways in which phenomenology broke through so many barriers of philosophical thought but then ran into its own limitations. Crucial in this was a certain conception of language: 'Intuition, in the straightforwardness of a consciousness that welcomes data, remains the source of all meaning, whether these data be ideas, relations, or sensible qualities. The meanings conveyed by language have to be justified in a reflection on the consciousness that aims at them' (Levinas, 1996, p. 35). Husserl himself returns everything to the given (ibid., p. 36), with data and meaning ascriptions minutely inventoried as though one were dealing with an investment portfolio. We have data and we have consciousness, and it is the latter that confers meaning.[12] The recalcitrant metaphoricity of language, however, threatens to infect this pure authenticity. And so, 'Every metaphor that language makes possible has to be reduced to the data, which language is suspected of abusively going beyond. The figurative meaning has to be justified by the literal meaning supplied in intuition' (ibid., p. 35). The phenomenological reduction is then a reduction of language too.

There is a certain mythification of literal meaning here, extending from empiricism into phenomenology, that subtly shores up an unquestioning relation to the given. It is a mythification as language can never be so pure. Exposure of the metaphor discreetly submerged in 'con*cept*' and *Begriff* unsettles the credibility of the literal: the muscular movements of the hand make of the given something solid—to be picked up and grasped, or to be pointed at. '*These metaphors*', Levinas emphasises, '*are to be taken seriously and literally*' (ibid., p. 152). The greedy hand of the hegemonic ego reaches for the satisfaction promised by truth as adequation, and casts as unintelligible whatever surpasses its measure. In taking *this* as *that* neither the *this* nor the *that* is first given outside of discourse. Thus, our taking what is given can never happen within an exclusively literal language, for there is no such thing. Levinas refers approvingly to Bruno Snell's comment on *The Iliad*, that:

> when . . . the resistance to an attack by an enemy phalanx is compared to the resistance of a rock to the waves that assail, it is not necessarily a matter of extending to the rock, through anthropomorphism, a human behavior, but of interpreting human resistance petromorphically. Resistance is neither a human privilege, nor a rock's, just as radiance does not characterize a day of the month of May more authentically than the face of a woman. The meaning precedes the data and illuminates them. (ibid., p. 37)

Is it language then that gives meaning? If this is true for Heidegger, if this is something more than cultish aphorism, for Levinas this giving is less redolent of the solid grounding of Being: it derives from something that exceeds Being. With the idea of infinity Levinas deepens radically and intensifies the notion of the background. But his account of this must be traced through a further stage. On a Heideggerian view then, the background, theatricalised as the backstage of being, is evident in the way that language comes to be understood not as representational but as revealing in the manner of art: truth, that is, as *aletheia*[13]. Language is not communication, where this is in service of adequation or the satisfaction of needs: it exemplifies rather culture's otherness to our present being. Of Merleau-Ponty and Heidegger in this respect Levinas writes:

> Language qua expression is, above all, the creative language of poetry. Art is then not a blissful wandering of man, who sets out to make something beautiful. Culture and artistic creation are part of the ontological order itself. They are ontological par excellence, they make the understanding of being possible . . . The artistic expression would assemble being into a meaning and thus provide the original light that scientific cognition itself would borrow from. (ibid., p. 41)

But this backstage, so construed, is just another stage on from the phenomenological reduction. The priority that is given to ontology in Western philosophy generally is still there: it is there in Heidegger's central preoccupation with the question of being. Art—language itself—draws the curtains from the props of that backstage; it sets new scenes. But, Levinas seeks to show, the ethical is beyond this, beyond truth as adequation *or* as alethaic. The light that characterises Heidegger's piety towards Being—a piety tainted with nostalgia—contrasts in Levinas with the insomniac darkness of the *il y a*, a night in the alienation and meaninglessness of which responsibility to the Other (person) comes to disturb. This stage back from being, and from being's backstage, is nothing other than ethics itself.

It is through the account of metaphor then that Levinas' resistance to language as alethaic is developed in 'Meaning and Sense'. This goes beyond the appeal to a horizon or the recognition that any word must be 'at the confluence of innumerable semantic rivers' (ibid., p. 37). It is metaphor—understood not as the application of an other image to decorate literal meaning, but as a *carrying away* (the word's literal meaning)—it is metaphor that animates the given. And this carrying away, towards what *is not*, towards something beyond being, points to the fact that language is produced only through the relation to the face, the relation in all its asymmetry: it is the Other that teaches me, in a discourse that cannot be converted into interiority, that cannot figure in totality. My responsibility to the Other is impetus to language. Hence the background from which the given comes is not a stage of being but ethics itself.

Arising from what cannot be known, the given leaves us, as we saw, in debt. This past orientation, absolute in kind, is to a debt never to be settled, and it is matched by a future bearing: a responsibility to the *to-come* (*l'à-venir*) that deepens the more I answer to it. The sense of this, this direction, is not found in the robust data sets (for so they are imagined) of a much vaunted 'objectivity' but in traces that call us beyond the present and beyond our needs—traces, that is, that cannot be Heidegger's pathways to further clearings in the forest, but must be markers of something unreachable, immemorial. As Edith Wyschogrod eloquently puts this:

> Traces are clues, tracks, or trails that cannot be integrated into the order of the world wherever transcendence transcribes and erases itself, preeminently in the human face. The effort to coerce transcendence into appearing assures its loss; it can only be glimpsed in and through another as Other. (Wyschogrod, 1995, p. 142)

### WORKS, BEYOND NEED

There is, is there not, something scandalous about this? Unlike the returning movement of circularity, this direction is a *sens unique*, a one-way street with no return, no appropriation into the Same. Its way of thinking and acting, its 'work', Levinas will say, is not an operation on the world, but a movement towards that which is other or beyond. Other than presence, other than being at all, this is a direction that *gives* meaning: 'Does not sense as orientation indicate a leap, an outside oneself toward the *other than oneself*, whereas philosophy wants to reabsorb every Other into the Same and to neutralize alterity?' (ibid., p. 48). To philosophy so conceived, to a certain conceptualisation of educational research, Levinas' thought must indeed come as a scandal: that there is in human life the possibility of a different kind of activity, one that is necessarily orientated to that which is beyond what is present or what is to be made present. And this is misconstrued as a movement along a continuum towards a further point that will become present along that continuum. Such would be the thinking of goals to be realised and targets to be hit. In contrast the movement imagined here is diachronous to the common time that locates points in the continuum. The relation to this time of the Other is ethics.

Work then, so construed, is not the labour of exchange which remains within the circle of the natural. It does not arise from need or open onto a world that is *for me* (ibid., p. 51). While data are situated within an economy of returns, of profit and loss, work aims at a possibility of the good that is not datable, that is impervious to targeting and audits. Work, an orientation that goes *freely* away from the Same, is tied to ethics itself: 'It is an action for a world to come, a going beyond one's epoch—a going beyond oneself which requires the epiphany of the Other—such is the fundamental thesis which underlies these pages' (ibid., p. 50). I expend myself, give myself up. My work goes beyond me in ways I cannot foresee, and with effects I cannot know. Without this all is limited. And this movement is crucially related to the operation of the gift:

> Now *the work conceived radically is a movement of the Same toward the Other which never returns to the Same.* The Work thought through all the way requires a radical generosity of the movement which in the Same goes toward the Other. It consequently requires an *ingratitude* of the Other; gratitude would be the *return* of the movement to its origin. (ibid., p. 49)

This is not then the return of Ulysses but Abraham's leaving of his fatherland for ever, to depart for a land as yet unknown, for a land that he will not, cannot reach.

The turning towards the Good that Plato sees to be at the heart of education—a turning 'to the truth with one's whole soul' (*Phaedo*)— requires not (only) sincerity and supreme effort; it requires humility, where this is not a self-negation, and the ego-burdened reflection on oneself that this so commonly entails, but an absorption in work directed to what is beyond. Humility is 'the necessary condition for a "beyond the given" which dawns in every meaning, for the metaphor which animates it' (Levinas, 1996, p. 56). Language's abusive going beyond the given is something that the empiricist tradition has sought to overcome. But this is the very marvel of language: 'Whatever be its psychological, social, or philological history, the *beyond* which the metaphor produces has a sense that transcends this history; the power to conjure up illusions which language has must be recognized, but lucidity does not abolish the beyond of these illusions' (ibid.).

Plato directs our attention to something other than being. We can return to Plato in a new way, Levinas suggests, by catching sight in meaning of something that precedes culture, by envisioning language out of 'the revelation of the Other (which is at the same time the birth of morality) in the gaze of a human being looking at another human precisely as abstract human disengaged from all culture, in the nakedness of his face' (ibid., p. 58).

## RESPONSIBILITY, BEYOND THE GIVENS OF EDUCATIONAL RESEARCH

RoutledgeFalmer's 2001 Educational Research catalogue lists a new collection edited by Olwen MacNamara entitled *Becoming an Evidence-based Practitioner*. The book, the blurb tells us, provides:

> case studies which show teachers how to 'do' and 'use' research and how to 'do' effective pedagogy [and explains] how a group of teachers set out to

observe, describe, analyse and intervene in areas of the '*primary recipe book*'. The book can be raided for insights into research methods as well as generic professional issues about teaching and learning. . .

Of course, this is nothing more than a publicity leaflet but the text betrays a kind of anxiety. Why, for a start, these inverted commas here? Do we do research or do we 'do' research? Is research used or 'used'? Can pedagogy, effective or otherwise, be something that, like drugs, is 'done'? And how odd the mixed metaphors of recipes and raids! It is as if there is in this self-consciousness some returning sense of the strangeness of this language. In the play of the inverted commas here (or perhaps, put otherwise, in their inability to rein in these words), language abusively—*marvellously!*—goes beyond the sound practitioner evidence-based common-sense to which the book no doubt aspires.

It must be self-evident how the picture unfolding in this chapter is massively at odds with prevailing aspects of the contemporary world in which educational research is undertaken, aspects that shape the way in which it is conceived. The régime of totality is everywhere in evidence in instrumentalism and performativity. Our empiricist traditions are high points in the metaphysics of presence. And contemporary ethics speaks the language of naturalism, the language of needs, desires and their satisfaction.

The examples raised at the start of this essay were each connected with a brief criticism. Those criticisms collectively can now be seen as related to the broader movement of this essay: to the critique of a thinking within totality. It scarcely needs saying that the preoccupation with efficiency and effectiveness, with performativity, is on this view a malaise with deep causes in the totalising ways of thinking sketched here. The vocabulary of contemporary educational research—of policy and practice also—makes it difficult, if not impossible, to think differently about these matters. It is then a severe curtailment of the possibilities of research and of the potential of education.

There are implications here at the most practical level—for example, in matters of curriculum and assessment. The tidy specification of curriculum content, no less than the tightly-specified research project, makes possible a highly systematic approach to its delivery within the circle of exchange: clearly specified learning outcomes or competencies are assessed in a tidy correlation with curriculum objectives ('framing the question'). The transparency of what is learned, for customers or other stakeholders, imposes the expectation that all must be made present. Ease of access to what is studied encourages the learner to think of the curriculum as something to consume and dispense with in order 'the better to move on (just as the efficient research professor progressively despatches her 'boxes of data'). Such is the *lingua franca* of policy and planning today. Matters such as these are expected to be the focus of educational research.

Research is expected to contribute to the development of a set of techniques that are then to be applied in the delivery of the curriculum, to a technology of teaching and learning. The idea of evidence-based policy and practice again assumes this model of research findings that are then to be applied ('technological and proud'). That research in education should be transparent and accessible to end-users furthers this (and this will, of course, be 'the latest research'). Such a requirement may well, on the face of it, suggest a kind of humility, but there can be hubris in the demand for clarity and transparency—in our confident assumptions that we can get things taped. Similarly, there is here the danger of a dumbing down, the 'seam of anti-intellectualism' of which David Blunkett has complained.[14] Obscurantism is never to be excused, but neither should it be confused with inherent difficulty. If research texts are difficult, perhaps the reader should consider how far the failure in comprehension is her own. If the policy maker or practitioner is too busy to read and comprehend research that is not simply transparent, or to listen to someone who can understand, there may be an obligation to make them less busy—the better to improve policy and practice.

Even questions of the ethics of educational research tend to be asked at the operational level—ethics is 'applied'—in apparent obliviousness to the deeper all-pervasiveness of the ethical as it is, for example, delineated in this essay. Moreover, the tendency towards a normalisation of research forever blunts the edge of ethical enquiry. Earnest self-consciousness about research methodology, professionalisation and orthodoxy ('research methods for all'), may ironically be complicit in this. And the self-consciousness we noted in the publicity blurb extends in other ways, again at odds with the present argument. Narrative research and reflective practice are inevitably egocentric in some degree. Given undue emphasis, they can stand in the way of the humility that ethics, the relation to infinity, requires.

In contrast to these limiting forms of research, conceived within the realm of totality, is it possible to say something about a more ethical conception of educational practice and research (and so again to risk 'the examiner's dismay')? This needs to be understood especially in the light of an orientation to the future. Such an orientation, as we have seen, is a responsibility. I shall not rehearse the ways in which a curriculum might be designed to foster an attention to what is other—in the relation to people but also in things studied, where these are not simply materials to be mastered and then cast aside but objects of a certain mystery and impenetrability. If educational practice is committed in some way to such goods, research that aims at effectiveness and improvement—what works—is cast in a rather different light. It seems very much to miss the point.

Does the present argument perhaps indicate the need for a different kind of writing? There are no simple answers here. Certainly it is true that some of the texts that have most influenced education are of genres within which it is scarcely possible to write today. Think of the Utopian writings of Plato and Rousseau. Think even of the discursive essay, not commonly seen today save *outside* the channels of educational research as it is currently practised.[15] The paradigm discourses do not welcome works of this kind. Yet such works may open to a *to-come* or to an *as if*. They may realise ways of thinking that break with the circle of expectations.

How can this cast light on the aims of educational research, on what it is in fact doing and on what it might do? It would be a serious misreading of the present argument to suppose that it is against empirical research. Of course, there are innumerable empirical projects that are eminently worthwhile. (The complaint here has been against empiric*ism*, and this is also, let us remember, a distortion and misconstrual of empirical work itself.) But the view that this is the only or the best way to understand and improve education, prevalent though this indeed is, comes to seem oddly parochial in the light of the ways education has been studied and understood in other places and at other times. In refreshing comments in the above-mentioned speech Blunkett asked educational researchers to think the unthinkable.[16] Taking Blunkett at his word will require not 'boxes of data' but the realisation of a different language in education, of different kinds of discourse in research. Without this we remain within the realm of the exchange of values in the thought of totality and calculable returns.

We saw how the provocations from Weil and Kierkegaard led us to the kind of paradoxical ways of thinking and approach that Eliot's words suggest. But it was the more searching analysis of the background and the given that laid the way for the deeper account of meaning that Levinas provides. The force of this reveals the significance of the logical givens upon which any research must depend; and it also shows something of the implications of the kinds of discourse in which prescriptive givens are conceived and in which educational research is undertaken. There is a political and ethical obligation to question the nature of education, to be open to such a questioning, and this requires a different language. The point of the argument advanced here is not to safeguard a corner of educational research for the kind of philosophical enquiry that this essay attempts. It is to suggest that without the possibility of a rich language, educational practice and research will be forever constrained within what have become the parochialisms of the present age.

*Correspondence*: Paul Standish, IELL, University of Dundee, Dundee DD1 4HN, UK.
Email: p.standish@dundee.ac.uk

## NOTES

1. The naturalism of such a view is brought into view in a helpful way in Jan Masschelein's recent exploration of Hannah Arendt's distinction between *zoe* (bare life) and *bios* (human life as a form of life) in relation to the discourse of lifelong learning (Masschelein, 2001).
2. How unlike much research in physical science this is! Contrary to the popular image, it is the unexpected and the role of the imagination in responding to the unexpected that are of crucial importance there. *Having ideas*, as Peter Medawar suggests, is the scientist's highest achievement; there is no 'scientific method'; and a scientist is before anything else a person who *tells stories*, albeit stories that there is a duty to verify.
3. For a developed discussion of this fetish character, see Standish, 2000.
4. See, for example, the essay 'Language' in Heidegger, 1971.
5. For a superb account of possibilities in higher education along the lines envisaged here, see Bearn, 2000.
6. Not to mention the fact that research gurus have sometimes built their careers upon the development of innovative quasi-technical vocabularies. Not to mention the ways in which success in journal publishing and on the conference circuit can sometimes depend on the emulation of such vocabularies—with appropriate citation, of course!
7. For a discussion of the operation of such a veto see Smith and Standish, 1997.
8. For a more detailed discussion of the relevance of Derrida's thoughts here to education, see Blake *et al.*, 1998, Ch. 6.
9. See especially Heidegger, 1972. On Heidegger's account the unconcealing of being is to be understood in large part in terms of the giving of language.
10. Levinas' usage of terms denoting otherness is more complex than can be readily explicated in this essay. For present purposes it is worth distinguishing *Autrui*, which has no plural form and which Levinas thinks of in human terms, from *autre*, meaning other or alterity in general.
11. This is not, it must be stressed, a 'theory of ethics'. It is not to be contrasted with other theories in the manner that utilitarianism contrasts with deontological views. The contrast here is with ontology: ethics is the order of responsibility, other than and prior to the order of being.
12. Of course, Husserl's position is far more complex than these brief remarks suggest. Levinas sees a perhaps fertile ambiguity in Husserl's accounting for meanings by a return to the given (ibid., p. 35). What after all is a return?
13. *Aletheia* is the notion of truth as unconcealedness or revealing. Central to Heidegger's thought is the idea that the early Greek understanding of truth in this way came to be obscured by notions of truth as correctness, adequation or representation.
14. In a speech made on 2 February 2000 to an Economic and Social Research Council seminar, according to the press release on the DfEE website, Minister for Education David Blunkett 'called upon social science researchers to join with policy-makers in breaking down the "seam of anti-intellectualism" running through society'. He also stressed the importance of 'sound, relevant and intelligible research'.
15. Of course, there are notable exceptions, the *Journal of Philosophy of Education* being one.

16. Blunkett went on to say that 'the policy process itself also has to undergo a radical change' and that politicians and civil servants were becoming 'more relaxed about welcoming radical thinking'. There was a need for academics to think the unthinkable since if they did not, no one else would.

## REFERENCES

Bauman, Z. (1990) *Thinking Sociologically* (Cambridge, MA, Blackwell).

Bearn, G. (2000) Pointlessness and the University of Beauty, in: P. Dhillon and P. Standish (eds) (2000) *Lyotard: Just Education* (London, Routledge), pp. 230–258.

Blake, N. Smeyers, P., Smith, R. and Standish, P. (1998) *Thinking Again: education after postmodernism* (Westport, CN, and London, Bergin & Garvey).

Borgmann, A. (1992) *Crossing the Postmodern Divide* (Chicago and London, University of Chicago Press).

Derrida, J. (1992) *Given Time: 1. Counterfeit Money*, trans. P. Kamuf (Chicago and London, University of Chicago Press).

Dreyfus, H. (1980) Holism and Hermeneutics. Symposium with Richard Rorty and Charles Taylor, *Review of Metaphysics*, 34, pp. 3–23.

Eliot, T. S. (1968) *The Four Quartets* (London, Faber).

Heidegger, M. (1968) *What is Called Thinking?*, trans. J. Glenn Gray (New York and London, Harper & Row).

Heidegger, M. (1971) *Poetry, Language, Thought* (New York, Harper & Row).

Heidegger, M. (1972) *Time and Being*, trans. J. Stambaugh (New York, Harper & Row).

Heidegger, M. (1991), *The Principle of Reason*, trans. R. Lilly (Bloomington and Indianapolis, Indiana University Press).

Kierkegaard, S. (1996) *Papers and Journals: a selection*, trans. A. Hannay (Harmondsworth, Penguin).

Levinas, E. (1996) *Basic Philosophical Writings*, A. T. Peperzak, S. Critchley and R. Bernasconi (eds) (Bloomington and Indianapolis, Indiana University Press).

Levinas, E. (1998a) *Collected Philosophical Papers*, trans. A. Lingis (Pittsburgh, PA, Duquesne University Press).

Levinas, E. (1998b) *Otherwise than Being*, or, *Beyond Essence*, trans. A. Lingis (Pittsburgh, PA, Duquesne University Press).

Masschelein, J. (2001) The discourse of the learning society and the loss of childhood, *Journal of Philosophy of Education*, 35.1, pp. 1–20.

Reynolds, D. (1997a) *Times Educational Supplement*, 27 June, p. 21.

Reynolds, D. (1997b) School effectiveness: retrospect and prospect. *Scottish Educational Review*, 29.2, pp. 97–113.

Sellars, W. (1963) *Sense, Perception and Reality* (London, Routledge & Kegan Paul; New York, The Humanities Press).

Smith, R. and Standish, P. (1997) *Teaching Right and Wrong: moral education in the balance* (Stoke-on-Trent, Trentham Books).

Standish, P. (2000) Fetish for effect, in: N. Blake and P. Standish (eds) (2000) *Enquiries at the Interface: philosophical problems of online education, Journal of Philosophy of Education*, Special Issue, 34.1, pp. 167–186.

Weil, S. (1977) *Waiting on God*, trans. E. Craufurd (London, Collins, Fount Paperbacks).

Wittgenstein, L. (1958) *Philosophical Investigations*, trans. G. E. M. Anscombe (Oxford: Blackwell).

Wittgenstein, L. (1980) *Culture and Value*, trans. P. Winch (Oxford, Blackwell).

Wyschogrod, E. (1995) The art in ethics: aesthetics, objectivity, and alterity in the philosophy of Emmanuel Levinas, in: A. T. Peperzak (ed.) *Ethics as First Philosophy: the significance of Emmanuel Levinas* (New York and London, Routledge), pp. 137–148.

# Appendix A

## British Sociological Association: Statement of Ethical Practice

This statement is one of a set of Guidelines on a variety of fundamental aspects of professional sociology.

The British Sociological Association gratefully acknowledges the use made of the ethical codes and statements of the Social Research Association, the American Sociological Association and the Association of Social Anthropologists of the UK and the Commonwealth.

1) The purpose of the statement is to make members aware of the ethical issues that may arise throughout the research process and to encourage them to take responsibility for their own ethical practice. The Association encourages members to use the Statement to help educate themselves and their colleagues to behave ethically.

2) The statement does not, therefore, provide a set of recipes for resolving ethical choices or dilemmas, but recognises that it will be necessary to make such choices on the basis of principles and values, and the (often conflicting) interests of those involved.

3) Styles of sociological work are diverse and subject to change, not least because sociologists work within a wide variety of settings. Sociologists, in carrying out their work, inevitably face ethical, and sometimes legal, dilemmas which arise out of competing obligations and conflicts of interest.

4) The following statement advises members of the Association about ethical concerns and potential problems and conflicts of interest that may arise in the course of their professional activities. The statement is not exhaustive but summarises basic principles for ethical practice by sociologists. Departures from the principles should be the result of deliberation and not ignorance. The strength of this statement and its binding force rest ultimately on active discussion, reflection, and continued use by sociologists. In addition, the statement will help to

communicate the professional position of sociologists to others, especially those involved in or affected by the activities of sociologists.

## PROFESSIONAL INTEGRITY

5) Sociological research is a valuable activity and contributes to the well-being of society.Members should strive to maintain the integrity of sociological inquiry as a discipline, the freedom to research and study, and to publish and promote the results of sociological research including making data available for the use of researchers in the future.

6) Members have a responsibility both to safeguard the proper interests of those involved in or affected by their work, and to report their findings accurately and truthfully. They need to consider the effects of their involvements and the consequences of their work or its misuse for those they study and other interested parties. Sociologists should note that there are national laws and administrative regulations (for example Data Protection Acts, the Human Rights Act, copyright and libel laws) which may affect the conduct of their research, data dissemination and storage, publication, rights of research subjects, of sponsors and employers etc.

7) While recognising that training and skill are necessary to the conduct of social research, members should themselves recognise the boundaries of their professional competence. They should not accept work of a kind that they are not qualified to carry out. Members should satisfy themselves that the research they undertake is worthwhile and that the techniques proposed are appropriate. They should be clear about the limits of their detachment from and involvement in their areas of study. (Also see 45–47).

8) Social researchers face a range of potential risks to their safety. Safety issues need to be considered in the design and conduct of social research projects and procedures should be adopted to reduce the risk to researchers.

9) In their relations with the media, members should have regard for the reputation of the discipline and refrain from offering expert commentaries in a form that would appear to give credence to material which, as researchers, they would regard as comprising inadequate or tendentious evidence. (Also see 20–24).

## RELATIONS WITH AND RESPONSIBILITIES TOWARDS RESEARCH PARTICIPANTS

10) Sociologists, when they carry out research, enter into personal and moral relationships with those they study, be they individuals, households, social groups or corporate entities.

11) Although sociologists, like other researchers are committed to the advancement of knowledge, that goal does not, of itself, provide an entitlement to override the rights of others.

12) Members should be aware that they have some responsibility for the use to which their data may be put and for how the research is to be disseminated. Discharging that responsibility may on occasion be difficult, especially in situations of social conflict, competing social interests or where there is unanticipated misuse of the research by third parties.

### Relationships with research participants

13) Sociologists have a responsibility to ensure that the physical, social and psychological well-being of research participants is not adversely affected by the research. They should strive to protect the rights of those they study, their interests, sensitivities and privacy, while recognising the difficulty of balancing potentially conflicting interests.

14) Because sociologists study the relatively powerless as well as those more powerful than themselves, research relationships are frequently characterised by disparities of power and status. Despite this, research relationships should be characterised, whenever possible, by trust and integrity.

15) In some cases, where the public interest dictates otherwise and particularly where power is being abused, obligations of trust and protection may weigh less heavily. Nevertheless, these obligations should not be discarded lightly.

16) As far as possible participation in sociological research should be based on the freely given informed consent of those studied. This implies a responsibility on the sociologist to explain in appropriate detail, and in terms meaningful to participants, what the research is about, who is undertaking and financing it, why it is being undertaken, and how it is to be disseminated and used.

17) Research participants should be made aware of their right to refuse participation whenever and for whatever reason they wish.

18) Research participants should understand how far they will be afforded anonymity and confidentiality and should be able to

reject the use of data-gathering devices such as tape recorders and video cameras.

19) Sociologists should be careful, on the one hand, not to give unrealistic guarantees of confidentiality and, on the other, not to permit communication of research films or records to audiences other than those to which the research participants have agreed.

20) Where there is a likelihood that data may be shared with other researchers, the potential uses to which the data might be put must be discussed with research participants and their consent obtained for the future use of the material. (iv) When making notes, filming or recording for research purposes, sociologists should make clear to research participants the purpose of the notes, filming or recording, and, as precisely as possible, to whom it will be communicated. It should be recognised that research participants have contractual and/or legal interests and rights in data, recordings and publications.

21) The interviewer should inform the interviewee of their rights under any copyright or data protection laws.

22) Researchers making audio or video recordings should obtain appropriate copyright clearances.

23) Interviewers should clarify whether, and if so, the extent to which research participants are allowed to see transcripts of interviews and field notes and to alter the content, withdraw statements, to provide additional information or to add glosses on interpretations.

24) Clarification should also be given to research participants regarding the degree to which they will be consulted prior to publication. Where possible, participants should be offered feedback on findings, for example in the form of a summary report.

25) It should also be borne in mind that in some research contexts, especially those involving field research, it may be necessary for the obtaining of consent to be regarded, not as a once-and-for-all prior event, but as a process, subject to renegotiation over time. In addition, particular care may need to be taken during periods of prolonged fieldwork where it is easy for research participants to forget that they are being studied. In some situations access to a research setting is gained via a 'gatekeeper'. In these situations members should adhere to the principle of obtaining informed consent directly from the research participants to whom access is required, while at the same time taking account of the gatekeepers' interest. Since the relationship between the research participant and the gatekeeper may continue long after the sociologist has left the

research setting, care should be taken not to compromise existing relationships within the research setting.

26) It is, therefore, incumbent upon members to be aware of the possible consequences of their work. Wherever possible they should attempt to anticipate, and to guard against, consequences for research participants which can be predicted to be harmful. Members are not absolved from this responsibility by the consent given by research participants.

27) In many of its forms, social research intrudes into the lives of those studied. While some participants in sociological research may find the experience a positive and welcome one, for others, the experience may be disturbing. Even if not harmed, those studied may feel wronged by aspects of the research process. This can be particularly so if they perceive apparent intrusions into their private and personal worlds, or where research gives rise to false hopes, uncalled for self-knowledge, or unnecessary anxiety.

28) Members should consider carefully the possibility that the research experience may be a disturbing one and should attempt, where necessary, to find ways to minimise or alleviate any distress caused to those participating in research. It should be borne in mind that decisions made on the basis of research may have effects on individuals as members of a group, even if individual research participants are protected by confidentiality and anonymity.

29) Special care should be taken where research participants are particularly vulnerable by virtue of factors such as age, disability, their physical or mental health. Researchers will need to take into account the legal and ethical complexities involved in those circumstances where there are particular difficulties in eliciting fully informed consent. In some situations proxies may need to be used in order to gather data. Where proxies are used, care should be taken not to intrude on the personal space of the person to whom the data ultimately refer, or to disturb the relationship between this person and the proxy. Where it can be inferred that the person about whom data are sought would object to supplying certain kinds of information, that material should not be sought from the proxy.

30) Research involving children requires particular care. The consent of the child should be sought in addition to that of the parent. Researchers should use their skills to provide information that could be understood by the child, and their judgement to decide on the child's capacity to understand what is being proposed. Specialist advice and expertise should be

sought where relevant. Researchers should have regard for issues of child protection and make provision for the potential disclosure of abuse.

### Covert Research

31) There are serious ethical and legal issues in the use of covert research but the use of covert methods may be justified in certain circumstances. For example, difficulties arise when research participants change their behaviour because they know they are being studied. Researchers may also face problems when access to spheres of social life is closed to social scientists by powerful or secretive interests.

32) However, covert methods violate the principles of informed consent and may invade the privacy of those being studied. Covert researchers might need to take into account the emerging legal frameworks surrounding the right to privacy. Participant or non-participant observation in non-public spaces or experimental manipulation of research participants without their knowledge should be resorted to only where it is impossible to use other methods to obtain essential data.

33) In such studies it is important to safeguard the anonymity of research participants. Ideally, where informed consent has not been obtained prior to the research it should be obtained post-hoc.

### Anonymity, privacy and confidentiality

34) The anonymity and privacy of those who participate in the research process should be respected. Personal information concerning research participants should be kept confidential. In some cases it may be necessary to decide whether it is proper or appropriate even to record certain kinds of sensitive information.

35) Where possible, threats to the confidentiality and anonymity of research data should be anticipated by researchers. The identities and research records of those participating in research should be kept confidential whether or not an explicit pledge of confidentiality has been given.

36) Appropriate measures should be taken to store research data in a secure manner. Members should have regard to their obligations under the Data Protection Acts. Where appropriate and practicable, methods for preserving anonymity should be used including the removal of identifiers, the use of pseudonyms and other technical means for breaking the link between data and identifiable individuals. Members should

also take care to prevent data being published or released in a form which would permit the actual or potential identification of research participants without prior written consent of the participants. Potential informants and research participants, especially those possessing a combination of attributes which make them readily identifiable, may need to be reminded that it can be difficult to disguise their identity without introducing an unacceptably large measure of distortion into the data.

37) Guarantees of confidentiality and anonymity given to research participants must be honoured, unless there are clear and overriding reasons to do otherwise, for example in relation to the abuse of children. Other people, such as colleagues, research staff or others, given access to the data must also be made aware of their obligations in this respect. By the same token, sociologists should respect the efforts taken by other researchers to maintain anonymity.

38) Research data given in confidence do not enjoy legal privilege, that is they may be liable to subpoena by a court and research participants should be informed of this.

39) There may be fewer compelling grounds for extending guarantees of privacy or confidentiality to public organisations, collectivities, governments, officials or agencies than to individuals or small groups. Nevertheless, where guarantees have been given they should be honoured, unless there are clear and compelling public interest reasons not to do so.

40) During their research members should avoid, where they can, actions which may have deleterious consequences for sociologists who come after them or which might undermine the reputation of sociology as a discipline.

41) Members should take special care when carrying out research via the Internet. Ethical standards for internet research are not well developed as yet. Eliciting informed consent, negotiating access agreements, assessing the boundaries between the public and the private, and ensuring the security of data transmissions are all problematic in Internet research. Members who carry out research online should ensure that they are familiar with ongoing debates on the ethics of Internet research, and might wish to consider erring on the side of caution in making judgements affecting the well-being of online research participants.

## RELATIONS WITH & RESPONSIBILITIES TOWARDS SPONSORS AND/OR FUNDERS

42) A common interest exists between sponsor, funder and sociologist as long as the aim of the social inquiry is to

advance knowledge, although such knowledge may only be of limited benefit to the sponsor and the funder. That relationship is best served if the atmosphere is conducive to high professional standards.

43) Members should ensure that sponsors and/or funders appreciate the obligations that sociologists have not only to them, but also to society at large, research participants and professional colleagues and the sociological community. The relationship between sponsors or funders and social researchers should be such as to enable social inquiry to be undertaken professionally. In research projects involving multiple funders or inter-disciplinary teams, members should consider circulating this Statement to colleagues as an aid to the discussion and negotiation of ethical practice.

44) Research should be undertaken with a view to providing information or explanation rather than being constrained to reach particular conclusions or prescribe particular courses of action.

*Clarifying obligations, roles and rights*

45) Members should clarify in advance the respective obligations of funders and researchers where possible in the form of a written contract. They should refer the sponsor or funder to the relevant parts of the professional code to which they adhere. Members should also be careful not to promise or imply acceptance of conditions which are contrary to their professional ethics or competing research commitments.

46) Where some or all of those involved in the research are also acting as sponsors and/or funders of research the potential for conflict between the different roles and interests should also be made clear to them.

47) Members should also recognise their own general or specific obligations to the sponsors whether contractually defined or only the subject of informal and often unwritten agreements. They should be honest and candid about their qualifications and expertise, the limitations, advantages and disadvantages of the various methods of analysis and data sources, and acknowledge the necessity for discretion with confidential information obtained from sponsors.

48) They should also try not to conceal factors which are likely to affect satisfactory conditions or the completion of a proposed research project or contract.

*Pre-empting outcomes and negotiations about research*

49) Members should not accept contractual conditions that are contingent upon a particular outcome or set of findings from a proposed inquiry. A conflict of obligations may also occur if the funder requires particular methods to be used.

50) Members should clarify, before signing the contract, how far they are entitled to be able to disclose the source of their funds, the personnel, aims and purposes of the project.

51) Members should also clarify their right to publish and disseminate the results of their research.

52) Members have an obligation to ensure sponsors grasp the implications of the choice between alternative research methods.

*Guarding privileged information and negotiating*
*problematic sponsorship*

53) Members are frequently furnished with information by the funder who may legitimately require it to be kept confidential. Methods and procedures that have been utilised to produce published data should not, however, be kept confidential unless otherwise agreed.

54) When negotiating sponsorships members should be aware of the requirements of the law with respect to the ownership of and rights of access to data.

55) In some political, social and cultural contexts some sources of funding and sponsorship may be contentious. Candour and frankness about the source of funding may create problems of access or co-operation for the social researcher but concealment may have serious consequences for colleagues, the discipline and research participants. The emphasis should be on maximum openness.

56) Where sponsors and funders also act directly or indirectly as gatekeepers and control access to participants, researchers should not devolve their responsibility to protect the participants' interests onto the gatekeeper. Members should be wary of inadvertently disturbing the relationship between participants and gatekeepers since that will continue long after the researcher has left.

*Obligations to sponsors and/or Funders*
*During the Research Process*

57) Members have a responsibility to notify the sponsor and/or funder of any proposed departure from the terms of reference

of the proposed change in the nature of the contracted research.

58) A research study should not normally be undertaken -where it is anticipated that resources will be inadequate.

59) When financial support or sponsorship has been accepted, members must make every reasonable effort to complete the proposed research on schedule, including reports to the funding source.

60) Members should, wherever possible, disseminate their research findings as widely as possible and where required make their research data available to other researchers via appropriate archives.

61) Members should normally avoid restrictions on their freedom to publish or otherwise broadcast research findings.

*At its meeting in July 1994 the BSA Executive Committee approved a set of Rules for the Conduct of Enquiries into Complaints against BSA members under the auspices of this Statement, and also under the auspices of the BSA Guidelines on Professional Conduct.*

**If you would like more details about the Rules, you should contact the BSA Office.**

*It is additionally proposed that:*

- *the revised Statement should no longer stand alone as written advice to BSA members, but that it should be accompanied by a development programme of activities including workshops and training sessions at the events sponsored by BSA (annual conference, postgraduate schools etc.) and additional free-standing BSA ethics training opportunities.*
- *the printed and web versions of the final text of the Statement will have an attached Appendix which will list further sources of information, advice and support (web sites, agencies, publications etc.) for particular issues, identified in the numbered paragraphs. These are not included in the text presented here, but will be added once the text is finalised.*

# Appendix B

## British Psychological Society Code of Conduct: A Code of Conduct for Psychologists

Under the terms of its Royal Charter, the Society is required to 'maintain a code of conduct'. In 1985 the Society adopted a code of conduct prior to the introduction of the Register of Chartered Psychologists with provision for an Investigatory Committee and Disciplinary Board to consider complaints of professional misconduct against members of the Society. In the light of experience dealing with several dozen allegations of misconduct these committees recommended some amendments to the code. After extensive consultations the following revised Code of Conduct was approved by the Council in February 1993 and adopted forthwith.

Statute 15 (12) states that a Disciplinary Committee shall be 'guided by the Code of Conduct, but that mention or lack of mention in the Code of Conduct of a particular act or omission shall not be taken as conclusive on any question of professional conduct'. Nevertheless, the Code sets out certain minimum standards for conduct with which psychologists are required to comply. However, the Code is also supplemented by several other guidelines and statements on matters of ethics and conduct published by the Society and its sub-systems. These frequently set out standards of good practice at which psychologists should aim. Some of these other statements give detailed guidance on matters such as advertising and descriptions, research with human or animal participants and some are relevant to specific fields of professional practice or concern the special provisions of law and practice on such matters as confidentiality and the disclosure of information. Members and contributors of the Society, many of whom will be Chartered Psychologists, must also take account of these further guidelines issued from time to time by the Society and its sub-systems, but especially those relevant to their own specialist fields of practice or research.

## 1. General

In all their work psychologists shall conduct themselves in a manner that does not bring into disrepute the discipline and the profession of psychology. They shall value integrity, impartiality and respect for persons and evidence and shall seek to establish the highest ethical standards in their work. Because of their concern for valid evidence, they shall ensure that research is carried out in keeping with the highest standards of scientific integrity. Taking account of their obligations under the law, they shall hold the interest and welfare of those in receipt of their services to be paramount at all times and ensure that the interests of participants in research are safeguarded.

## 2. Competence

Psychologists shall endeavour to maintain and develop their professional competence, to recognise and work within its limits, and to identify and ameliorate factors which restrict it.

Specifically they shall:

2.1 refrain from laying claim, directly or indirectly, to psychological qualifications or affiliations they do not possess, from claiming competence in any particular area of psychology in which they have not established their competence, and from claiming characteristics or capabilities for themselves or others which they do not possess;

2.2 recognise the boundaries of their own competence and not attempt to practise any form of psychology for which they do not have an appropriate preparation or, where applicable, specialist qualification;

2.3 take all reasonable steps to ensure that their qualifications, capabilities or views are not misrepresented by others, and to correct any such misrepresentations;

2.4 if requested to provide psychological services, and where the services they judge to be appropriate are outside their personal competence, give every reasonable assistance towards obtaining those services from others who are appropriately qualified to provide them;

2.5 take all reasonable steps to ensure that those working under their direct supervision comply with each of the foregoing, in particular that they recognise the limits of their competence and do not attempt to practise beyond them.

## 3. Obtaining consent

Psychologists shall normally carry out investigations or interventions only with the valid consent of participants, having taken all reasonable steps to ensure that they have adequately understood the nature of the investigation or intervention and its anticipated consequences.

Specifically they shall:

3.1 always consult experienced professional colleagues when considering withholding information about an investigatory procedure, and withhold information only when it is necessary in the interests of the objectivity of the investigatory procedure or of future professional practice;

3.2 where it is necessary not to give full information in advance to those participating in an investigation, provide such full information retrospectively about the aims, rationale and outcomes of the procedure as far as it is consistent with a concern for the welfare of the participants;

3.3 refrain from making exaggerated, sensational and unjustifiable claims for the effectiveness of their methods and products, from advertising services or products in a way likely to encourage unrealistic expectations about the effectiveness of the services or products offered, or from misleading those to whom services are offered about the nature and likely consequences of any interventions to be undertaken;

3.4 normally obtain the consent of those to whom interventions are offered, taking all reasonable steps to ensure that the consent obtained is valid, except when the intervention is made compulsorily in accordance with the provisions and safeguards of the relevant legislation;

3.5 recognise and uphold the rights of those whose capacity to give valid consent to interventions may be diminished including the young, those with learning disabilities, the elderly, those in the care of an institution or detained under the provisions of the law;

3.6 where interventions are offered to those in no position to give valid consent, after consulting with experienced professional colleagues, establish who has legal authority to give consent and seek consent from that person or those persons;

3.7 recognise and uphold the rights of recipients of services to withdraw consent to interventions or other professional procedures after they have commenced and terminate or recommend alternative services when there is evidence that those in receipt of their services are deriving no benefit from them.

## 4.   Confidentiality

Psychologists shall maintain adequate records, but they shall take all reasonable steps to preserve the confidentiality of information acquired through their professional practice or research and to protect the privacy of individuals or organisations about whom information is collected or held. In general, and subject to the requirements of law, they shall take care to prevent the identity of individuals, organisations or participants in research being revealed, deliberately or inadvertently, without their expressed permission.

Specifically they shall:

4.1 endeavour to communicate information obtained through research or practice in ways which do not permit the identification of individuals or organisations;

4.2 convey personally identifiable information obtained in the course of professional work to others, only with the expressed permission of those who would be identified, (subject always to the best interests of recipients of services or participants in research and subject to the requirements of law and agreed working practices) except that when working in a team or with collaborators, they shall endeavour to make clear to recipients of services or participants in research, the extent to which personally identifiable information may be shared between colleagues or others within a group receiving the services;

4.3 in exceptional circumstances, where there is sufficient evidence to raise serious concern about the safety or interests of recipients of services, or about others who may be threatened by the recipient's behaviour, take such steps as are judged necessary to inform appropriate third parties without prior consent after first consulting an experienced and disinterested colleague, unless the delay caused by seeking this advice would involve a significant risk to life or health;

4.4 take all reasonable steps to ensure that records over which they have control remain personally identifiable only as long as is necessary in the interests of those to whom they refer (or, exceptionally, to the general development and provision of psychological services), and to render anonymous any records under their control that no longer need to be personally identifiable for the above purposes;

4.5 only make audio, video, or photographic recordings of recipients of services or participants in research (with the exception of recordings of public behaviour) with the expressed agreement of those being recorded both to the recording being made and to the subsequent conditions of access to it;

4.6 take all reasonable steps to safeguard the security of any records they make, including those held on computer, and, where they have limited control over access to records they make, exercise discretion over the information entered on the records;

4.7 take all reasonable steps to ensure that colleagues, staff and trainees with whom they work understand and respect the need for confidentiality regarding any information obtained.

## 5. *Personal conduct*

Psychologists shall conduct themselves in their professional activities in a way that does not damage the interest of the recipients of their services or participants in their research and does not inappropriately undermine public confidence in their ability or that of other psychologists and members of other professions to carry out their professional duties.

Specifically they shall:

5.1 refrain from improper conduct in their work as psychologists that would be likely to be detrimental to the interests of recipients of their services or participants in their research;

5.2 neither attempt to secure or to accept from those receiving their service any significant financial or material benefit beyond that which has been contractually agreed, nor to secure directly from them any such benefit for services which are already rewarded by salary;

5.3 not exploit any relationship of influence or trust which exists between colleagues, those under their tuition, or those in receipt of their services to further the gratification of their personal desires;

5.4 not allow their professional responsibilities or standards of practice to be diminished by considerations of religion, sex, race, age, nationality, party politics, social standing, class, self-interest or other extraneous factors;

5.5 refrain from practice when their physical or psychological condition, as a result of for example alcohol, drugs, illness or personal stress, is such that abilities or professional judgement are seriously impaired;

5.6 value and have respect for all relevant evidence and the limits of such evidence when giving psychological advice or expressing a professional opinion;

5.7 value and have respect for scientific evidence and the limits of such evidence when making public statements that provide psychological information;

5.8 refrain from claiming credit for the research and intellectual property of others and give due credit to the contributions of others in collaborative work;

11.1 take steps to maintain adequate standards of safety in the use of all procedures and equipment used in professional practice or research;

11.1 bring allegations of misconduct by a professional colleague to the attention of those charged with the responsibility to investigate them, doing so without malice and with no breaches of confidentiality other than those necessary to the proper investigatory processes and when the subject of allegations themselves, they shall take all reasonable steps to assist those charged with responsibility to investigate them.

# Appendix C

## British Educational Research Association Ethical Guidelines

*The British Educational Research Association adopted the following set of ethical guidelines at its Annual General Meeting on 28 August 1992. These are based on guidelines developed at a BERA seminar in March 1988 (published in Research Intelligence, February 1989) and the proposed ethical standards of the American Educational Research Association as published in Educational Researcher, December 1991. (We are grateful to the AERA Committee on Standards for permission to adapt their guidelines.)*

1. The British Educational Research Association believes that all educational research should be conducted within an ethic of respect for persons, respect for knowledge, respect for democratic values, and respect for the quality of educational research.

### RESPONSIBILITY TO THE RESEARCH PROFESSION

2. Educational researchers should aim to avoid fabrication, falsification, or misrepresentation of evidence, data, findings, or conclusions.
3. Educational researchers should aim to report their findings to all relevant stakeholders and so refrain from keeping secret or selectively communicating their findings.
4. Educational researchers should aim to report research conceptions, procedures, results, and analyses accurately and in sufficient detail to allow other researchers to understand and interpret them.
5. Educational researchers should aim to decline requests to review the work of others when strong conflicts of interest are involved or when such requests cannot be conscientiously fulfilled on time. Materials sent for review should be read in their entirety and considered carefully, with evaluative comments justified with explicit reasons.
6. Educational researchers should aim to conduct their professional lives in such a way that they do not jeopardize

251

future research, the public standing of the field, or the publication of results.

## RESPONSIBILITY TO PARTICIPANTS

7. Participants in a research study have the right to be informed about the aims, purposes and likely publication of findings involved in the research and of potential consequences for participants, and to give their informed consent before participating in research.
8. Care should be taken when interviewing children and students up to school leaving age; permission should be obtained from the school, and if they so suggest, the parents.
9. Honesty and openness should characterize the relationship between researchers, participants and institutional representatives.
10. Participants have the right to withdraw from a study at any time.
11. Researchers have a responsibility to be mindful of cultural, religious, gendered, and other significant differences within the research population in the planning, conducting, and reporting of their research.

## RESPONSIBILITY TO THE PUBLIC

12. Educational researchers should communicate their findings and the practical significance of their research in clear, straightforward, and appropriate language to relevant research populations, institutional representatives, and other stakeholders.
13. Informants and participants have a right to remain anonymous. This right should be respected when no clear understanding to the contrary has been reached. Researchers are responsible for taking appropriate precautions to protect the confidentiality of both participants and data. However, participants should also be made aware that in certain situations anonymity cannot be achieved.

## RELATIONSHIP WITH FUNDING AGENCIES

14. The data and results of a research study belong to the researchers who designed and conducted the study unless alternative contractual arrangements have been made with respect to either the data or the results or both.
15. Educational researchers should remain free to interpret and publish their findings without censorship or approval from

individuals or organizations, including sponsors, funding agencies, participants, colleagues, supervisors, or administrators. This understanding should be conveyed to participants as part of the responsibility to secure informed consent. This does not mean however that researchers should not take every care to ensure that agreements on publication are reached.

16. Educational researchers should not agree to conduct research that conflicts with academic freedom, nor should they agree to undue or questionable influence by government or other funding agencies. Examples of such improper influence include endeavours to interfere with the conduct of research, the analysis of findings, or the reporting of interpretations. Researchers should report to BERA attempts by sponsors or funding agencies to use any questionable influence, so that BERA may respond publicly as an association on behalf of its members thereby protecting any individual or contract.

17. The aims and sponsorship of research should be made explicit by the researcher. Sponsors or funders have the right to have disclaimers included in research reports to differentiate their sponsorship from the conclusions of the research.

18. Educational researchers should fulfil their responsibilities to agencies funding research, which are entitled to an account of the use of their funds, and to a report of the procedures, findings, and implications of the funded research.

19 The host institution should appoint staff in the light of its routine practices and according to its normal criteria. The funding agency may have an advisory role in this respect, but should not have control over appointments.

20. Sponsored research projects should have an advisory group consisting of representatives from those groups and agencies which have a legitimate interest in the area of inquiry. This advisory group should facilitate access of the researcher(s) to sources of data, other specialists in the field and the wider educational community.

21. The funding agency should respect the right of the researcher(s) to keep his or her sources of data confidential.

22. In the event of a dispute between the funding agency and researcher(s) over the conduct of the research, or threatened termination of contract, the terms of the dispute and/or grounds for termination should be made explicit by the funding agency or researcher and be open to scrutiny by the advisory group. If either party feels that grounds for termination are unreasonable then there should be recourse

to arbitration by a body or individual acceptable to both parties.

## PUBLICATION

23. Researcher(s) have a duty to report both to the funding agency and to the wider public, including educational practitioners and other interested parties. The right to publish is therefore entailed by this duty to report. Researchers conducting sponsored research should retain the right to publish the findings under their own names. The right to publish is essential to the long-term viability of any research activity, to the credibility of the researcher (and of the funding agency in seeking to use research findings) and in the interests of an open society. The methodological principle of maximising the dissemination of information to all interested parties is an integral part of research strategy aimed at testing on a continuous basis the relevance, accuracy and comprehensiveness of findings as they emerge within the process of inquiry.

24. The conditions under which the right to publish might be legitimately restricted are:

   • general legislation (e.g. in the area of libel or race relations);
   • undertakings given to participants concerning confidentiality and generally not to cause unnecessary harm to those affected by the research findings; and
   • failure to report findings in a manner consistent with the values of inquiry i.e. to report findings honestly, accurately, comprehensively, in context, and without undue sensationalisation.

25. Publications should indicate whether or not they are subject to reporting restrictions.

26. The researcher(s) should have the right, as a last resort and following discussions with the funding agency and advisory group, to publicly dissociate themselves from misleadingly selective accounts of the research.

27. Funding bodies should not be allowed to exercise restrictions on publication by default, e.g. by failing to answer requests for permission to publish, or by undue delay.

28. Resources need to be made available for dissemination and publication and should be built in to funding.

29. In the event of a dispute over publication, the researcher should seek recourse first to the advisory group and secondly to an independent arbitration body or individual.

# INTELLECTUAL OWNERSHIP

30. Authorship should be determined on the basis that all those, regardless of status, who have made a substantive and/or creative contribution to the generation of an intellectual product are entitled to be listed as authors of that product. (Examples of creative contributions are: writing first drafts or substantial portions; significant rewriting or substantive editing; contributing generative ideas or basic conceptual schema or analytic categories; collecting data which requires significant interpretation or judgement; and interpreting data.)
31. First authorship and order of authorship should be the consequence of relative leadership and creative contribution.

# RELATIONSHIP WITH HOST INSTITUTION

32. Institutions should both develop their own codes of practice which govern ethical principles and establish appropriate standards of academic freedom, including the freedom to disseminate research findings. While such codes should be observed within all research, including non-contract research, they are particularly important in respect of contract research. Such codes should be honoured by institutions and researchers in the negotiation of contractual arrangements put forward by funding agencies, and in the carrying out of these obligations once they have been agreed.
33. While academic staff should not engage in contract research without agreement by the institution, the latter should not be allowed to compel academic staff to engage in particular contract research.
34. It is assumed that contracts will in all cases be interpreted reasonably and with regard to due process. However, should a legitimate disagreement arise between the funding agency and the researchers engaged on it, then the researchers' institutions should give the researchers full and loyal support in resolving this disagreement.

# Appendix D

## Social Sciences and Humanities Research Council of Canada
## Tri-Council Policy Statement: Ethical Conduct for Research Involving Humans

Please note that only a summary version of the full Policy is reproduced here by kind permission of the Social Sciences and Humanities Research Council of Canada.

This section outlines the standards and procedures to be used by Research Ethics Boards (REBs) for ethics review.

### A. Research Requiring Ethics Review

Article 1.1

a. All research that involves living human subjects requires review and approval by an REB in accordance with this Policy Statement, before the research is started, except as stipulated below.

b. Research involving human remains, cadavers, tissues, biological fluids, embryos or foetuses shall also be reviewed by the REB.

c. Research about a living individual involved in the public arena, or about an artist, based exclusively on publicly available information, documents, records, works, performances, archival materials or third-party interviews, is not required to undergo ethics review. Such research only requires ethics review if the subject is approached directly for interviews or for access to private papers, and then only to ensure that such approaches are conducted according to professional protocols and to Article 2.3 of this Policy.

d. Quality assurance studies, performance reviews or testing within normal educational requirements should also not be subject to REB review.

## B. Research Ethics Boards (REBs)

### B1. Authority of the REB

Article 1.2
The institution in which research involving human subjects is carried out shall mandate the REB to approve, reject, propose modifications to, or terminate any proposed or ongoing research involving human subjects which is conducted within, or by members of, the institution, using the considerations set forth in this Policy as the minimum standard.

### B2. Membership of the REB

Article 1.3
The REB shall consist of at least five members, including both men and women, of whom:

    a.  at least two members have broad expertise in the methods or in the areas of research that are covered by the REB;

    b.  at least one member is knowledgeable in ethics;

    c.  for biomedical research, at least one member is knowledgeable in the relevant law; this is advisable but not mandatory for other areas of research; and

    d.  at least one member has no affiliation with the institution, but is recruited from the community served by the institution.

### B3. Number of REBs within an Institution and Relationships among REBs

Article 1.4

    a.  REBs shall be established by the highest levels of the institution, and cover as broad a range of research as is consistent with manageable workloads. Departmental REBs normally are not acceptable (except as discussed below for review of undergraduate research within course requirements). A multiplicity of REBs with small workloads within the same institution should be avoided.

    b.  Large institutions may find it necessary to create more than one REB, usually to cover different areas of research. The jurisdiction of each REB should be clearly defined by the normal processes of governance within the Institution, and a mechanism should be established to coordinate the practices of all REBs within the Institution.

    c.  Small institutions may wish to explore regional cooperation or alliances, including the sharing of REBs.

# C. Analysis, Balance and Distribution of Harms and Benefits

## C1. Minimal Risk

The standard of minimal risk is commonly defined as follows: if potential subjects can reasonably be expected to regard the probability and magnitude of possible harms implied by participation in the research to be no greater than those encountered by the subject in those aspects of his or her everyday life that relate to the research then the research can be regarded as within the range of minimal risk. Above the threshold of minimal risk, the research warrants a higher degree of scrutiny and greater provision for the protection of the interests of prospective subjects. There is a similar threshold regarding undue or excessive offers of benefit. As an offer of payment in relation to research participation exceeds the normal range of benefits open to the research subject, it is increasingly likely to amount to an undue incentive for participation (see Section 2B).

## C2. Scholarly Review as Part of Ethics Review

Article 1.5
   a. The REB shall satisfy itself that the design of a research project that poses more than minimal risk is capable of addressing the questions being asked in the research.
   b. The extent of the review for scholarly standards that is required for biomedical research that does not involve more than minimal risk will vary according to the research being carried out.
   c. Research in the humanities and the social sciences which poses, at most, minimal risks shall not normally be required by the REB to be peer reviewed.
   d. Certain types of research, particularly in the social sciences and the humanities, may legitimately have a negative effect on public figures in politics, business, labour, the arts or other walks of life, or on organizations. Such research should not be blocked through the use of harms/benefits analysis or because of the potentially negative nature of the findings. The safeguard for those in the public arena is through public debate and discourse and, in extremis, through action in the courts for libel.

# D. Review Procedures

## D1. A Proportionate Approach to Ethics Assessment

Article 1.6
The REB should adopt a proportionate approach based on the

general principle that the more invasive the research, the greater should be the care in assessing the research.

## D2. Meetings & Attendance

Article 1.7
REBs shall meet regularly to discharge their responsibilities.

## D3. Record Keeping

Article 1.8
Minutes of all REB meetings shall be prepared and maintained by the REB. The minutes shall clearly document the REB's decisions and any dissents, and the reasons for them. In order to assist internal and external audits or research monitoring, and to facilitate reconsideration or appeals, the minutes must be accessible to authorized representatives of the institution, researchers and funding agencies.

## D4. Decision-making

Article 1.9
REBs shall meet face-to-face to review proposed research that is not delegated to expedited review. REB review shall be based upon fully detailed research proposals or, where applicable, progress reports. The REB shall function impartially, provide a fair hearing to those involved and provide reasoned and appropriately documented opinions and decisions. The REB shall accommodate reasonable requests from researchers to participate in discussions about their proposals, but not be present when the REB is making its decision. When an REB is considering a negative decision, it shall provide the researcher with all the reasons for doing so and give the researcher an opportunity to reply before making a final decision.

## D5. Reconsideration

Article 1.10
Researchers have the right to request, and REBs have an obligation to provide, reconsideration of decisions affecting a research project.

## D6. Appeals

Article 1.11
a.  In cases when researchers and REBs can not reach agreement

through discussion and reconsideration, an institution should permit review of a REB decision by an appeal board, provided that the board's membership and procedures meet the requirements of this Policy. No ad hoc appeal boards are permitted.

b.  Small institutions may wish to explore regional cooperation or alliances, including the sharing of appeal boards. If two institutions decide to use each other's REB as an appeal board, a formal letter of agreement is required.

c.  The Councils will not entertain any appeals of REB decisions.

## E. Conflicts of Interest

Article 1.1

If an REB is reviewing research in which a member of the REB has a personal interest in the research under review (e.g., as a researcher or as an entrepreneur), conflict of interest principles require that the member not be present when the REB is discussing or making its decision. The REB member may disclose and explain the conflict of interest and offer evidence to the REB provided the conflict is fully explained to the REB, and the proposer of the research has the right to hear the evidence and to offer a rebuttal.

## F. Review Procedures for Ongoing Research

Article 1.13

a.  Ongoing research shall be subject to continuing ethics review. The rigour of the review should be in accordance with a proportionate approach to ethics assessment.

b.  As part of each research proposal submitted for REB review, the researcher shall propose to the REB the continuing review process deemed appropriate for that project.

b.  Normally, continuing review should consist of at least the submission of a succinct annual status report to the REB. The REB shall be promptly notified when the project concludes.

## G. Review of Multi-Centred Research

Principles of institutional accountability require each local REB to be responsible for the ethical acceptability of research undertaken within its institution. However, in multi-centred research, when several REBs consider the same proposal from the perspectives of their respective institutions, they may reach different conclusions on one or more aspects of the proposed research. To facilitate coordination of ethics review, when submitting a proposal for multi-centred research, the researcher may wish to distinguish between core elements of the research—which cannot be altered without invalidating the pooling of data from the participating institutions—and those elements that can be altered to comply with local requirements without invalidating the research project. REBs may also wish to coordinate their review of multi-centred projects, and to communicate any concerns that they may have with other REBs reviewing the same project. The needed communication would be facilitated if the researcher provides information on the institutional REBs that will consider the project.

## H. Review of Research in Other Jurisdictions or Countries

Article 1.14
Research to be performed outside the jurisdiction or country of the institution which employs the researcher shall undergo prospective ethics review both (a) by the REB within the researcher's institution; and (b) by the REB, where such exists, with the legal responsibility and equivalent ethical and procedural safeguards in the country or jurisdiction where the research is to be done.

# Index

Printed in the United States
118015LV00003B/25-42/P

9 780631 231677